CW00504936

£2-50

(27

` FAMILY

Jane Austen's Family

Through Five Generations

MAGGIE LANE

Maggie Lane

ROBERT HALE · LONDON

To Paul

ISBN 0 7090 1744 8

Robert Hale Limited
Clerkenwell House
Clerkenwell Green
London EC1R 0HT

Photoset in North Wales by
Derek Doyle & Associates, Mold, Clwyd
and printed in Great Britain by
St Edmundsbury Press, Bury St Edmunds, Suffolk
and bound by Woolnough Bookbinding Ltd

Contents

Illustrations

Acknowledgements

To the delight of dwelling in the Austens' world, which has constituted my primary satisfaction in writing this book, has been added another, quite unlooked-for gratification: the generosity and friendly interest with which my enquiries and pleas for help have invariably been met. Books, like babies, bring out the best in people; it seems that everybody takes pleasure in contributing towards a safe delivery.

I would like to record my sincere gratitude to Brian Southam, for his early advice and encouragement; to G.P. Hoole, local historian of Tonbridge, for so generously putting his researches at my disposal; to Lt-Col J.H. Smart, Clerk to the Governors of Sevenoaks School, for lending me his only copy of the school's history; and to the Reverend Mervyn Smith, Rector of Horsmonden, for sharing his knowledge of the parish.

Among the descendants of the Austen family I am warmly grateful to Diana (née Hubback) and David Hopkinson for their friendly assistance and hospitality, for allowing me to read and make notes from their manuscript biography of Catherine Hubback and from other family papers, and for permission to reproduce the two portraits of and sketch by Catherine; to Mr and Mrs Lawrence Impey for showing me many family documents, and allowing me to reproduce the sketch of Emma Smith and quote from the *Austen Papers*; and to Joan Austen-Leigh (Mrs Mason Hurley) for supplying me with much useful information, for allowing me to reproduce the picture of Caroline Austen, and above all, for instigating a correspondence which is an unfailing inspiration. I am also grateful to Miss Helen Lefroy for permission to reproduce the drawing by and portrait of Anna Lefroy and to the descendants of Sir

Francis Austen for allowing me to quote from his *Memoirs*.

For permission to use and quote from her invaluable work *Jane Austen's Kindred* I am deeply indebted to Joan Corder. Quotations from *Jane Austen's Letters* and *Minor Works* are made by kind permission of the Oxford University Press. I am grateful to Douglas Maloney and Partners of Cranbrook, Kent, for allowing me to reproduce the photograph of Broadford House, and to the Robert Harding Picture Library and Geoff Goode for that of James Edward Austen-Leigh.

I would like to thank James Butler-Kearney for so efficiently supplying the majority of illustrations in this book and the Jane Austen Memorial Trust for permission to reproduce them, as well as to quote from Caroline Austen's *Reminiscences* and *My Aunt Jane Austen*. Sir Hugh Smiley, Honorary Secretary of the Jane Austen Society, deserves my special thanks for the unwearied way he has answered all my correspondence.

The manuscript poem of James Austen is quoted by kind permission of the Warden and Fellows of Winchester College, and I am grateful to the Librarian, Paul Yeats-Edwards, for his assistance. I would also like to record my thanks to Susan Garland of Kent County Archives for transcribing parish register entries and to the staff of Bristol Central Library for acquiring rare books and helping to direct my researches.

Finally, to Keith Goddard who made prints from negatives or originals loaned to me, to Elizabeth Smart who typed the manuscript, to my ex-husband Paul Lane who was ungrudging of his time and help in countless ways, and to all the friends and relations who have interested themselves in the progress of the work, and kindly borne with my obsession with the Austens, I offer my sincere appreciation.

An elegant sufficiency, content,
Retirement, rural quiet, friendship, books,
Ease and alternate labour, useful life,
Progressive virtue, and approving Heaven!

Thomson, *The Seasons*: 'Spring', 1.1161

Introduction

Few detailed records exist of ordinary family life in the century and a half which can roughly be said to comprise the Georgian age. Before the explosion of middle-class numbers and the spread of education which occurred in Victorian times and which resulted in a rich crop of letters and memoirs of that period, such documents as survive tend to concern only families who were aristocratic or otherwise famous.

The Austen correspondence, tracing the lives of five or six generations, from the beginning of the eighteenth century to the middle of the nineteenth, therefore possesses a rarity value in addition to its intrinsic interest. No comparable record remains which is at once so early, so continuous and so descriptive of everyday matters for the 'middling people' of Georgian England, to use Walpole's phrase. Their surviving letters, though only a fraction of what must have passed between the many members of this highly literate and affectionately united family, are so fortunately spread over a span of 150 years that they succeed in bringing vividly to life a whole saga of shifting generations and subtly changing fortunes. From them, and other evidence, we gain a composite picture of talented, vigorous and attractive individuals, and a unique insight into the age in which they lived.

The Austens were not an over-worldly or ambitious race. They did not seek to found a great dynasty or to achieve power or public honours. Simple private happiness, a set of duties marked out and performed, and sufficient income to enjoy a fair share of the comforts and elegancies of life in which their period so much excelled, formed the height of Austen ambition.

Few of them were born to ease and affluence. Mostly they had to make their own ways in a world which they did not see as owing them a living; for some there were long struggles, for others moments of panic. A bank failure, a threatened lawsuit, a disappointing will, the premature death of a parent: all these things could and did bring disaster very close, and with no state safety-net, only the solidarity of the extended family gave the individual any protection.

So it was with a mixture of mutual help and self-reliance that the Austens succeeded not only in creating agreeable lives for themselves, but, in their various roles – as doctor and lawyer, banker and clergyman, soldier and sailor, farmer and landowner – in contributing significantly to the safety and prosperity of their country.

They were a remarkably united family. Not only prudence but real attachment bound them together. They lived in times of increasing mobility; during the Georgian period the Austens spread from Kent, where they had long been settled and from which they are never known to have ventured before, to seek their livings and their pleasures in Hampshire and Bath, London and Paris, in India and on the high seas of Nelson's navy. Yet even when separated by long distances, they kept in touch with each other, despite the difficulties of travel and communications: embarking on family visits, writing affectionate letters and assisting one another financially according to their various circumstances.

In their snug parsonages, their improved cottages, their elegant town houses and their tranquil country estates, they led what may seem to us an idyllic existence. The poverty of the majority of the people and the exploitation of their labour which enabled the few to live in comfort, they were happily able to view in all sincerity as the God-given order of things. This is not to say that they were negligent in relieving distress; they took their obligations to those less fortunate than themselves very seriously, and treated their own servants with uncommon humanity. But they could enjoy their privileges, having worked hard to secure them, untroubled by what we should today call a social conscience. In any case, though bad enough, conditions for the labouring poor before the Industrial Revolution was underway were not so horrifying as they were later to become.

Both the man-made and the natural world were at the height of their beauty and their harmony one with the other. Builders and craftsmen seemed incapable of producing anything ugly, and the countryside was tamed but not despoiled. Dr A.L. Rowse has said that the England of this time 'makes the heart ache to think of'. The tyranny of nature was at last becoming sufficiently subdued for her glories to be appreciated, rather than her caprices endured; for the first time a sizeable proportion of the population had the leisure and the learning to lead truly cultivated lives. Not many can have been better mentally equipped to do so than the Austens.

There was a refreshing intellectual liberty in the air. The eighteenth-century way of thinking was balanced, rational, robust. Free alike from the bigotry and coarseness of the preceding ages, and the hypocrisy and repression of the one which followed, the Georgian period had also the advantage over our own of looking with cheerful confidence to the future. Individual life may have been more precarious, but the continuity of society as a whole was unquestionable, whilst their belief in the benefits of gradual progress must have conferred a peace of mind which we today can only yearn for.

Against this background, then, successive generations of the Austen family lived out their lives, uniting, we may well feel, 'some of the best blessings of existence'. They were handsome, they were clever, and if only some of them were rich, none of them was very poor. They were happy together, sharing a lively sense of humour, and their circle of friends and acquaintances, not to mention their family ramifications by marriage, was exceptionally large. They were strong and healthy, many of them living into their eighties or nineties, and mercifully few of their children being lost in infancy – an all too common occurrence in, and the darker side of, their age. When one considers that Dr Johnson's friend Hester Thrale raised only four of her twelve children, it appears all the more remarkable that George and Cassandra Austen, whose marriage occurred the year after the Thrales', should have seen all eight of their offspring survive to adulthood. Sadly death in childbirth was not so unfamiliar to the Austens, and certainly the barbaric state of medicine is sufficient to cloud for a moment the sunlit picture we have been painting of Georgian life. So too is the harsh state of justice, witness to which is the terrifying ordeal of Jane Leigh Perrot, described in Chapter 7. That a respectable and innocent woman could face the very real threat of transportation is a severe indictment indeed.

But society was mellowing; the early eighteenth-century struggles of the widow Elizabeth Austen to maintain her children, and the frightening experience of her young granddaughter Philadelphia, who was obliged to undertake a hazardous voyage to India uncertain of what awaited her there, were to find no parallels among the Austens of the nineteenth century. In that latter period, it is true, the sea-faring brothers Frank and Charles experienced dangers and privations enough; but these were voluntarily encountered and brought their own rewards. Both rose to the rank of Admiral.

Indeed it could be said that life grew tamer as well as safer. Not to any later Austen was vouchsafed anything comparable to the heady success enjoyed by Eliza Hancock at the glittering French court of Louis XVI. Pleasures were becoming more domestic – more Victorian. Girls were increasingly sheltered from life, and neither Eliza's indulgences nor Philadelphia's risks would any more be tolerated for a young woman.

In the matter of educating their sons, too, the period under examination shows a discernible pattern. In the first half of the eighteenth century the Austen boys received the same type of education as Shakespeare had known – that provided by the local grammar school. The next generation was either prepared at home for university or sent at a tender age to begin a career at sea. Towards the end of the eighteenth century and thereafter, however, Austen youths were being sent as a matter of course to one of the famous public schools. The sons of landowners and clergymen alike are to be found attending Winchester and Eton. It is symptomatic of the establishment of the family.

In a history of several generations, as in no study of a single individual, the workings of heredity, the movements up and down the social scale, the reflections of the changing world beyond (which may not appear to be changing at all at the time) become clearly apparent. The opportunity to observe the effects of the passage of a century and a half upon one family is as instructive as it is entertaining. It is hoped that the general reader of biography and social history will find rewarding study in this portrait of the Austens.

At the same time, it attempts to satisfy those admirers of the novelist Jane Austen who wonder 'who exactly were her forbears' and 'what became of the family afterwards'. For Jane, of course, was the one famous member of this large family of fascinating individuals. Since her fame was considerably belated, it in no way diminishes the value of the Austen record as a picture of ordinary Georgian life; its effect, however, has been to cause more papers to be preserved, more reminiscences to be written, more researches to be made, than if none of their number had achieved celebrity.

I have deliberately left mention of her until last because this is not primarily a book about Jane Austen. She figures in the family saga only as one among many, not as the person on whom the spotlight is exclusively trained. Much has been written about her life, and even the lives of her immediate family as they overlap hers; my object has been to take the story back three generations before the one to which she belonged, and to carry it forward fifty years or so after her death. By the close of the Georgian era, the direct descendants of William Austen – whose birth coincided neatly with the start of the eighteenth century – numbered nearly seventy: most of them characterized by the energy and resourcefulness which made their age so enterprising, many of them gifted, charming, witty and agreeable. These people, whose lives were of considerable variety and interest, deserve a full-length study, and the wonder is that one has not been undertaken before.

Several very informative books have been published, but all have been long out of print, and in any case, each has told only part of the story. I am particularly indebted to *The Austen Papers* for much source material; but though covering a great deal of ground, there is little attempt in this to provide a continuous and intelligible narrative thread. For the details of the later branches of the family I have relied heavily on *Chawton Manor and its Owners*, *Jane Austen's Sailor Brothers* and *A Memoir of James Edward Austen Leigh*. These works, which were all published in the early part of the present century, contain much that is invaluable but are somewhat outdated and diffuse in their approach. Particulars of all these books will be found in the bibliography. My task has been to collate and weld together information from these and other sources, including later researches which have not been published before, or at least not in book form. For the sake of clarity, when quoting I have modernized spelling and printed abbreviated words in full.

A certain amount of quotation has been made from Jane Austen's own letters. Of these every word (naturally) is well worth reading, but I have tried to make sparing use of them for the reasons mentioned above: to avoid giving one member undue prominence in this general study of the Austen family. As all subsequent Austen biographers must be, I am under a great obligation to Dr Chapman for his marvellous elucidation of the family connections, friends and acquaintances contained in the notes to his edition of the letters. His claim for these letters that 'they yield a picture of the life of the upper middle classes of that time which is surely without a rival' I would extend to embrace the whole of the Austen correspondence.

For many, including myself, it has been but two short steps from enjoyment of Jane Austen's novels, to interest in her life, to curiosity about and affection for her entire family. Perhaps certain readers of the present work may make the same steps in the other direction. At all events, I fancy Jane, who would surely be astonished and embarrassed by the quantity of books inspired by herself, would appreciate, for once, having her beloved family take first place.

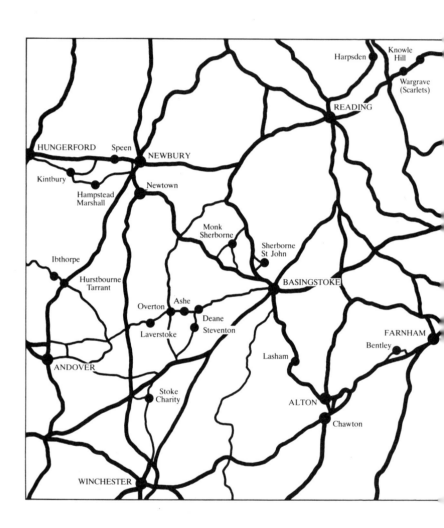

1

So unkindly dealt with

1701-21

At the very beginning of the eighteenth century, a child was born into the Austen family of west Kent, receiving the name of William at his baptism in Horsmonden church on 18 February 1701. For the infant, as for the infant century, the prospects appeared fair. England was emerging from the civil and religious strife of former ages to begin a long run of stability at home and supremacy abroad; whilst William, whose father was the only son of a wealthy man, seemed born to the comfortable life of the minor English gentry.

William was the fifth child and fourth son of John and Elizabeth Austen, whose home was Broadford, a medium-sized Tudor manor house standing in the scattered parish of Horsmonden, about seven miles to the south-east of Tonbridge, and not far from the county border with Sussex. With its massive oak frame, its many gables, lattice windows and exposed half-timbering, Broadford was typical of the period of its construction and, although by the time of William's birth already a little old-fashioned in appearance, was still able to boast every comfort which could make life tolerable in those days of difficult supply and transportation. Self-contained and self-sufficient, it was its own little world of production and consumption.

An inventory taken in 1708[1] details parlour, hall, little parlour, brewhouse, milkhouse, kitchen, pantry, bakehouse, wash-house, small beer cellar, best drink cellar, staircase, best chamber, little parlour chamber, great parlour chamber, brewhouse chamber, men's garret and stable. Yard, kitchen garden, orchards and meadows sloped away to the pleasant rolling countryside of the Weald of Kent.

As evidence of Broadford's longstanding prosperity, one principal room was completely panelled in oak, with the Tudor rose carved over the fireplace and elsewhere. As evidence of the source of that prosperity, attached to the ceiling of one of the upper rooms were the old rollers once used in the manufacture of woollen cloth.

For the Austens, like almost all the landowners in the Weald, derived their fortune from the industry which had been established by Edward III in 1331 when he invited a Flemish clothworker, John Kemp, to settle in Kent and to instruct the local workers in his craft. Before this time the native product was of very inferior quality, for the English workers knew 'no more what to do with their wool than the sheep that made it'.[2] As a result of this ignorance, the advantage of having abundant wool was wasted, most of it being sent to the Netherlands to be made up into cloth and re-imported.

Edward's contrivance to secure this important trade for his own kingdom was successful, and the Austens were among those with the enterprising spirit to profit from it, employing labour and becoming early examples of capitalists. It was a gentle form of capitalism, however, grounded in the cottage industry system, which allowed each skilled worker his measure of independence and dignity and which bound a whole neighbourhood in a community of interest. For each broadloom eighteen women were required to spin a week's consumption of wool, while twenty-seven craftsmen were occupied in the various stages of production.[3]

The masters of this trade were known as 'clothiers', and there were 'clothier' Austens scattered throughout west Kent, allowing for variations in the spelling of their name, which possibly derived from their having once rented lands from the Augustinian order. One such was William Astyn, who was buried in 1522 at Yalding, the next parish north of Horsmonden. His son Stephen had a large family by two wives; it was almost certainly one of *his* sons, Robert, who was the first Austen to reside at Broadford. Robert's first two children, John and Stephen, were baptized in the neighbouring village of Goudhurst, in 1560 and 1561 respectively. Between 1561 and 1565 the family took possession of Broadford, and Robert's subsequent children, Martha, Judith, Elizabeth, Benjamin and Joan, born between 1565 and 1582, were all baptized at Horsmonden.[4]

On Robert's death in 1603 John inherited the property, and the following year his own wife, Joan, died in giving birth to twin sons, her eighth confinement. The status of the family is evident from the charming effigy of her, in ruff, hat and gown, which her husband caused to have placed inside the church.

At the time of his own death in 1620, the nine children were all alive, but when the eldest, John, died childless in 1650, he was succeeded by his next surviving brother, the fifth son, Francis. A highly successful 'clothier', possessing perhaps the greatest business acumen of any Austen, Francis had already amassed sufficient money by 1647 to purchase for himself another lovely old manor house in the same parish. This was Grovehurst, standing about three quarters of a mile further up the valley from Broadford, and if anything even more imposing. Francis Austen bought it from Henry Whetenhall, a descendant of the de Grofhursts, and adapted it as a 'hall' for his trade. When, three years later, his old family home came into his possession too, Francis retained Grovehurst as his principal residence, and Broadford was relegated to the use of a grown-up son or other dependant.

Francis Austen appears to have become sufficiently wealthy to retire from trade altogether towards the end of his long life, or at least to enable his son to do so, since it is uncertain exactly when the Austen homes ceased to function partially as business 'halls'. Most likely such retirement was a gradual process, the shrewd clothmasters retaining some interest in the trade but growing less and less inclined (as they grew less and less needful) to allow its trappings to intrude into their private lives, which were increasingly being led in the style of the gentry.

On the death of Francis Austen in 1688, all his property passed to his son John, who was William's grandfather and who was still living at Grovehurst, a crusty and capricious old man of seventy-two, when William was born.

This John Austen had three surviving children: William's father, John, who had married Elizabeth, daughter of Thomas Weller, gentleman of Tonbridge; Anne, married to John Holman, of Tenterden, and mother of nine daughters and one son; and Jane, whose husband, Stephen Stringer, was the descendant of another 'clothier' family. Jane and Stephen Stringer lived at Triggs, in the parish of Goudhurst, and had five daughters, two of whom, through their marriages, were to influence the later history of the Austens.

Meanwhile it was natural that William's father, John Austen, as the only son of a wealthy gentleman, should look forward confidently to almost certain future affluence. By the terms of his father's will his two sisters were to inherit the sum of £4,000 apiece; all the remainder of a considerable fortune and extensive property must devolve upon him.

On the strength of such expectations John had contracted debts even before his marriage, incurring the displeasure of his father and beginning a train of events which was to result in much hardship and struggle for his wife Elizabeth and six of her seven children. Whether the whole of the blame should be attached to the young man's extravagance, or whether some of it was due to the impossibly small allowance his father made him, is arguable. No doubt there were aggravations on both sides. Mr Austen deplored the careless squandering of money his ancestors had painstakingly amassed, whilst John chafed at his protracted state of dependence.

Though his inheritance continued to elude him, his marriage to Elizabeth Weller, which took place in Tonbridge on 29 December 1693, did much to improve John's situation. His father was obliged to allow him a separate establishment at Broadford and, to clear the slate before the marriage articles were drawn up, promised to pay off all outstanding debts. Overpowered, perhaps, by the generosity of such a promise, and in any case accustomed to having his own way in everything, Mr Austen insisted on dictating the terms of the marriage settlement, whereby Elizabeth's jointure, should she become a widow, fell short of the interest payable on the amount of her dowry – an injustice to which her father, Thomas Weller, made no opposition, trusting to John's fairness to set matters straight when he became master of his own concerns.

In addition to her dowry, Elizabeth brought with her wedding gifts from her family and friends including silver plate and linen which were valued at above £50. But most importantly, in his wife John found a fiercely loyal ally, one who was appreciative of his good intentions and who, by providing him with domestic peace and a family of his own to cherish, exercised a steadying influence.

Elizabeth Austen was a woman of remarkable strength of character, as later events were to prove; and although the full measure of her tenacity and courage remained to be called forth, even in the early years of her marriage, when she had nothing worse to contend with than the meddling and meanness of her father-in-law, she possessed a quiet determination and an uncrushable spirit.

Such qualities did nothing to conciliate old Mr Austen, of course, and the two generations lived, within a mile of one another, on uneasy terms. If they thought him bad-tempered and unfeeling, he probably thought them still improvident, for as Elizabeth confesses in a document[5] written in 1708 explaining her affairs to her children, 'I never proposed the saving of money, knowing my father Austen's estate so large, that I thought, if we could live and enjoy ourselves on that little he allowed us, was sufficient but I was ever uneasy to be in debt, which made my husband keep his debts the more private, and also was not willing his father should know of them, fearing his displeasure, and it seemed most likely the son to be the longest liver.' However, she adds that she is sure they had no extravagance after they were married and that it was her husband's debts contracted before the marriage, and still unpaid by his father, despite the promise, which kept him in debt.

Meanwhile the family at Broadford was rapidly increasing. The first child was a daughter, named after her mother and always known as Betty. Six sons followed in quick succession.

But before his seventh child was eight months old, John Austen was dead. His not unreasonable hope of outliving his own father had proved a vain one. He died of consumption on 21 September 1704, after a long illness during which he had been tormented by worry for the future of his wife and children.

Everything he had meant to do for their security when he came into his inheritance must now be left to the mercy of his father, on whose justice and generosity he could place no reliance. Favouritism towards the eldest grandson, another John, was already much in evidence, and John was afraid that the others would not be given a fair share of the family wealth. He considered an estate of £500 a year ample provision for his eldest boy, and about half that figure for all the younger ones, on which, 'with education and employments', they could live in modest comfort and be no disgrace to their brother. As for Betty, it was essential that she should have a good dowry to attract a husband of suitable standing.

All the lands which John had brought into the marriage were settled equally among his sons, amounting to very little for each one, and nothing at all for his daughter, whilst, as he was not at liberty to dispose of any property, his own outstanding debts would have to be paid by selling personal effects. Elizabeth assured him that the outdoor goods and stock could be sold without material loss of comfort or convenience to her; but he had reason to fear that she might have to relinquish some furniture and indoor things as well.

On his deathbed John begged his father to ensure that all his children were well provided for, and Mr Austen, not unmoved, promised that he would do more for the younger ones in his will than he had previously intended. He promised too that the debts should be discharged without recourse to the sale of Elizabeth's household goods.

Much relieved, John made his will, leaving the education of the children in Elizabeth's hands, the rents from the lands held in trust for them providing for their maintenance until they came into their grandfather's legacies, with any surplus for Elizabeth's own use. His sisters' husbands, Holman and Stringer, were appointed executors, with power to demand yearly accounts of income and expenditure on the children's behalf from Elizabeth, who, if she remarried, would forfeit her management of their affairs. Some of this sounds like Mr Austen's conditions; at any rate, he gave his approbation, and John died in the belief that everything was properly and fairly settled.

Disagreement between daughter and father-in-law, however, was not long in arising, and concerned the funeral. Mr Austen was obliged to meet the expense but baulked at paying for mourning clothes for the widow and children. So soon after her bereavement, this was a cruelly distressing predicament for Elizabeth, who had no ready money to call on, and definite ideas about what was and was not respectful to her late husband's memory. She was driven to contemplate borrowing to keep up appearances, when at last, after great entreaty on the part of the executors, the tight-fisted old man was induced to part with £10 for the purpose. Elizabeth contrived to buy mourning for herself, Betty and all the boys who were old enough to wear it, for the sum of £9.6s.1d.

Shortly afterwards the outdoor goods and stock were offered for sale, and the sum of £522.7s.11d. realized was used to discharge some of John's debts. Unfortunately, as he had suspected, more remained, and Mr Austen was applied to to fulfil the deathbed promise to his son. With a perversity which must have been very trying to Elizabeth, he replied that, if any of her relations would put up half the money, he would meet the other half.

She writes: 'I had no relation to expect this favour from, neither indeed would I desire it of any, for I thought my father Austen had the greatest obligation of any person, to lay down the money not only for his promise sake, but in all other respects the greatest obligation to pay his son's debts, for all knew he must have many hundred pounds by him.'

She offered to have her possessions transferred to his name in return for the advance of money, but still he refused, and the executors felt they had no alternative but to arrange a further sale. They had actually fixed a day, when, on the plea of many friends and in accordance, Elizabeth suspected, with his own secret inclinations, Mr Austen ordered his sons-in-law to stop the sale.

He rode over to Broadford to meet Holman and Stringer and to inspect all Elizabeth's possessions, which he declared he did not want for his own use but for which after some prevarication he agreed to advance £200, provided they were settled on the eldest son and that Elizabeth continued to take as good care of them, while in her use, as if they had still been her own. Mr Austen would not increase his offer above £200, though Holman and Stringer told him the debts amounted to £20 or £30 more.

The sum of £200, of which the promise had been so painfully extracted, was at present put out to a money-lender at Wadhurst and was ordered in. There was some slight hindrance, and then, in Elizabeth's own words,

... it pleased God my father Austen was taken ill, but was thought not dangerous, then notice was given the £200 would be brought to Goudhurst the next day, but my father continuing worse, he was not capable of receiving money, but in a day or two more he died: his illness soon seized his brains, so that he never was sensible of his death, which happened the 13th day of the next July after his son.

His housekeeper informed where his will was, which was opened in the presence of his daughter and son Stringer, his daughter and son Holman, and also myself. We heard it read though I think myself the only stranger to any former knowledge of it. My then knowledge I could not bear but with great concern, nay yet I can seldom think on't without a tear, for as to myself I were never mentioned unless as it seemed necessitated to make me appear as no friend, nay rather an enemy to the family, but that did not so much concern me as to see my children so unkindly, nay I may say unnaturally dealt with. ... Now I found my poor husband's fears concerning his children too unhappily come to pass, one a large estate, the others but as if servants ... and as to my daughter ... I will own I did not forbear saying 'sure my father takes her for a bastard' when I heard how he had cut her off from any prospect of future hopes.

Elizabeth had further cause for alarm when she found that Holman and Stringer were no longer disposed to allow her the £200 out of old Mr Austen's estate, saying that no mention of it was made in the will or in his handwriting anywhere, and that to fulfil a promise made by word of mouth only might leave them open to legal action, should the young heir, when he grew up, choose to claim that they had been outside their rights in robbing his inheritance of £200.

In vain did Elizabeth protest that her son could never object to having his father's debts honourably discharged, to the promise made by his grandfather being fulfilled, to his mother's being spared the humiliation of being forced to sell her furniture. Even the gentleman appointed to audit the accounts, Sir Thomas Roberts, told Holman and Stringer that he would permit the payment, but still they would not make it. Elizabeth was helpless, having no resources to take her case to Chancery.

The circumstance was made even more aggravating from Stephen Stringer's admitting to her that the younger children's small legacies had been further reduced by £10 each, after the promise of the advance had been made by Mr Austen, for he declared that by giving away £200 he was depriving his heir of his rightful fortune, so the younger children should be made to pay for it. This wilful bias in favour of young John was unpardonable in Elizabeth's view, and she could only hope that when he came of age he would see the injustice of it and make his brothers and sisters amends.

Until then she must struggle along as she could. Her total household goods were valued at £203.2s.4d., but if she was to keep a home intact for her young family, not much of this could be spared. In the end she sold most of her silver plate, and her best bed and hangings, raising the sum of £46.10s.11d. Her husband's debts amounted to £224.1s.6d.; she had £24.5s.0d. in hand from rents received, and the balance of £153.19s.7d. she was forced to borrow.

For three more years she continued at Broadford, managing her affairs to the best of her judgement, keeping careful accounts for the scrutiny of Holman and Stringer, and never free from the worry of being continually in debt. Her chief concern, however, was for the education of her sons, and as they grew older, this pressed more and more on her mind.

Even if her eldest son turned out to be well disposed towards his brothers, he would not be old enough to do anything for them until they were past the age when they must be launched into the world. Deprived by their grandfather's caprice of their proper position in society, they were entitled at least to the good classical education that would stamp them indisputably as gentlemen, and thereafter to apprenticeships that would enable them to earn their own livings.

There were no schools in Horsmonden, and many of Elizabeth's well-wishers, and her brother-in-law Holman, advised her to leave Broadford and take up residence in one of the small neighbouring towns which possessed its own grammar school – Tonbridge or Sevenoaks, for example. Willing to do whatever was best for her sons, her only demur was that the cost of living in a town, where all food had to be bought in, would be greater than at Broadford, where she was already finding it difficult enough to maintain the family on the rents which she received for their lands. She was desperately worried about sinking further and further into debt, and could foresee only increasing expense. Beside food, schooling, clothes and pocket money would all cost more as her boys grew older, and though she could let Broadford, they would have to pay rent for a house in town.

It had already occurred to her that she might make some small increase in her income by taking in boarders, once she had removed to a house in town, when a situation came to her notice which seemed particularly suitable to her circumstances. The Master of

Sevenoaks School was looking for a housekeeper for the schoolhouse and was prepared to let Elizabeth and her children live there rent free and, most important of all, to give the boys a free education, in return for her looking after him and the other boy boarders. In addition there was the possibility of making a little profit from what these pupils paid for their board.

Elizabeth felt she could not do better than to accept such an offer. It would secure her prime object, a good education for her sons, and although running such a large establishment, and looking after other people's children, was not what she had been brought up to expect, she was only too thankful to have some honest means of working for her family's benefit.

She concludes her account:

> These considerations with the thoughts of having my own boys in the house, with a good Master (as all represented him to be) were the inducement that brought me to Sevenoaks, for it seemed to me, as if I could not do a better thing for my children's good, their education being my great care, and indeed all I think I were capable of doing for them, for I always thought if they had learning, they might the better shift in the world, with that small fortune was allotted them. I was also in hopes it might be an inducement for my brothers to let my eldest son live with me, as they paid for his board. I thought it might be a help in my housekeeping, which would have been a great kindness. My brothers at first did seem to say it might be so, but afterwards resolved to put him to another place, which I confess I took unkindly of them, yet I will be content, and hope it may be all for the best.

So Elizabeth left her comfortable and dignified country house, where she had lived for fourteen and a half years, and where all her children had been born – where she had enjoyed the position of lady of the neighbourhood, and mistress of her own home – to live in a town and work for a Master. The removal was made on 27 June 1708, and from the following Michaelmas Broadford was let to one Thomas Yorkton. Elizabeth had hoped to receive £40 per annum for the lease but had to be satisfied with £36.

One of the oldest grammar schools in the country, Sevenoaks School owed its existence to Sir William Sevenoke, a fine example to the Austen boys and other scholars of how far hard work and determination could get an apprentice lad. A foundling who had been given as a surname the name of the town where he was discovered as an abandoned infant by a passing horseman, Sevenoke was apprenticed to a London ironmonger and in 1397 admitted into the Grocers' Company, becoming Master of that guild in 1408. Seven years later he was elected an Alderman of the City of London, and in 1418 Lord Mayor. Thus 'the foundling boy became the chief magistrate of the greatest city in the world.'⁶

He always recalled with gratitude the little town where he had so unpropitiously started life and in his will, made in 1432, stipulated that the rents and profits of certain of his London property should be used to found and maintain a grammar school in Sevenoaks. Subjects to be taught were Greek, Latin, English, writing and arithmetic. Prayers were to be said three times a day; on Fridays the boys were 'to go orderly to the Parish Church of Sevenoaks, and hear the Litany (or Procession) sung or said, and thank God for the benefits bestowed on them by their benefactors'. From 25 March to 29 September school hours were 6 to 11 and 1 to 6. In the winter months these were reduced to 7 to 11 and 1 to 5, which was just as well, since the boys had to provide their own candles.

When the Austens arrived at the school, the Master was Elijah Fenton, then aged twenty-five and already the author of a volume of poetry. Later he was to distinguish himself by helping Pope to translate the *Odyssey* and to be mentioned by Dr Johnson in his *Lives of the Poets* as 'an excellent versifier and a good poet'.⁷ It was his influence which brought the school into good repute and in view of the Austens' residence in his house, it is pleasing to note that his character was as much praised by his contemporaries as his academic abilities. The Earl of Orrery, who was privately tutored by Fenton for six years, says that, 'He was never named but with praise and fondness, as a man in the highest degree amiable and excellent,' and other accounts confirm this. Elizabeth must have had a considerate employer, then, and her sons a brilliant teacher. Unfortunately he left the school in 1710, lured by the promises of various high-born patrons impressed by his wit.

Despite the undoubted advantages to the family of the move to Sevenoaks, their meagre finances were perpetually overstretched, and Elizabeth was never to be totally free from debt again. Her annual accounts were meticulously kept. As she had feared, food was expensive, and clothes, books and pocket money were continually rising items, though the rents from which they had to be met were static, whilst any emergency, such as the large amount of 'physic' required in 1715 at £11.18s.8d., made a serious impression on her budget.

The cost of Betty's upkeep rose dramatically when, at the age of nineteen, and now a young woman whose only hope of provision was to attract a husband, she was allocated a separate dress allowance. Thus in the accounts for 1714-15 her clothes cost £8.11s.0d., and in 1715-16 £16.4s.3d. At Michaelmas 1717 Betty was of age to receive her grandfather's small legacy, and thereafter paid her own board and expenses. Happily, her mother's fears that she would never marry well were unfounded. Betty eventually made a very respectable alliance with George Hooper, a practising Tonbridge attorney who belonged to the fifth generation of his family's law firm. Thus Betty's married status was very much on a par with that of all her younger brothers, though her husband's future was more assured than theirs, which remained to be made.

Having seen them well taught, Elizabeth's next duty to her sons was to find the money to launch each one upon a professional career which would support him for the remainder of his life. In January 1714 the second son Francis was bound apprentice to George Tilden, an attorney in Bedford Row, London, for a premium of £140. Unfortunately Francis caught smallpox that year, and the cost of this, together with the clothes required to set him up in his new life, amounted to £29.10s.6d. The following year, too, his clothes and pocket money cost Elizabeth £28.18s.8d.

Such expenses were repeated with all the sons. Just after his sixteenth birthday, on 11 November 1715, Thomas was apprenticed for a fee of £60 to Henry Wells, citizen and haberdasher. Medicine was the profession chosen for William, whose apprenticeship to the surgeon William Ellis of Woolwich on 20 February 1718 cost his mother £115.10s.0d.

No indentures are recorded for Robert, but he left home in the latter half of the year 1718, perhaps to follow some trade at Tenterden, where he died of smallpox in January 1728, unmarried.

He was the only one of Elizabeth's children to have no family of his own.

Finally, £105 was found on 1 June 1719 to bind Stephen apprentice to William Innys, a London stationer. The apprenticeship fees – which interestingly reflect the status, or perhaps the money-making potential, of the various trades and professions chosen, law being regarded most highly, and medicine scarcely above bookselling – were possibly advanced out of each son's legacy, on the authority of their uncles. Even so, their mounting expense left Elizabeth by 1719 £137 in debt.

John, brought up separately from his brothers and sister and away from his mother's influence, seems to have inherited something of his grandfather's disposition and to have guarded against allowing the poorer members of his family to regard him as a soft touch. The same year Elizabeth noted against her accounts: 'My son John desires the rent at Broadford may be allowed to him as an equivalent for the expenses he has been at this year on his brothers' account, and repairs, and for his own part in the rents.' Whilst the other boys were working out their apprenticeships, John was at Pembroke College, Cambridge, where he had been admitted as a fellow commoner on 4 May 1713, preparing to be a gentleman of leisure and squire of Grovehurst and Broadford. Shortly after his return he married his cousin Mary Stringer; he was evidently well in with his uncles, who had possibly set him against his mother.

Less than two years after seeing the last of her sons safely out into the world, Elizabeth died. Her body was taken from Sevenoaks, where she had worked so bravely, back to Tonbridge, where she had been born to very different expectations, and was buried there on 25 February 1721.

2

A country surgeon

1722-51

Having completed his apprenticeship, William Austen returned to
Kent, where he set up as a surgeon in the busy little market town of
Tonbridge.[1] Here, in East Street, lived his sister Betty with her three
small children and her husband, George Hooper, who, as an
attorney and a native of the town, was not without influence in
local affairs. Here too, occupying the substantial house known as
'Chauntlers', was William's uncle Robert, eldest brother of
Elizabeth Austen and head of the long-established and highly
respected Weller family, five generations of which are com-
memorated in Tonbridge parish church.

Such connections were of the utmost value to William in gaining
acceptance amongst the townspeople. In a small and mostly static
community, who you were was at least as important as what you
knew; and the recommendations which his brother-in-law and
Weller cousins were able to make helped establish him in his
practice.

A 'surgeon', in the eighteenth century, was the term for a
superior, or apprenticeship-trained, general practitioner, rather than
denoting one who specialized in performing operations – though
this was certainly part of his stock-in-trade. The other type of
country doctor was called an apothecary and usually restricted his
activities to prescribing and making up medicines – somewhat
resembling our present-day pharmacist, though directly involved
with diagnosis. When he had ascertained that there was 'business'
enough for them both, William invited his brother Thomas to join
him in Tonbridge as an apothecary and undertook to pass on
sufficient knowledge for the purpose. With the quickness of

learning characteristic of the Austens, and the experience of helping to treat William's patients, Thomas probably soon knew as much as his brother of the primitive methods of their day, though he was never entitled to term himself surgeon.

Presumably Thomas had not found the haberdashery trade sufficiently congenial or lucrative. With his wife Elizabeth and son Henry, who had been born in 1726, he settled at 186 High Street. William's own timber-framed house stood on the opposite side of the High Street, at its junction with Bank Street and almost facing the short lane which led up to the church.

The brothers were soon absorbed into the professional life of the town and taking an active part in local affairs. They were frequently required to witness legal documents – in years to come Thomas would even be doing well enough to stand sponsor to the Medway navigation scheme. It was a tribute to the power of education, when education was the preserve of a very small minority. 'A country surgeon would not be introduced to men of their rank,' William's granddaughter Jane was to write of the aristocracy nearly a hundred years later;[2] but though country doctors were unlikely to be on social visiting terms with the landed gentry, in their own spheres they were men of substance and some influence. In addition to the house in which he lived, William was buying up parcels of property in Tonbridge whenever he had cash to spare. Involved, busy, respected and steadily growing in prosperity, it was, on the whole, an agreeable life, and all the more agreeable for the sense of belonging to a community.

By the age of twenty-six William felt able to support a wife, and he chose one highly suited to the position in society which he could offer her. Rebecca Walter was the widow of one medical man, and the daughter of another. Her father, Sir George Hampson, had earned his living as a physician in Gloucester until 1719, when he had inherited the baronetcy from a cousin, together with property near Maidstone and at Taplow, Buckinghamshire. He had died in 1724 and Rebecca's brother, another Sir George, was now the fifth baronet.

Her first husband had been William Walter MD of Frant, just over the border in Sussex – one of the few country doctors of that time to hold a degree in medicine. It is possible that the widow met

William Austen through his uncle Henry Weller, who was also a resident of Frant and who, when he died, left the sum of £400 to be divided between the children of his sister Elizabeth Austen.

Rebecca was four years older than her second husband and of slightly higher rank. From her first marriage she had a little son, William Hampson Walter, and with *his* future to consider, it seems doubtful that she would have accepted William Austen's proposal had he not been prospering.

For their own first child Rebecca and William decided upon the name of Hampson, and even though the baby was a girl, that was what she was christened, on 11 September 1728. A second daughter received the almost equally unusual name of Philadelphia at her baptism on 15 May 1730.

Whatever William's professional skills may have been, they were of little avail against the harsh physical realities of the time, and he could not save little Hampson from dying in July of that year. She was the first of the family to be buried in Tonbridge parish church.

The Austens' only son was born on 1 May 1731. As there was already a young William in the household, he could not be called after his father, and so the Hampson name of George was chosen for him. Another daughter, Leonora, was born in January 1733. This fourth experience of childbirth in as many years was too much for Rebecca, and she died on 6 February, aged thirty-six.

Left with three motherless infants of his own, as well as a stepson entrusted to his care, William Austen had need of a second wife. After a decent interval had elapsed, he found one in Mrs Susan Kelk, a woman twelve years older than himself. When they married, on 20 May 1736, she was forty-eight, which would then have been considered quite old, though in fact she lived to be eighty. Was William attracted towards older women, did plucky widows remind him poignantly of his mother, or was it simply that they represented more prudent, more sensible choices? Did he perhaps deliberately choose a stepmother for his children who was unlikely to produce any of her own?

To match the 'messuages' in Tonbridge now in William's posses-sion, Susan Kelk brought into the marriage settlement two fields, with the picturesque names of 'The Old Hopgarden' and 'School Mead', both situated in Tonbridge parish and totalling seven acres.

But William's second marriage was destined to be even briefer than the first, for he died on 7 December 1737, just short of his thirty-seventh birthday. He was buried in Tonbridge church next to his first wife and infant daughter, and his name was added to the slab in the north aisle commemorating theirs.

If William had remarried solely or chiefly for his children's benefit, the measure appears to have been counter-productive, for there is no record of their stepmother caring for the family after his death, and indeed, her very existence prevented their inheriting his carefully acquired property for thirty years. She continued to live in the Tonbridge house until her death in 1768.

The three little Austens and their half-brother were thus left to the protection of their various relations. It was natural that the Hampsons, as the more affluent side of the family, should do most for the orphans; but George, whose lovable disposition and aptitude for learning made him a most engaging boy, was selected by his uncle Francis to be educated at his expense.

As yet unmarried, Francis was already becoming the most successful, in worldly terms, of all Elizabeth's younger sons. Whilst all prospered in their various professions, Francis grew extremely rich. (John, the privileged eldest son, had died in 1728, leaving Broadford to the next generation in the person of his own son John, who inherited at the age of twelve. No help was forthcoming from *that* quarter.)

Like his brothers Thomas and William, Francis had returned from apprenticeship in London to the county of his birth. Only Stephen continued to earn his livelihood in the capital, as a bookseller in St Paul's Churchyard where he kept the shop known as 'The Angel and Bible' – but even he came back to Kent towards the end of his life and was buried at Horsmonden. Perhaps to avoid competition with his brother-in-law Hooper, Francis decided to practise law at Sevenoaks. Here, in his great-nephew Henry Austen's happy turn of phrase, composed more than a hundred years later, he 'set out in life with £800 and a bundle of pens, as attorney, and contrived to amass a very large fortune, living most hospitably, and yet buying all the valuable land round the town'.[3]

In addition to building up a private practice, Francis won the confidence of the Duke of Dorset, whose seat, Knole, adjoined the town of Sevenoaks, frequently acting for him in the capacity of agent. He was also appointed Clerk of the Peace for Kent.

Francis possessed exactly the right qualities to succeed as a lawyer, being always quick to seize the initiative, able to inspire trust in those for whom he acted, and to gain ascendancy over those who threatened to oppose. Upright and industrious, shrewd without being petty or mean, the qualities of his mind were given outward expression in the correctness at all times of his dress and manners. Had Elizabeth foreseen all this when she purchased on his behalf the most expensive of all her sons' apprenticeships? Or was it his own ambition which directed him towards the law? As the eldest of the disinherited boys – old enough, at the time of the disaster, to suffer with his mother from insecurity, fear and rage – he may well have been fired with an early determination to retrieve the family status and prosperity.

He certainly had good reason to feel satisfied with his achievement so far when in 1743 he purchased the Red House in Sevenoaks. This was to be his home for the rest of his life, a home which reflected his own solidity and importance in the town. As imposing a building as either Broadford or Grovehurst, the Red House was also more fashionable, with its rosy brick façade and Queen Anne symmetry. Built in 1686, it had been inhabited during Francis' schooldays by Thomas Fuller, doctor and writer of some local celebrity.[4] An engraving was made of the property in 1719, showing Knole as its nearest neighbour – showing vividly, too, the contemporary taste in garden design, upon which later 'improvers' were to work with so much relish, restoring the look of untamed nature as eagerly as their predecessors had striven to tidy it away. Order and formality were agreeable to early eighteenth-century eyes as proof of the controlling power of wealth. As this ability to control became taken for granted, later generations could afford to take a more relaxed and romantic view of natural beauty.

Writing in his own old age, Henry Austen paints a charming portrait of his great-uncle Francis as a man of his times: 'All that I remember of him is, that he wore a wig like a Bishop, and a suit of light grey ditto, coat, vest and hose. In his picture over the chimney the coat and vest had a narrow gold lace edging, about half an inch broad, but in my day he had laid aside the gold edging, though he retained a perfect identity of colour, texture and make to his life's end – I think he was born in Anne's reign, and was of course a smart man of George the First's. It is a sort of privilege to have seen and conversed with such a model of a hundred years since.'

There was both kindness and duty in Francis Austen's sponsorship of George. That he was genuinely fond of his nephew was shown by acts of generosity towards him over a period of many years, even after Francis had acquired closer claims on his affection. At the same time, he felt it an obligation to equip the fatherless boy to earn an honourable living, just as he had been equipped by his mother's struggles; and in George's exceptional intellect, he saw promising material for enhancing the standing of the family as a whole. For George it was not a soft option; a boy so helped was expected to make the most of the advantages he had been given, and to help on others in his turn.

So George entered Tonbridge School in 1740, at the age of nine. He joined his cousin Henry, son of Thomas Austen the apothecary, who was already a pupil there and who, indeed, was to become Head Boy three years later.

Dating from 1553, Tonbridge School was not so ancient a foundation as its counterpart at Sevenoaks but had been similarly endowed by a successful and grateful merchant son of the town – in this case, Sir Andrew Judde. Governed by the Worshipful Company of Skinners, the school offered the usual classical education to a small number of boys – anything between twenty and sixty in the middle part of the eighteenth century. The pupils were the sons of local clergy, lawyers, doctors, well-to-do tradesmen and farmers – and occasionally of the minor gentry. Brighter than most of his companions, George was by the age of sixteen ready to matriculate.

He was lucky. Among Sir Andrew Judde's friends in the City had been Sir Thomas White, founder of the Merchant Taylors' School and of St John's College, Oxford. As a mark of regard for his friend, Sir Thomas had established at St John's College one fellowship to be held exclusively by an old Tonbridgian, with the stipulation that at the time of the award the scholar must be under nineteen years of age. The first three years were always probationary, while the holder took his degree; after that the fellowship was for life, to be relinquished only upon marriage or upon obtaining ecclesiastic preferment above a certain value. In 1747 this fellowship fell vacant for the first time since 1720, most fortuitously for George Austen, whose application for the award was successful.

George must have been particularly gratified to be granted this assistance towards his living expenses at Oxford and the beginnings of some security for the future; not only because it justified his uncle's faith in him but because it was a welcome first step towards self-support in a year which saw a notable increase in Francis Austen's responsibilities.

The cautious lawyer had waited until he was nearly fifty before taking a wife, by which time he was rich enough to attract further riches in the shape of the dowry of Anne Motley, twenty years his junior. Unhappily the lady died in bringing their only child into the world, in November 1747 – a son, christened Francis Motley and always known in the family by his mother's maiden name.

It was the second birth among George's nearest relations that year. His half-brother, William Walter, had married Susanna Weaver, and their first child was born on 16 August and baptized Weaver at Shipbourne church, near Tonbridge, precisely one month later. No profession was followed by William Walter; he had been brought up on Hampson charity and either received a small annuity from them or had inherited sufficient property from his father to enable him to live without working. He occupied a succession of rented houses in west Kent and was never very satisfied with any of them; many were unwanted parsonages where the clergyman was a pluralist. It seems a pity that William was not, like the Austens, equipped to practise one of the professions, which would have injected some purpose and satisfaction into his life besides increasing his income. Money appears to have been always short, and he lived with his growing family in a very quiet way. Nevertheless, despite such differences, and an age gap of at least eight years, not to mention long periods of separation in their childhoods, he and George retained an affectionate interest in one another and kept in contact for the whole of their lives.

George's other boyhood companion, his cousin Henry, also took an important step in his career in this eventful year of 1747. A brilliant and forceful individual, Henry had crowned an exemplary academic progress by obtaining his degree at Queens' College,

Cambridge. Now, at the age of twenty-one, he was ordained deacon, requiring special dispensation from the Archbishop of Canterbury as he was two years short of canonical age. He was immediately appointed to the parish of Shipbourne, as perpetual curate – the equivalent of vicar, though as only a deacon he was not yet authorized to perform all the functions of a parish priest.

The patron of the living was William Vane, Duke of Cleveland, whose seat, Fairlawne, stood in the parish. It was possibly his influence that had procured the dispensation, though how he came to be acquainted with Henry Austen and so impressed by his merits is not known.

There is an unproved but not implausible theory that it was at Fairlawne that a friendship was formed between the young Austen cousins and a contemporary of theirs as yet as obscure as themselves but destined to achieve great national importance: Warren Hastings.

Between 1740 and 1749 the orphan Warren lived with his uncle and guardian, Howard Hastings, in Westminster, at which school he was a pupil. Officially employed at the Customs House, Howard Hastings derived a good proportion of his income, and spent a great deal of his time, as companion and business adviser to the Duke of Cleveland. Frequent visits were paid to Fairlawne, Warren often accompanying his uncle.[5]

Born in 1732, Warren was just eighteen months younger than George Austen, and of a very similar rank and education, resembling him too in having his fortune to seek by his own efforts. It is certainly possible that from the time of Henry's appointment to Shipbourne in 1747 the three clever youths occasionally met and conversed together.

A personal knowledge of George Austen, who seemed effortlessly to inspire the friendship and regard of all who knew him, does appear a better foundation for Warren Hastings' later act of faith in sending his beloved only son home from India to be cared for and educated by George, than the mere recommendation of her brother by Philadelphia, with whom Warren was by that time intimately acquainted.

Howard Hastings died in 1749. His will stated that he was entitled to £200 a year from the Duke, and £2,000 on his death;

and it recommended his nephew to the protection of the Duke and the Duke's heir, Henry Vane. But Howard's trust was misplaced, and the Vanes having declined to do anything for him, the eighteen-year-old Warren Hastings set sail for India to try his fortune in January 1750.

Exactly two years later, Philadelphia Austen was embarking on the same perilous sea voyage, even more uncertain than Hastings could have been as to what her future held.

3

Splendidly, yet unhappily married

1752-63

Between her baptism in 1730 and her petition to the Directors of the East India Company in November 1751,[1] seeking permission to sail by the *Bombay Castle* (ostensibly to join friends at Fort St David), no documentary evidence exists to prove where Philadelphia Austen spent her childhood. The only clue comes in a letter written by her husband many years later, referring to the kindness shown by her Freeman relations early in life. It seems probable therefore that Philadelphia was cared for chiefly by her mother's sister Catherine, who was married to John Hope Freeman.

But the Freemans had children of their own, and Philadelphia's future was unprovided for. Unlike her brother George, she could not be equipped to earn her own living; she could only be helped to get a husband, and therefore a maintenance for life.

Philadelphia grew into a very pretty woman, as her miniature shows, but her lack of dowry discouraged suitors – in England, at any rate. In India, it was known, things were differently balanced. There, a shortage of unmarried white women virtually guaranteed that any such arriving on the scene would be eagerly sought by one of the many Englishmen toiling on the sub-continent year after year, lacking the time or the money to return home in search of a wife.

So it was decided that the best assistance which could be given Philadelphia was to pay her fare out to India. It was a daunting prospect from almost any point of view, and could hardly have been welcome to her. Not only was the voyage itself long, uncomfortable and dangerous – enough to deter all but the most determined husband-hunter or devoted new bride – but at the end of it a proposal of marriage would have to be attracted and accepted, the likelihood of its being very congenial seeming remote. The whole enterprise was humiliating in the present, and not very promising of happiness for the future.

Philadelphia had, for a woman, an adventurous spirit and an independent nature, which was just as well – although possibly if she had been a more helpless type her relations would never have contemplated India for her. As a wife she was never clinging, and as a widow she cheerfully journeyed abroad when she could have chosen to stay safely at home. She seems to have inherited her grandmother Austen's pluck. Her sister-in-law was to write of her 'courage' and marvel at her self-possession in the face of mishaps which would have fluttered most of her sex. But this was much later, after her Indian experiences had helped build her character. When she embarked for India she was not yet twenty-two years of age, and even Philadelphia must have quaked at the perils which lay before her.

We can perhaps gauge her feelings from a passage written by her niece Jane Austen forty years later, in which she makes use – rare for her – of family history for fictional purposes. It occurs in *Catharine*, one of her earliest fragments, written when she was not yet seventeen; she must often have heard her parents talking of the past.

> The eldest daughter had been obliged to accept the offer of one of her cousins to equip her for the East Indies, and though infinitely against her inclinations had been necessitated to embrace the only possibility that was offered to her, of a maintenance; yet it was *one*, so opposite to all her ideas of propriety, so contrary to her wishes, so repugnant to her feelings, that she would almost have preferred servitude to it, had choice been allowed her. Her personal attractions had gained her a husband as soon as she had arrived at Bengal, and she had now been married nearly a twelvemonth. Splendidly, yet unhappily married. United to a man of double her own age, whose disposition was not amiable, and whose manners were unpleasing, though his character was respectable.[2]

The *Bombay Castle* sailed on 18 January 1752 and docked at Madras on 5 August. Six months later, on 22 February 1753, Philadelphia Austen married Tysoe Saul Hancock, a surgeon of Fort St David. He was forty-two.

The age difference is echoed in the passage from *Catharine* already quoted, and possibly, but by no means certainly, the character of the bridegroom too. From his surviving letters Tysoe Hancock appears to have been most tenderly disposed towards his wife, grudging her nothing. His worst trait was self-pity, but it is only fair to state that when these letters were written he did have much to pity himself for – ill health, financial insecurity, separation from his wife and daughter, uncertainty as to whether he would ever see them again. References to his sister and sister-in-law, and remembrance of the former in his will, as well as his deep care and solicitude for the welfare of his wife and child, show him to have been both affectionate and dutiful in his personal relationships. And he was able to gain and to maintain the sincere friendship of Warren Hastings. Possibly the case was that he was a good man but simply not to Philadelphia's taste.

For the first eight years of her marriage she had no child. Separated from all her natural ties both of place and of person, with no family to care for nor any work to fill her time, she must have led an empty existence, and the socializing in which she indulged for want of anything better to do held no appeal to her busy husband and produced some disagreement between them. It was not a satisfying life.

It was, however, probably preferable to her sister Leonora's. She never married, and all we know of her is that she was still alive in 1770, when Tysoe Hancock wrote to his wife; 'I think Mr Hinton has behaved very nobly to poor Leonora for he certainly had not the least obligation to do anything for her. My parts shall be always done by her with great cheerfulness. I am not the least surprised that Mrs Hinton left nothing to her.'[3]

From this it appears likely that Leonora had been placed as a companion to a Mrs Hinton, but what happened to her subsequently is not known. Possibly Tysoe Hancock and George Austen each spared a little from their income to maintain her. From the tone in Tysoe's letter, and from the complete lack of other references to Leonora elsewhere in the Austen correspondence, it may be inferred that she was simple-minded. Nothing else can explain the disparity between the exclusion of this sister from family visits and correspondence, and the warm attachment which existed for the whole of their lives between the other siblings, George, Philadelphia and their half-brother William.

Such exclusion of the feeble-minded from normal family life was to the Georgian way of thinking merely rational and realistic and, since the poor sufferer had his or her wants provided for, certainly not inhumane. The tragedy was to recur in the Austen history, as was the treatment it received.

In 1759, Philadelphia and Tysoe Hancock moved to Bengal, at the request of Clive, and either began or renewed their acquaintance with Warren Hastings. Three years previously Hastings had married Mary Buchanan, née Elliot, whose sponsors when she first came out to India as the bride of Captain Buchanan were the same gentlemen who had sponsored Philadelphia; possibly the two girls were friends. Captain Buchanan became a victim of the Black Hole of Calcutta. The marriage between his widow and Warren Hastings produced a son, George, in 1757, and a daughter, Elizabeth, the following year. Elizabeth lived only two months, however, and her mother never recovered fully from the birth, dying in July 1759.

The tragedy drew Philadelphia and Hastings together. She could supply the female sympathy he craved, and he was always to feel indebted to her from this time on. Hancock had not been Hastings' choice for the position of surgeon at Kasimbazaar, but he rapidly grew reconciled to him, and the two men of such disparate ages were soon embarking on a variety of commercial ventures in partnership – salt, timber, carpets, opium and rice being among the commodities they dealt in.[4]

In 1761, after eight years of childless marriage, Philadelphia gave birth to a daughter. She was given the name that Hastings' own daughter had briefly borne, and he stood godfather to her. Indeed, he was to take a warm and generous interest in her all her life, either from mere goodwill and gratitude towards her parents or from some closer tie. Certainly Philadelphia did not escape the breath of scandal. 'It is beyond a doubt that she abandoned herself to Mr Hastings,' wrote Clive to his wife four years later.[5] However, Tysoe Hancock appeared to entertain no such suspicions and was devoted to his little Betsy.

Hastings' legitimate child, George, had recently been sent home to England for the sake of his health. With no close relations of his own, Hastings chose to entrust his beloved son to George Austen. Whether Philadelphia loyally sang her brother's praises (although it was nine years since she had seen him), or whether Hastings valued his memory as a personal friend, is unknown. A bachelor with no home of his own seems a strange choice of guardian for a four-year-old boy; but there is every indication that George Austen cared tenderly for his little namesake.

Whilst Philadelphia had been establishing some sort of a life for herself in India, her brother had progressed steadily in his chosen clerical and academic career. In October 1753 George had been awarded a Smythe Exhibition, worth £10 a year for seven years. Instituted in the early seventeenth century by Sir Thomas Smythe, Governor of the East India Company and grandson of Sir Andrew Judde, there were six such exhibitions designed to enable old Tonbridgians to study at Oxford with a view to taking holy orders. The poverty of the parents and scholarship of the youth were both to be taken into account in awarding the exhibitions. George Austen's application made mention of the fact that he was an orphan, had obtained his degree and was already a Fellow of his college.[6]

The following year he obtained his MA and was ordained deacon in Oxford and simultaneously appointed to the positions of perpetual curate at Shipbourne (Henry Austen having obtained preferment to nearby Chiddingstone) and second master, or Usher as it was called, at his old school, Tonbridge.

To fulfil his new duties George was allowed leave of absence by his college, but he returned to Oxford each summer holiday and resided there as Fellow from July to September each year. Evidently he felt no scruples about leaving his Shipbourne parish unattended for such a length of time. Ordination to the priesthood came in 1755, at Rochester.

Gradually George was establishing a pattern that was to fit him comfortably for the rest of his life. These years at Tonbridge and Oxford as a young man without family responsibilities were a sort of prologue to his life's role as eighteenth-century parson and paterfamilias. He was sampling both teaching and ministering, and finding them both to his taste. Busy, hard-working, always alive to

honourable ways of augmenting his income, never shirking labour –
he yet avoided sacrificing the life of the spirit or intellect to mere
mercenary advantage.

During the period at Tonbridge he obtained his maintenance
from a variety of sources: the Usher's salary and free lodging; any
profit he could make out of the boarders at his house, of whom he
was allowed to take up to eight; an obligatory Christmas box of half
a guinea from the parents of each boy he taught;[7] his Smythe
exhibition; the money from his fellowship (in 1757 for example this
was £12.10s.4d.); and his stipend as perpetual curate of
Shipbourne. Insufficient to support a family, such means were
perfectly adequate for a single man living in school or college.

Among the pupils at Tonbridge was Motley Austen, and it is
pleasing to think that George was able to repay in some measure
the kindness of his uncle Francis, by teaching and watching over the
motherless boy. Indeed, perhaps George's presence there was the
deciding factor when Francis chose to send his son to Tonbridge,
rather than the more obvious Sevenoaks School.

In 1758, at the age of sixty, Francis Austen married the second of
his 'two wealthy wives', as his great-nephew explained:

Wickham estate and advowson was the property of a Mr Lennard some
ninety years ago. He left it to his widow for life, and afterwards to his
and her only child, a Miss Lennard. The widow was legally attacked by
the nearest male relations of the defunct – she flung the cause into the
hands of my Great-Uncle, old Frank Austen: he won the cause and the
wealthy widow's heart and hand. A very pleasing amiable woman she
was; I remember her about 1780, and thought her a great deal
handsomer than her daughter, who always lived with her and my Uncle
till her death. She (the widow) was the second wife, and mother of two
sons, John and Sackville.[8]

The latter took his name from the family at Knole.

George Austen resigned his post of Usher in 1757 and took up
full time residence again in Oxford at the beginning of the following
year. He became assistant chaplain of St John's College in March
1758 and proctor in 1759; the next year he was awarded his BD.
He is said to have been known as 'the handsome proctor' at this
period of his life. His miniature shows his bright, intelligent dark
eyes to have been perhaps his chief personal attraction – features

that were to be inherited by all his children, giving them a remarkable and pleasing family resemblance.

His future was now about to be decided for him, as the result of a long and somewhat complex chain of events. In November 1759, his cousin Henry Austen had been appointed to the living of Steventon, in Hampshire, which was in the gift of a distant cousin, Thomas Knight. Since Henry still retained the living of Chiddingstone, however, and continued to reside in Tonbridge, where he was courting a local girl, Mary Hooker, he never did duty at Steventon. This was left to the curate, who since 1754 had been Thomas Bathurst, another young relation of Thomas Knight.

In 1761 the living of West Wickham, which as we have seen was at the disposal of the second Mrs Francis Austen, and which was much more conveniently placed to be held in conjunction with that of Chiddingstone, only a horse-ride away, was offered to Henry – possibly on condition that he resign Steventon to his deserving younger cousin George. It would be more precise to say that Mrs Austen invited Henry to hold West Wickham until her own son, Sackville, for whom it was ultimately intended, took holy orders; but as Sackville was only just born, this 'keeping warm' period promised to last more than twenty years. Henry married his Mary in 1763, and of their five children, all were baptized at West Wickham and one was buried there.

Upon Henry's resignation of Steventon, it was offered by Thomas Knight to George Austen, who was instituted rector on 11 November 1761 – beginning, albeit hesitatingly, a forty-year association with the place. Perhaps George, like Henry before him, regretted that Steventon was not in Kent, for he did not reside there immediately. There is reason to suppose that he had rather hankered after West Wickham for himself and would have been better pleased had his cousin not always, through mere virtue of primogeniture, been offered first choice in every good thing that was going.

But however much he might have preferred a rectory in Kent, it was not possible for George to feel less than grateful that he had now a home and an income that were his for life, to replace those attaching to his fellowship which would have to be relinquished should he marry. At the age of thirty, with a secure livelihood and a mature judgement, 'the handsome proctor' was at liberty to look for a wife.

Who was this Thomas Knight who proved such a benefactor to George? He was related to him only by marriage, and then only distantly – but in those days family ramifications ran deep.[9]

It will be recalled that one of the brothers-in-law who harassed the widowed Elizabeth Austen was Stephen Stringer. By his wife Jane he had five daughters, of whom Mary married her cousin, John Austen of Broadford; Elizabeth married Edward Bathurst, a barrister (it was their son who was curate at Steventon); and Hannah married the very rich William Monke of Shoreham in Sussex, a relation of the Duke of Albermarle.

The only child and consequently the heiress of this couple was Jane Monke. In July 1729 she became the wife of Thomas May, formerly Thomas Brodnax, whose family home was at Godmersham near Canterbury in east Kent. The son of Colonel William Brodnax and his wife Anne May, Thomas had taken the arms and surname of May by Act of Parliament in 1727, on succeeding to the Sussex property of his mother's cousin Sir Thomas May, who died childless.

Enriched therefore from all sides, Thomas was able to rebuild the house at Godmersham in a very much grander style. Work began in 1732. He had the grace to embellish his fine new mansion with three shields of arms commemorating his triple fortune: those of Brodnax to the west, Monke to the east, and May quartered with Brodnax in the centre.

But, incredibly, there was to be yet another accession of wealth and change of surname. One of his second cousins was the formidable Elizabeth Knight of Chawton in Hampshire. This lady had inherited property at Steventon through her maternal grandfather, Sir Christopher Lewkenor, and at Chawton through her paternal grandmother, Dorothy Martin, née Knight. There had been Knights at Chawton since the reign of Edward II, and all who inherited the property took that surname. Not only Elizabeth herself, but both the men who married her, were obliged to take the name of Knight.

The two Hampshire estates in Elizabeth's possession were separated by some thirty miles. Chawton was considerably the better property, and it was there that she lived and ruled over her domains with a benevolent despotism. Childless and twice widowed, as she approached old age she fretted about what would happen to Chawton after her death. Deeply attached to the place and conscious of the duties as much as the dignities of her position, she looked for a successor who would care for the welfare and traditions of Chawton as sincerely as she did herself.

With such a prize, there was no shortage of eager and sycophantic claimants, but she fixed on her kinsman Thomas May because, as a landlord, he had proved himself conscientious, and as a wealthy man already, he was disinterested and honourable. Having settled the question of succession rather in the manner of her queenly namesake, Elizabeth Knight died in 1737, after a reign of thirty-five years.

What she had failed to consider was that Thomas May was, hardly surprisingly, extremely fond of his comfortable new dwelling at Godmersham and had no intention of living permanently elsewhere. So although he was by no means negligent of his Hampshire estates, he had never the close involvement with them that Elizabeth had desired. Indeed, from the time of her death, a hundred years were to pass before Chawton House enjoyed a settled family of owner-occupiers in residence again.

To accept this latest legacy it was necessary to adopt the name of Knight, and so in 1738 Thomas had to go to Parliament again for an Act to change his name for a second time. The obvious remark was made in the House: 'This gentleman gives us so much trouble, that the best way would be to pass an Act for him to use whatever name he pleases.'

To make his possessions more manageable, Thomas Knight sold his Sussex property and purchased instead Neatham and Colmer near Chawton. His several manor houses in Hampshire were let to tenants; he was truly a Kent man at heart, fulfilling at different times the duties of High Sheriff for the county and Member of Parliament for Canterbury.

Of the children born to him and his wife Jane, several died in infancy, and three daughters grew up but never married. The sole surviving son, another Thomas, was a contemporary of George Austen – he was educated at Eton and at Magdalen College, Oxford, where he received his MA in 1759. Afterwards he made the Grand Tour of Europe and on his return became Member of Parliament for New Romney, and as such one of the Barons of the Cinque Ports.

As George Austen gratefully accepted the living of Steventon, it was beyond his imaginings that one day all his benefactor's vast riches would devolve upon a son of his own.

4

We have now another girl

1764-76

On 26 April 1764, at Walcot church in the city of Bath, George Austen married Miss Cassandra Leigh.

His twenty-four-year-old bride was well chosen. In her distinguished good looks, her spry intelligence and her 'habit of active exertion and hardihood', she was a perfect match with himself – ideally suited by nature and upbringing to be the wife of a cultured but hardworking country parson. Intellectually his equal, if inevitably less learned, she possessed a ready wit and a realistic judgement, in useful counterpoint to his own mild manners and serenity of disposition.

Explaining the happiness of the marriage, a granddaughter described her as 'quick, lively, matter-of-fact, with excellent sense and a good education', and him as 'a most amiable and excellent man, a most highly accomplished scholar, with exquisite taste'. She also praised his 'gentleness of temper, and his steadiness of principle'.[1]

Born on 26 September 1739, Cassandra was one of the four surviving children of the Reverend Thomas Leigh and his wife Jane. Both sides of the family had Oxford connections. Jane Leigh was the daughter of Dr John Walker and sister of William Walker, Principal of New Inn Hall, while Thomas himself had been elected Fellow of All Souls so early in life that he was nicknamed 'Chick Leigh'. He was subsequently holder of the college living of Harpsden, near Henley-on-Thames, where Cassandra's childhood was spent.

In the early 1760s Thomas Leigh retired to Bath, with his wife and two daughters – perhaps with one eye on the marriage prospects of the latter, or perhaps on account of his health. Bath was

at the height of its popularity as a fashionable resort of health and
pleasure: its elegant terraces, crescents and squares in the process of
encroaching their golden stone on the seven green hills which
surrounded the medieval city. Hither well-bred people from all
parts of the kingdom flocked to enjoy the civilized pleasures of
urban life, to take the waters, to mix and meet one another and not
infrequently to find marriage partners.

Thomas Leigh died just a few months before the wedding of
Cassandra and George, and it is possible that the one event had
waited upon the other. In the strictly snobbish sense, George was
marrying above himself, and Thomas may have doubted whether
the surgeon's son was good enough for his daughter.

The Leighs were a family of aristocratic as well as academic
connections. A celebrated ancestor was Sir Thomas Leigh, the Lord
Mayor of London behind whom Elizabeth rode to be proclaimed
Queen. The younger son of Sir Thomas founded the branch of the
family who were to be ennobled into successive Lord Leighs and
whose seat was the magnificent Stoneleigh Abbey in Warwickshire.
Meanwhile the elder son married the daughter of the Earl of
Berkeley and settled at Adlestrop in Gloucestershire. Cassandra's
grandfather was his great-grandson, Theophilus Leigh, and her
grandmother was Mary Brydges, sister of the great Duke of
Chandos whose ostentatious display of wealth provoked the satire
of Alexander Pope.

Among the twelve children of Theophilus and Mary were two
younger sons who distinguished themselves at Oxford, Thomas and
Theophilus. Master of Balliol for half a century, Theophilus was
noted for his witticisms, many of which were preserved in the
memoirs of his wide acquaintance. He seems to have been a most
original character, given to saying the unexpected thing. Mrs Thrale
wrote of him to Dr Johnson: 'Are you not delighted with his gaiety
of manners and youthful vivacity now that he is eighty six years of
age?'[2]

Although it is possible that Cassandra first met George in Bath, it
is more likely that she came to know him in the Oxford home of
this uncle, where intellectual affinity counted for more than strict
social equality. Cassandra would have been there visiting her
cousins, Theophilus' daughters – another Cassandra, and Mary –

from whom the removal to Bath had recently separated her and with whom she was to remain on visiting terms all her life.

Four years after Cassandra's marriage her elder sister Jane married another clergyman, Edward Cooper. Two other sisters, Anne and Mary, had died in infancy.[3] Of her two brothers the younger, Thomas, was another of those sad imbeciles who was boarded out and rarely mentioned in the family again.

But Cassandra's elder brother, James, of whom she was very fond, as he of her, was more fortunate in every sense of the word, inheriting from his mother's side of the family a considerable estate, and doing so at such a young age that his life was early marked out for leisure and independence. He was only fourteen when his great-uncle Thomas Perrot died, bequeathing him the estate of Northleigh in Oxfordshire, on condition he took the arms and surname of Perrot. It was stipulated that James must reach the age of twenty-one before coming into his inheritance; as soon as he did so, he pulled down Northleigh, sold the land to the Duke of Marlborough and built for himself a mansion more to his liking, on land he had purchased in the parish of Wargrave, near Maidenhead in Berkshire.[4] He called his new house Scarlets.

In the same year that his sister Cassandra married George Austen, James Leigh Perrot took a wife. She was Jane Cholmeley, the twenty-year-old daughter of a barrister who had spent almost his entire working life on the island of Barbados. Jane had been born on the island and sent back to school in England at the age of six, never to see her immediate family again. When not at school she lodged with her Cholmeley relations, until she had the early good luck to captivate the wealthy James Leigh Perrot. Becoming mistress of Scarlets amply compensated for former deprivations, and the couple settled happily in their country home. When gout began to trouble James, he also bought a house in Bath, where they spent part of each year.

Meanwhile, the financial circumstances in which the young Austens began *their* married life were much less comfortable. To the marriage settlement, dated 15 March 1764, George brought certain freehold lands situated in Tonbridge, and the third part of certain messuages in the same town, expectant on the death of Susan Austen, his stepmother. His two sisters, of course, were entitled to the other two thirds. Cassandra's property likewise depended on the death of her mother, and consisted of some leasehold houses in Oxford and the sum of £1,000.[5]

As it happened, both ladies died in 1768 – Mrs Leigh on 29 August at Steventon. The Tonbridge properties were sold by public auction for £1,285, those in Oxford for £1,065. Together with the legacy of £1,000, this money was invested in South Sea Annuities.

This investment represented practically the only equity which the Austens were to possess during the whole of their married lives, and the only estate – by then somewhat devalued – which they were able to leave their children. George Austen worked hard to supplement his income, and his wife was an excellent manager, but with a large growing family it was constantly swallowed up, and there was no doubting that any daughters they had would be dowerless, and any sons would have to make their own ways in the world. As their brother-in-law Hancock wrote, 'I fear George will find it easier to get a family than to provide for them.'

But George and Cassandra Austen themselves possessed a capacity for contentment, and a cheerful confidence in the future, far removed from Tysoe Hancock's habitual pessimism. If they only provided their children with a happy home life, with good food and fresh air, with physical and mental liberty, with affection, stimulation and, above all, a sound education (and in their father they would have a ready-made teacher), the young parents were willing to put their trust in God for the rest.

And anyway, between them, were they not possessed of a goodly number of very rich relations?

Steventon Rectory might have been habitable to the bachelor curate Bathurst, but as it stood it was not a fit residence for a lady, or for the child that was soon expected. While it was being improved for them at Thomas Knight's expense, the Austens occupied the neighbouring parsonage-house of Deane, where the first three of their children were born and baptized.

This accommodation was available to them through the further generosity of Francis Austen, who, not to be outdone by Thomas Knight, had purchased the right of presentation to the two livings adjoining that of Steventon – Ashe and Deane – in order that the first which happened to fall vacant might make a useful addition to his nephew's income at a period when his family expenses would probably be increasing.

Deane it was which eventually George came to hold, in tandem with Steventon. But this was not until 1773; on the Austens' arrival in Hampshire the Rector of Deane was William Hillman. A wealthy man, he chose to live in some splendour at Ashe Park (and to quarrel, incidentally, with the squire of his parish, Mr Harwood), which was how the Austens came temporarily to occupy Deane Rectory.

The three children born there were all boys. First came James, on 13 February 1765, named in honour of Cassandra's rich brother. The next son, born on 26 August 1766, was given his father's name, and Tysoe Hancock was asked to stand godfather to him. Then came Edward, on 7 October 1767, called after another brother-in-law, Edward Cooper.

The original parsonage-house at Steventon was described by a later Austen as 'a few miserable rooms of lathe and plaster'. She implies that it was completely rebuilt for the Austens, but whether so or merely 'improved' and extended, by the time they took occupation in 1768, 'the parsonage consisted of three rooms in front on the ground floor, the best parlour, the common parlour and kitchen; behind were Mr Austen's study, the back-kitchen and stairs; above were seven bedrooms, and three attics. The rooms were low-pitched, but not otherwise bad.'[6]

This rather grudging estimation must have accorded with the general nineteenth-century view that the Georgian improvers still had not got it right, since the rectory was pulled down and rebuilt yet again, sixty years later. To modern eyes, however, there is a homely simplicity and fitness for purpose about Steventon Rectory as sketched and painted during the Austens' occupancy. Four-square and solid, with symmetrically placed windows – latticed below, dormers above – and a central front door sheltered by a trellised porch, it looks like a house that was easy to love and that, for all its plainness and lack of luxury, possessed every comfort that unostentatious people could require.

To the south of the house was an old-fashioned garden where vegetables and flowers intermingled, bounded by a thatched mud wall and some fine elms. Beyond this was the home farm, source of abiding interest to both master and mistress, as well as of abundant

fresh food for the family, and some profit. The Austens employed a
farm bailiff, but George supervised the wheat, the hay and the pigs,
while Cassandra's responsibilities included the poultry and the
dairy. Theirs was a life rooted in the country and the seasons.

Cassandra, for all her cleverness and polish, was not too fine a
lady to interest herself in the practical management of the
household, or to take an active part in its day-to-day running. At
various periods of her life we chance to hear of her doing the family
mending in the drawing-room, and not putting it away even if
visitors called; planting and digging up her own potatoes, clad in a
green workman-like smock; and rising from her bed in the middle
of the night to walk a mile and a half along a pitch-black, muddy
country lane to help a daughter-in-law in childbirth. Such doings
appear to have astonished (and somewhat ashamed) her Victorian
descendants, trapped in their sheltered drawing-room lives.

Partly it was that Cassandra was a child of her time, when nature
still had to be wrestled with and when none but the very, very rich
were exempt from the effort; before the realities of life could be
hidden behind folds of drapery and plush, or a plethora of servants.
And partly that she was, as an individual, enormously energetic and
capable. One feels that had she had the misfortune to be born a
hundred years later, she would have suffered the frustrations of a
Florence Nightingale, and many another. Happily Cassandra's
abilities and her lot in life slotted together to perfection, so that, in
exercising the one, she had the satisfaction of fulfilling the other.

She found time to educate seven children until they reached the
age of classical studies, when their father took over; she wrote
charades and light verse for family entertainment and kept up
correspondence with numerous relations; she mixed with ease
among the neighbouring gentry and even aristocracy. The Austens'
circle of such acquaintance was large; a considerable portion of life
was occupied by social pleasures, or social duties. Because the
landowner, Thomas Knight, lived in a distant county and rented
out Steventon Manor to the Digweed family, George Austen, as his
representative, enjoyed a higher standing in the neighbourhood
than many a contemporary parson.

Not that George any more than Cassandra was ever idle, or
above his work. He began at Steventon as he intended to go on,
making a copy in his own neat handwriting of one of the church

registers from its beginnings in 1738, which he then continued for the period of his incumbency.[7] In addition to his clerical and pastoral duties, and the supervision of the farm, he took in to board and educate a succession of pupils, the sons of gentlemen – chiefly in order to augment his stipend, but also to keep in his hand at teaching until his own boys were old enough to start on Latin and Greek.

In the first year of the Austens' marriage, the Hancocks had returned to England, anxious for the health and education of their daughter Betsy, then aged four. The voyage home cost them £1,500. Warren Hastings sailed with them, arriving only to find his little son dead of a 'putrid sore throat', to the grief, not only of himself but of George and Cassandra Austen, who had loved him like a child of their own.

Tysoe Hancock hoped to retire permanently to England but before long made the unhappy discovery that it was impossible to keep his family in the style he would wish on the interest of the moderate fortune he had painfully accumulated in India. By the summer of 1768 he felt himself obliged to return to that country in an effort to make more money. Now a rather elderly man, and never in good health, as he sailed away he had little hope of ever seeing his wife and child again.

They corresponded regularly, but with letters taking months in passage, news was stale and advice given in the knowledge that it would arrive too late to be acted upon. Henceforward Philadelphia could, without breach of conjugal duty, go her own way, and the inference is that she relished her new liberty. Beyond the occasional obligatory expression of regret, there is nothing to indicate that either wife or daughter missed him. Unlike his brother-in-law, whose 'benevolent smile'[8] cheered all who knew him, poor Mr Hancock seems to have been a constant purveyor of doom, which accorded ill with Philadelphia's zest for living and little Betsy's frivolous sense of fun.

In order that Betsy should benefit from the good masters available in town, Philadelphia took a house in Bolton Street, where she and her daughter lived with the help of two servants they had brought back from India, Peter and Clarinda. For part of the year she also rented a cottage in Surrey.

It is from Bolton Street, where George was evidently visiting his sister, that the first of a series of letters written by the Austens to Susanna, wife of William Walter, is dated. The Walters now had five children: Weaver, who went to Cambridge and was ordained; William, and George, both of whom at the appropriate age went out to Jamaica under the patronage of their uncle Sir George Hampson; James, and Philadelphia.

In this correspondence Mrs Austen refers to her practice of putting out each successive infant 'to nurse' with a village woman, which seems to have taken place at about three months and lasted roughly a year. In view of the high level of child mortality, and the inevitably inferior hygiene and living conditions of the labouring classes, it seems the Austens ran a terrible risk; but it was a risk that paid off, for their children came back remarkably hardy, and not one was lost at an early age.

But to temper their pride and delight in all the others, there was increasing anxiety about little George. His afflictions, acknowledged in this series of letters, were unhappily proving him to be another in the tally of family mental defectives. It is not clear to what extent he remained with his foster-parents, or how much of his childhood was spent at Steventon Rectory. In 1770 he appears to be away, and in 1772 to be at home; perhaps there had been an improvement in his condition, but if so it was not enduring, for he makes no further appearance in the family record and was boarded out for the remainder of his long life.

Of all the letters which George and Cassandra Austen must have written in the course of their lives to their various far-flung relations, it is happy that this little group,[9] at least, survives. It affords a charming glimpse of the family in its infancy, and of the day-to-day concerns which occupied the parents; and it culminates in the announcement of an event which was to result in the giving of more pleasure to more people all over the globe and down through the centuries than the writer of the letter could possibly have imagined.

The Bolton Street letter is dated 2 May 1770:

Understanding from my brother that he is soon to leave you for some weeks, I cannot help for many reasons wishing that you would pass the time of his absence at Steventon; I need not say you will make your sister Austen and myself very happy by such a visit, and I hope the change of air and place may be of some little service to you. I shall return home on Saturday sennight next, and as a chaise will hold you and I and Philly we may travel very commodiously. You must not refuse my request and I dare [say] you will not, I shall therefore expect you in town and will add no more at present than my love to George, James and Philly.

George wrote next from Steventon on 8 July:

The day I received your kind letter, for which accept my thanks, your sister set out for London to enter on her office of nurse in ordinary, and the same post likewise brought me intelligence that she was too late for the ceremony she intended being present at, for Mrs Cooper was happily brought to bed last Sunday morning of a boy and both well; he came, it seems, rather before his time, and of course the babe is a small one, but however very like to live; you may possibly have heard this from sister Hancock, but lest you should not I could not help mentioning it as I am sure the news will give you great pleasure. I don't much like this lonely kind of life, you know I have not been much used to it, and yet I must bear with it about three weeks longer, at which time I expect my housekeeper's return, and to make it the more welcome she will bring my sister Hancock and Betsy along with her. You may depend on it that if it is tolerably convenient we will return your visit another summer, and I say we, for I certainly shall not let my wife come alone, and I dare say she will not leave her children behind; I am much obliged to you for your kind wish of George's improvement. God knows only how far it will come to pass, but from the best judgement I can form at present, we must not be too sanguine on this head; be it as it may, we have this comfort, he cannot be a bad or a wicked child. I beg my love to my brother and tell him I shall hope to see him at Steventon this summer, though your impatience prevented his coming in the spring. The only news I have to send you, and the chief subject of conversation in our neighbourhood is the quarrels of Mr Hillman and Squire Harwood, they have commenced actions against each other and seem to promise good sport for the lawyers. My love to Weaver, George, James and Philly. My James joins me in this; he and his brothers are both well, and what will surprise you, bear their mother's absence with great philosophy: as I doubt not they would mine and turn all their little affections towards those who were about them and good to them; this may not be a pleasing reflection to a fond

parent, but is certainly wisely designed by Providence for the happiness
of the child.

Cassandra Austen then took up the correspondence, writing on
26 August:

I received your kind letter in town and should have thanked you for it
before now, but was so hurried while I was in town that I deferred it till
I got home, and then Mr Austen told me he had wrote to you very
lately, and so I thought I would stay a little longer. I was not so happy
as to see my nephew Weaver, suppose he was hurried in time as I think
everyone is in town; 'tis a sad place, I would not live in it on any
account: one has not time to do one's duty either to God or to man. I
had the pleasure of leaving my sister tolerably well and the child quite
so; they are now moved into the country: I hope change of air will
enable her to pick up her strength. We talk of going there and to
Scarlets in about three weeks' time, and shall be absent a full month. I
shall take both my boys with me ...

Sister Hancock staid with us only a few days, she had more courage
then you had, and set out in a post-chaise with only her little Bessy, for
she brought neither Clarinda or Peter with her, but believe she sincerely
repented, before she got to her journey's end, for in the middle of
Bagshot heath the postilion discovered that he had dropped the trunk
from off the chaise. She immediately sent him back with the horses to
find it, intending to sit in the chaise till he returned, but was soon out of
patience and began to be pretty much frighted, so began her walk to the
'Golden Farmer' about two miles off, where she arrived half dead with
fatigue, it being in the middle of a very hot day. When she was a little
recovered she recollected she had left all the rest of her things (amongst
which were a large parcel of India letters, which she had received the
night before, and some of them she had not read) in the chaise with the
door open, she sent a man directly after them and got them all safe and
after some considerable time the driver came with the trunk and
without any more misfortune got to Bolton Street about nine o'clock.
She is now settled in her cottage near Cobham, Surrey. The letters
brought good account both of my brother Hancock and Mr
Hastings ...

What luck we shall have with those sorts of cows I can't say. My
little Alderney one turns out tolerably well, and makes more butter
than we use, and I have just bought another of the same sort, but as her
calf is but just gone, cannot say what she will be good for yet ...

The next letter from Cassandra is dated 9 December:

Thank God we are all very well, and my little Neddy's cough seems entirely to have left him: he was so well that I ventured to leave him with his maid for a few days, while we went to Southcote, where we found my sister, Dr Cooper and the little boy quite well, I had not seen her before, since I left them in town last July. We went on Monday and returned last night and found Neddy quite well. The day after Christmas day we are to go to my brother Perrot's for about ten days, but there I shall take Neddy as well as Jemmy, there being no little ones there to catch anything bad of us ...

My poor little George is come to see me today, he seems pretty well, though he had a fit lately; it was near a twelvemonth since he had one before, so was in hopes they had left him, but must not flatter myself so now. I find my sister Hancock has been much incommoded by the waters, so fancy she won't be sorry when the time comes for her going to town, which I think she says is to be next month. I have a great notion she will soon be tired of Byfleet, as it seems to be a very bad winter place.

After a rather larger gap between her children than usual, Cassandra was again pregnant when she wrote this letter. Tysoe Hancock, on hearing the news from Philadelphia, responded gloomily: 'That my brother and sister Austen are well, I heartily rejoice; but I cannot say that the news of the violently rapid increase of their family gives me so much pleasure; especially when I consider the case of my godson, who must be provided for without the least hopes of his being able to assist himself.'

Henry Thomas was born on 8 June 1771 and was the first of the family to be baptized at Steventon. As the name of Mr Knight, George's benefactor, it is rather remarkable that 'Thomas' had failed to appear earlier and was even now relegated to second place. It was a well-established Leigh name, too; but perhaps it reminded Cassandra too painfully of her afflicted brother. Henry, of course, was named after George's cousin.

Little Henry was a toddler, and the next baby on its way, before Cassandra wrote again to Susanna Walter, on 8 November 1772:

My little boy is come home from nurse, and a fine stout little fellow he is, and can run anywhere, so now I have all four at home, and some time in January I expect a fifth, so you see it will not be in my power to take any journeys for one while ... Thank God we are all well in health; I begin to be very heavy and bundling as usual. I believe my sister

Hancock will be so good as to come and nurse me again, for which I am
sure I will be much obliged to her, as it will be a bad time of the year
for her to take so long a journey.

The Austens' fifth child was born on 9 January 1773 and was a
most welcome daughter in that very masculine household of father,
sons and pupils. She was given the names Cassandra Elizabeth; her
godmother was Elizabeth Leigh, a cousin of her mother. As Mrs
Austen had anticipated, she was assisted at the birth by Philadelphia
Hancock, and it was on hearing of this that Tysoe Hancock wrote in
the same vein as before: 'I must own myself sorry to hear of your
going to Steventon, and for the occasion of it: I fear George will
find it easier to get a family than to provide for them; pray give my
love to them.'

Cassandra wrote again on 6 June 1773:

We will not give up the hopes of seeing you both (and as many of your
young people as you can conveniently bring) at Steventon before the
summer is over; Mr Austen wants to show his brother his lands and his
cattle and many other matters; and I want to shew you my Henry and
my Cassy, who are both reckoned fine children. I suckled my little girl
through the first quarter; she has been weaned and settled at a good
woman's at Deane just eight weeks; she is very healthy and lively, and
puts on her short petticoats today. Jemmy and Neddy are very happy in
a new play-fellow, Lord Lymington, whom Mr Austen has lately taken
the charge of; he is between five and six years old, very backward of his
age, but good tempered and orderly: he is the eldest son of Lord
Portsmouth who lives about ten miles from hence. – My sister Cooper
has made us a visit this spring, she seems well in health, but is grown
vastly thin – her boy and girl are well, the youngest almost two years
old, and she has not been breeding since, so perhaps she has done. We
expect my brother and sister Perrot to-morrow for a fortnight, we have
not seen them near a twelvemonth. I have got a nice dairy fitted up, and
am now worth a bull and six cows, and you would laugh to see them;
for they are not much bigger than Jack-asses – and here I have got
jackies and ducks and chicken for Phylly's amusement. In short you
must come, and, like Hezekiah, I will shew you all my riches.

The next letter is dated 12 December 1773:

I thank you much for your kind letter, and the receipt for potato cakes,
I have not yet found time to try it, but dare say they will be very nice
and light ...

I thank God we are all quite well and my little girl is almost ready to run away. Our new pupil, Master Vanderstegen, has been with us about a month, he is near fourteen years old; he is very good tempered and well disposed. Lord Lymington has left us, his mamma began to be alarmed at the hesitation in his speech, which certainly grew worse, and is going to take him to London in hopes a Mr Angier (who undertakes to cure that disorder) may be of service to him.

The 'rapid increase' that Mr Hancock so much deplored continued. Francis William was born on 23 April 1774: he is the 'last boy' referred to in Cassandra's letter dated 20 August 1775 and was named (again somewhat belatedly, one would have thought) after kind uncle Francis Austen and William Walter.

Many thanks for your good wishes; we are all, I thank God, in good health, and I am more nimble and active than I was last time, expect to be confined some time in November. My last boy is very stout, and has run alone these two months, and he is not yet sixteen months old. My little girl talks all day long, and in my opinion is a very entertaining companion. Henry has been in breeches some months and thinks himself as good a man as his brother Neddy, indeed no one would judge by their looks that there was above three years and a half difference in their ages, one is so little and the other so great. Master Van is got very well again, and has been with us again these three months; he is gone home this morning for a few holidays. The wheat promises to be very good this year, but we have had a most sad wet time for getting it in, however, we got the last load in yesterday, just four weeks after we first began reaping. I am afraid the weather is not likely to mend for it rains very much today, and we want dry weather for our peas and oats; I don't hear of any barley ripe yet, so am afraid it will be very late before harvest is over.

The next letter was written by George on 17 December 1775:

You have doubtless been for some time in expectation of hearing from Hampshire, and perhaps wondered a little we were in our old age grown such bad reckoners but so it was, for Cassy certainly expected to have been brought to bed a month ago: however last night the time came, and without a great deal of warning, everything was soon happily over. We have now another girl, a present plaything for her sister Cassy and a future companion. She is to be Jenny, and seems to me as if she would be as like Henry, as Cassy is to Neddy. Your sister thank God is pure well after it, and sends her love to you and my brother, not forgetting James and Philly.

Jane (we never hear her called Jenny again) was named not only for her godmother, the wealthy second wife of old Francis Austen, but for her two aunts, Mrs Cooper, and Mrs Leigh Perrot, and in memory of her maternal grandmother. Having got into the habit of giving their children two names, it is rather curious that the Austens could think of no second one for Jane.

Concurrent with this correspondence is the sequence of letters[10] written by Tysoe Hancock to his wife from Calcutta, of which he made and kept careful, numbered copies. The extracts given below are either highly illustrative of his character or interesting on the subject of Betsy's education and future prospects.

At first the parents seemed agreed that it would be of benefit to Betsy to educate her in France. On 28 November 1769 Hancock wrote: 'Your sentiments of Betsy's going to France are exactly the same with mine, and I most heartily wish that you may have received so much encouragement as to be now in France and situated to your mind.' But by 7 September of the following year he was writing, 'Your letter mentions how little encouragement Mrs Mitchel gives you in your intention of going to France; I am sorry for it, as Betsy will soon be too old to risk her picking up the levity or follies of the French.'

This plan was shelved, and Philadelphia took a cottage in Byfleet, Surrey, in which she intended to live for part of the year. Her husband wrote on 18 March 1771: 'What effect your removal from London may have on Betsy's education you are the best judge; as she will probably (unless I should live long) have but little more to depend upon, it is of very great consequence; I am certain that you will readily give up the pleasure of the country for a month or two more than you proposed in the year, should you find it necessary to the child's better education. You do not mention her having begun to learn music.'

Possibly Philadelphia protested that the country cottage was an economy measure, for on 28 August he replied, 'I am a little surprised at your proposal that I should limit your expenses; did I ever accuse you of extravagance? Live comfortably and make yourself easy; take care of your own and the child's health. The improvement of Betsy gives me great pleasure, as I am on the subject, I must request you would get for her the best writing master to be procured by money and that she as soon as possible may begin to learn arithmatic – Her other accomplishments will be ornaments to her, but these are most absolutely necessary.'

Towards the end of the year Warren Hastings was appointed Governor of Bengal. 'This government will prove to him a crown of thorns,' prophesied Hancock. Hastings himself wrote to Philadelphia on 31 January 1772 from Fort St George, where he was about to embark for Bengal. The closing paragraph of his letter reads: 'Kiss my dear Bessy for me, and assure her of my tenderest affection. May the God of goodness bless you both! Before I close my letter let me gratify my present feeling by telling you that great as my obligations have been to you, you have increased them by a recent and disinterested instance of your friendship for me in your last letter. My next shall remind you of the subject. Till then, adieu, my dear and ever-valued friend. Remember me, and make my Bessy remember and love her godfather and her mother's sincere and faithful friend.'

Hancock's next letter mentioned that, 'Mr Hastings is arrived this day February 17th. He is thin and very grave; but in good health.' Two months later, with some satisfaction perhaps, he described to Philadelphia the woman with whom Hastings was having an affair and who was to become, after her divorce, his second wife:

'She is about twenty six years old, has a good person and has been very pretty, is sensible, lively and wants only to be a greater mistress of the English language, to prove she has a great share of wit. She came to Calcutta last October ... I should not have mentioned Mrs Imhoff but I knew everything relative to Mr Hastings is greatly interesting to you.'

Was it Warren Hastings' residence in Calcutta, or the presence of this rival for his affection, which induced Philadelphia to suggest, now, that she and Betsy join Mr Hancock there? It appears to have been the only time she made such a suggestion. Her husband replied at length on 23 September.

I will now give you my opinion concerning Betsy's coming to India. You say she will be so well accomplished at twelve as many are at fifteen years of age. I believe she will, but let me ask you if it be possible she would have any degree of judgement at that tender age. Her arrival here would be at that period of life when she will naturally form to herself false notions of happiness, most probably very romantic, the disappointment of which may greatly embitter the rest of her days. You know very well that no girl, though but fourteen years old, can arrive in India without attracting the notice of every coxcomb in the place, of whom there is very great plenty at Calcutta with very good persons and no other recommendation. You yourself know how impossible it is for a young girl to avoid being attached to a young handsome man whose address is agreeable to her. Debauchery under the polite name of gallantry is the reigning vice of the settlement. I scarcely know to whom I would wish my daughter married were she of a proper age; which she will not be for some years, as I am certain nothing shortens a woman's days so much as her being married when too young. The danger and inconvenience of a voyage to India are very great, but there is [a] still much greater objection, I mean the possibility of your dying in passage. If such an unhappy accident should happen, is it possible to reflect on the situation of the child without horror? It is very probable from my many dangerous ailments, to which the climate is most unfriendly, that I may not live to receive you. Paint to yourself the distresses you must suffer in a place where you are now a perfect stranger. Do not imagine there is the least of that friendly hospitality which was formerly so remarkable here; its place is supplied by self interest. I am certain no argument can ever induce me to give my consent to the introduction of my daughter to so lewd a place as Bengal now is, were all other objections removed.

I am glad to hear that Betsy has a good ear to music; if she attempts the guitar at all I beg she may have the best masters; otherwise she will get a wrong method of fingering which can never afterwards be rectified. As I hold myself to be a perfect judge of this matter, I shall not submit to have my opinion controverted, but insist on your compliance with my request.

On 11 December there was rare good news to convey:

What I am going to tell you will I am sure make you very happy. A few days ago Mr Hastings under the polite term of making his goddaughter a present made over to me a Respondentia bond for 40,000 rupees to be paid in China. I have given directions for the amount, which will be about £5,000, to be immediately remitted home to my attorneys. Let me caution you not to acquaint even the dearest friend you have with his circumstance. Tell Betsy only that her godfather has made her a great present, but not the particulars; let her write a proper letter on the occasion.

Despite this good fortune, Hancock continued in his pessimistic vein, writing to his wife on 29 March 1773:

You gave me great pleasure by saying that you are not of a melancholy disposition in your last letter; you have often told me that I am inclined to take the gloomy side of any question: I believe you are right in your judgement, but I am sorry to say that all my gloomy predictions have proved true: I have great reason to fear they will continue to do so. You seem to entertain great hopes of my returning to England soon: an event scarcely possible which you must acknowledge when you recollect what I formerly wrote you concerning my circumstances, and at the same time consider that twenty thousand pounds will afford no more than seven hundred per annum, which is much less than what we spent when we lived with the utmost frugality.

In fact he calculated that during the time they had been all together in England, a period of $3\frac{1}{2}$ years, they had spent £5,366.

'My not returning ought to be a comfort to you,' he wrote, 'as it prevents your having constantly before your eyes a wretch who can convey no idea but that of misery and sickness.' In the same style he responded to his wife's offer to send him a new waistcoat: 'I should be the most ridiculous animal upon earth could I put any finery upon such a carcase as mine worn out with age and diseases.' And when the waistcoat arrived nevertheless, 'I admire it very much; it is really elegant, but much, much too fine for my wearing; nothing can be more infamously ridiculous than an old carcase dropping into the grave with gout, gravel and many other disorders, wrapped and clothed in finery.'

Just once he reproached her about their financial situation, on 3 September 1773: 'You know how incapable you are of managing such complicated affairs. Oh Phila, had a very few of these hours which were formerly spent in dissipations been employed in acquiring the necessary and most useful knowledge of accounts, happy it would have been for us both. I do not mention this to excuse my not sending you money as you desire; for I will do in this as I have ever done since our connection, comply with your request.'

But two months later he was blaming a third person for the muddle in his affairs – Francis Austen, who acted for him in England: 'I am perfectly resolved to take my affairs out of your

Uncle's hands by the next despatch; it would be cruelty to you not to do it, for by his management I may be a fourth time ruined.' Considering Francis' track record, we may doubt it.

The details of Betsy's upbringing continued to occupy him; she was twelve when he wrote: 'I am glad that Betsy is happy with her horse; my intention in giving it to her is more on account of her health than to please her. I am convinced that riding is the most wholesome exercise in the world, and though I think fox-hunting not only dangerous but in some degree an indecent amusement for a lady, yet I wish my daughter to sit gracefully on a horse and to ride without fear.'

The following year the question of French arose again. He wrote on 26 August 1774: 'Undoubtedly your method of teaching Betsy French by giving her a French companion is the shortest – I can have no objection to it, till the child may be old enough to imbibe the spirit of intrigue, without which no French woman ever yet existed.'

In the same letter he told Philadelphia: 'Represent to yourself that I have lived many months without entertaining any company or ever going into company, that I have confined my diet to one dish a day and that generally salt fish or curry and rice, that I eat neither breakfast or supper: and all this that I may save a little for you.'

His trials were nearly over. In March of the following year Warren Hastings made Betsy the gift of a further £5,000. George Austen and Hastings' brother-in-law John Woodman were appointed trustees. Much relieved, Hancock wrote to Philadelphia: 'The interest of this money will produce to you while you shall live nearly £400 per annum; and the whole, should she marry, be a large fortune to Betsy after your death. As you and the child are now provided for, I may venture to tell you that I am not well enough to write a long letter ... Give my love and blessing to Betsy and remember me to Clarinda.'

Tysoe Saul Hancock died on 5 November 1775, aged sixty-four. It was the beginning of June 1776 before the news reached Philadelphia, who was supported by the presence of George and Cassandra, by chance staying with her at the time.

John Woodman wrote from London to Warren Hastings: 'I am sorry to find Mr Hancock's affairs are in so bad a situation: all his

effects will not more than clear his debts here.' Unable to provide
financially for his wife and daughter, by his will Hancock
bequeathed to Betsy 'a miniature picture of her mother painted by
Sharp and set in a ring with diamonds round it which I request she
will never part with as I intend it to remind her of her mother's
virtues as well as of her person'.

5

Great connections and expectations

1777-90

Restless, adventurous Philadelphia had once before entertained the idea of residing in France. Now economy chimed with inclination to make her revive the plan. It was possible to live more elegantly on the Continent than in England on a small income, and the benefits to Betsy would be considerable, enabling her to acquire a poise and a polish, not to mention a fluency in the French language, of value in themselves and highly advantageous on the marriage market.

That Betsy was now, in her sixteenth year, old enough to imbibe that 'spirit of intrigue' her father had wished her guarded from, was evidently no deterrent. Armed with introductions from their London friends, Philadelphia and her daughter – who henceforward adopted a more fashionable and ladylike diminutive of her name, and called herself Eliza – set out for the Continent in 1777. The faithful Clarinda went with them.

Lingering over their journey through Germany and Flanders, they were in Brussels in June 1778 and in Paris the following year. From there Philadelphia Hancock composed a letter[1] to her old but by now somewhat estranged friend Warren Hastings. There is a kind of hurt pride in her writing, a sense that she knew she had been paid off by his very generous gift to her daughter. The letter, dated 3 March 1780, begins:

'After a silence of so many years on your part, nothing should have prevailed on me to have troubled you with another letter but my earnest desire to have some information concerning Mr Hancock's affairs, and to whom can I apply but you? Let me therefore conjure you by your friendship for his memory and by those uncommon marks you have given of it to his family not to refuse me this request the last perhaps I shall ever make you ...'

Several people, including the servant Clarinda, had entrusted their money to Mr Hancock's care, and the purpose of Philadelphia's letter was to enquire whether there was any chance of repaying them. She then went on to describe a five-month illness Clarinda had suffered, necessitating three operations and the attendance of four doctors, concluding:

This has been a most unfortunate affair on all accounts and has cost me more anxiety than I can describe; the expense too has been and is still very heavy, it could not have happened at a worse time, but of that I shan't complain if the poor faithful creature can be restored to me.

I once thought to have confined this letter to business but knowing your heart as I know it and being convinced that in spite of appearances it is not changed for your friends, I cannot refuse you the satisfaction of knowing my daughter, the only thing I take comfort in, is in perfect health, and joins me in every good wish for your happiness – you may be surrounded by those who are happy in frequent opportunities of showing their attachment to you, but I will venture to say not one among them who can boast a more disinterested steady and unshaken friendship for you than that which for so many years has animated and will ever continue to animate the breast of, dear sir, your obliged friend Phila. Hancock.

Eliza now began to write to her half-cousin of much the same age as herself, the other Philadelphia in the family. Her correspondence with Philadelphia Walter, which was to endure for the next twenty years, affords us fascinating glimpses of French high life, of her Steventon relations and of her own attractively transparent personality: frivolous and flirtatious, perhaps, but lively, affectionate, open-hearted and generous too.

Our stay in Paris has been much longer than we at first intended [she wrote on 16 May]. Clarinda's long and dangerous illness has been in part the cause; she is at present much better and we think of soon moving; it will not be however in a great way; we propose spending the summer, or at least a part of it a small distance from this place, at a lady's country house about 20 miles from Paris. The country is pretty and I do not doubt spending some time agreeably, besides I shall not be sorry to quit for a little while the dissipations of the town, and to enjoy a little quiet. Paris is however the city in the world best calculated to spend the whole year in; it is not like London, where the summer months are insupportable. The walks and rides here, the amusements which continue the whole year round, the almost continual residence of people of fashion, all these things render it at all times agreeable.

We were a few days ago at Versailles and had the honour of seeing their Majesties and all the royal family dine and sup. The Queen is a very fine woman, she has a most beautiful complexion, and is indeed exceedingly handsome; she was most elegantly dressed, she had on a corset and petticoat of pale green lutestring covered with transparent silver gauze, the petticoat and sleeves puckered and confined in different places with large bunches of roses, and an amazing large bouquet of white lilac. The same flower, together with gauze, feathers, ribbon and diamonds intermixed with her hair. Her neck was entirely uncovered and ornamented by a most beautiful chain of diamonds, of which she had likewise very fine bracelets; she was without gloves, I suppose to show her hands and arms which are without exception the whitest and most beautiful I ever beheld. The King was plainly dressed, he had however likewise some fine diamonds. The rest of the royal family were very elegant, and indeed I may say the court of France is, I believe, upon the whole one of the most magnificent in all Europe.

There is perhaps no place in the world where dress is so well understood and carried to so great a perfection as in Paris, and no wonder it should be so since people make it the chief business and study of their lives. Powder is universally worn, and in very large quantities, no one would dare to appear in public without it. The heads in general look as if they had been dipped in a meal-tub. Hats likewise (which are called English but which do not bear the least resemblance to those of our nation) are much the fashion. The hair is cut in shades, not worn high at all. It was with reluctance, I conformed to the mode in this article, as my hair was very long on my arrival, and I was obliged to have it cut to half its length; but what will not all powerful fashion effect? and so much for the modes ...

I believe you will be troubled to read my letter as it is most abominably wrote, indeed I have been in such a hurry as I am obliged to go out and be dressed and send my letter before noon, that I hardly know what I have wrote. By the same gentlemen who are so good as to take charge of this, I send my picture in miniature done here to my Uncle G. Austen. He will most likely show it you. Pray tell me in your next if you think it at all like what you remember me. It is reckoned here like what I am at present. The dress is quite the present fashion and what I usually wear.

Philadelphia replied promptly to this letter, and Eliza wrote again
on 27 June:

I am happy my account of Versailles could afford you any amusement.
You wrong her Majesty however when you suppose her entirely
indebted to art for her complexion. She has really a beautiful natural
one; rouge is, I acknowledge, much worn here, but not so universally as
you imagine; no single ladies ever make use of it, and were they to do it
would be much disapproved of. When once married I own in general
they make themselves ample amends for this denial ...
   Mama has had a letter from my uncle G. Austen which informs us
the picture is safe arrived. I own I had not reflected on your distance
from Steventon, when I said you would see my picture ...
   You do not at all approve, then, of my settling in this country. I have
friends here as much for it as you can be against it. Was any such
arrangement however to take place it would not banish me from
England. I should certainly pay you a visit. How should you like it, my
dear, was I to introduce *un cousin françois* to your acquaintance?
Should you receive him very cordially, or are you persuaded like most
of our nation that nothing good can come from France? With all this,
be assured I only joke and am far from having any serious thoughts of
marrying in this country; no, no, you will most likely see me return to
England without having changed my name. True it is as I have already
said I have friends here who are so good as to desire to keep me with
them, and who therefore do everything in their power to prevail on me
to accept offers which would attach me to this country ...
   It will perhaps amuse you to have an account of a new manner of
dressing hair which is lately all the taste. The hind hair instead of being
turned up or plaited as usual, is curled at the ends, fastened with a small
comb, and suffered to wave over the shoulders in three or four large
curls. The hair in general is worn exceedingly low before; young people
who have good hair in an undress go without a cushion or anything to
raise it: hats of all sorts are worn, chip in particular of all colours
something in the form the English gentlemen wear them of a morning.
Large gold earrings, that is to say a ring with a single drop in the form
of a pear are much the *ton*: they are not at all like what I have seen in
England. In short was I to give you an account of all the different
modes I should never have done. They have more taste and more
whims in this country than in any other ...

Eliza's story is now taken up within two letters from John
Woodman to Warren Hastings. In a postscript to his letter dated 7
August 1781, he wrote: 'Mrs and Miss Hancock are yet in France

and likely to continue there, the young lady being on the point of marriage with a French officer which Mrs Hancock writes is of good family with expectation of good fortune, but at present but little. Her letter was to Mr Austen and self on the subject and she seems inclined to give up to them the sum which was settled on her for life, and wants the money to be transferred into the French funds which we have thought prudent for her sake to decline, and Mr Austen is much concerned at the connection which he says is giving up all their friends, their country, and he fears their religion.'

And on 26 December he wrote: 'Mrs Hancock ... is in France where I believe she intends to end her days, having married her daughter there to a gentleman of that country, I am afraid not very advantageously, although she says it is entirely to her satisfaction, the gentleman having great connections and expectations. Her uncle Mr Austen and brother don't approve of the match, the latter is much concerned at it; they seem already desirous of draining the mother of every shilling she has.'

Jean Gabriel Capotte, Comte de Feuillide, was ten years older than Eliza, proprietor of an estate at Gaboret in Gers, and a Captain of Dragoons in the Queen's Regiment. That it had been no love-match, on her side at least, but one with which Eliza was nevertheless highly satisfied, is evident from a letter she wrote to Philadelphia Walter from Paris on 27 March 1782:

As I know the affection you have borne me, I doubt not but you will expect and wish I should give you some account of myself. My Uncle Austen acquainted you with my marriage soon after its taking place. This event, the most important one of my life, was you may imagine the effect of a mature deliberation, and as it was a step I took much less from my own judgment than that of those whose councils and opinions I am the most bound to follow, I trust I shall never have any reason to repent it; on the contrary, if I may be allowed to judge of the future from the past and present I must esteem myself the most fortunate of my sex. The man to whom I have given my hand is everyways amiable both in mind and person. It is too little to say he loves, since he literally adores me; entirely devoted to me, and making my inclinations the guide of all his actions, the whole study of his life seems to be to contribute to the happiness of mine.

My situation is everyways agreeable, certain of never being separated from my dear Mama whose presence enhances every other blessing I enjoy, equally sure of my husband's affections, mistress of an easy fortune with the prospect of a very ample one, add to these the advantages of rank and title, and a numerous and brilliant acquaintance, amongst whom I can flatter myself I have some sincere friends, and you will unite with me in saying I have reason to be thankful to Providence for the lot fallen to my share; the only thing that can make me uneasy is the distance I am from my relations (among whom I beg you to be assured there is no one I regret more than yourself) and country, but this is what I trust I shall not have always to complain of, as the Comte has the greatest desire to see England, and even to make it his residence a part of the year ...

What you tell me of your brother James gives me great pleasure. I suppose he is much grown since I saw him; I do not think we should either of us know one another again, I fancy we are both a little altered since the time when he made verses on me in which he compared me to Venus and I know not what other Divinity, and played off fireworks in the cellar in honour of my charms. This happened as you may recollect in a visit I paid to Tonbridge some years ago ...

As for me I have danced more this winter than in all the rest of my life put together. Indeed I am almost ashamed to say what a racketing life I have led, but it was really most unavoidable, Paris has been remarkably gay this year on account of the birth of the Dauphin. This event was celebrated by illuminations, fireworks, balls etc. The entertainment of the latter kind given at court was amazingly fine.

The Court of France is at all times brilliant, but on this occasion the magnificence was beyond conception. The ball was given in a most noble saloon, adorned with paintings, sculpture, gilding etc, etc. Eight thousand lights disposed in the most beautiful forms showed to advantage the richest and most elegant dresses, the most beautiful women, and the noblest Assembly perhaps anywhere to be beheld; nothing but gold silver and diamonds and jewels of all kinds were to be seen on every side. Her Majesty, who is handsome at all times, had her charms not a little heightened by the magnificence of her adjustment. It was a kind of Turkish dress made of a silver grounded silk intermixed with blue and entirely trimmed and almost covered with jewels. A sash and tassels of diamonds went round her waist, her sleeves were puffed and confined in several places with diamonds, large knots of the same fastened a flowing veil of silver gauze; her hair which is remarkably handsome was adorned with the most beautiful jewels of all kinds intermixed with flowers and a large plume of white feathers.

The king had a gold grounded coat entirely embroidered with jewels, the Comte d'Artois and the Princesses were dressed with equal magnificence, and the persons of the Court by no means fell short of

them. In short altogether it was the finest sight I ever beheld, and I
cannot give you a better idea of it than the one which struck me at the
time, which was this: it answered exactly to the description given in the
Arabian Nights entertainments of enchanted palaces ...

Eliza's next letter was written more than a year later, on 1 May
1783:

I have some idea you may have my Uncle and Aunt Austen with you at
present, as in a letter Mamma has received from them they mention
their intention of paying you a visit about this time. They were to set
out on a little tour at Easter and to take Kent in their way ...
    I had some hopes of seeing England this autumn but I fear it will not
be in my power as I cannot well avoid making a journey into Guienne
before I leave France, the Comte's mother who inhabits that province
and who is far advanced in years having the greatest desire to see me:
my first project must therefore be subordinate to this latter and cannot
take place before it has been put into execution.'

The French aristocracy was still doing its best to provoke the rest
of the population into revolt. After mentioning a new opera-house
capable of mounting a production which included 'a troop of five
hundred horse', Eliza continued:

The gay world have lately been taken up with Longchamps, a kind of
fashion which I will endeavour to give you some account of.
Longchamps is a monastery situated in the Bois of Boulogne, a
delightful wood I have already mentioned to you, in the environs of
Paris. It was formerly the custom to go thither to hear vespers the three
last days of Passion week, but devotion has given place to vanity.
Everybody now goes to Longchamps not to say their prayers but to
show their fine clothes and fine equipages. They do not even enter the
convent but content themselves with parading in the Avenue that leads
to it in the style of the coaches in Hyde Park of a Sunday: their
appearance is however much finer for the number and magnificence of
the carriages are incredible. Most people have new and elegant ones on
this occasion with four or six fine horses, as many lackeys as possible
behind, sometimes to the number of eight, and often running footmen.
    The *élégants* or fashionable young men are in general either on
horseback or in open carriages. The Queen and Royal family are
generally there, and what much contributed to the beauty of the show
this year several of the princesses made their appearance in open
calashes drawn by six horses ...
    Whilst I am speaking of fashionable follies I cannot avoid

mentioning the changes in the *toilette*. The hair instead of being turned up behind has been worn for some time past in two or three clubs, but it is said this mode will not continue as it does not meet with her Majesty's approbation. Large yellow straw-hats such as I believe you may have seen worn by the hay-makers are universally adopted. They are called *à la Marlborough* as well as everything else of late. This great general certainly could never have imagined that so many years after his death his name would have been borrowed to set off all the frippery of dress, ribbands, silk. All is *à la Marlborough* and the prevailing colour is *la mort de Marlborough* which is a kind of Pompadour shot with black …

The cause of this Marlborough rage is the most curious in the world. The Dauphin's nurse was one day singing an old ballad to put him to sleep called the Death of Marlborough. The Queen happened to hear her, was pleased with it, and of course the whole court had it by heart the next day. The people who like to ape their betters followed their example. A pantomime appeared on the subject, verses without number were composed, and the fashion became general in a very short time …

On 23 June 1779 Cassandra Austen gave birth to her eighth and last child, Charles John. However, as Steventon Rectory gained one inmate, it lost another, for the very next month, at the early age of fourteen and having been educated entirely by his father, James matriculated at Oxford. Fortunate he was to be awarded a fellowship to St John's College under the ancient custom of Founder's Kin. The statutes of the college provided for the maintenance of six fellows who could prove their descent, not from Sir Thomas White, the founder, for he had been childless, but from his sister Mary.

Common among Oxford colleges, though non-existent at Cambridge, the custom persisted until Victorian sensibilities began to find it offensive, and abolished it by Act of Parliament in 1861. Nepotic and unfair though it appeared to them and must appear to us, the idea of the founders seems to have been that, since they were depriving their bodily heirs by diverting their fortunes into the creations of the colleges concerned, it was only just to compensate them in perpetuity in this way.

Founder's Kin had to matriculate, like any other student, but their fellowships were then theirs to enjoy for life, if they chose, only to be relinquished upon marriage.

To claim this privilege, James had to prepare a pedigree establishing the line from White through Leach, Dale, Perrot, Walker and Leigh.[2] Thus, by being his mother's son, James was able to become a fellow of his father's college – one of the lucky breaks that seemed to attend the Austens at all the really important junctures of their lives.

For the next six years George Austen made his eldest son a twice-yearly allowance of between £10 and £30[3] – according, presumably, to what he could afford. It was little enough for a young man to have as spending money, particularly a young man surrounded by others of his age many of whom were the scions of great families enjoying affluence and independence. The temptations for the poorer students to get into debt must have been considerable, but James was honest, sensible and sober, and no such trouble arose.

The education of the younger boys continued to occupy the rector of Steventon. The fifth son, Frank, in old age composed a memoir of his life which begins with a pleasing testimonial to the merits of his father as a teacher. Referring to himself – somewhat disconcertingly – in the third person throughout, Frank says he was 'educated at home under the immediate superintendance of his father, who was admirably calculated to the instruction of youth as he joined to an unusual extent of classical learning and a highly cultivated taste for literature in general, a remarkable suavity of temper and gentleness of manners'.[4]

James, whose degree in 1783 was the first such fruit of his father's efforts, and Henry, who was if anything even more precocious, were the two brothers most able to profit from George Austen's classical scholarship. Frank admits he was 'never remarkable for facility in acquiring languages', and Edward too made only moderate progress. He had, according to his mother, 'a most active mind, a clear head, and a sound judgment' but no academic bent.

Happily a stroke of fortune occurred to give a different turn to Edward's destiny, and a perfect outlet for his particular talents. Perhaps it was during a tour of Kent which the Austens made at Easter 1783 that Edward was first introduced to the Knights of Godmersham; he was then fifteen and a half.

Old Thomas Knight, George's benefactor, had died two years previously and had been succeeded by his son of the same name, who in 1779 had married Catherine Knatchbull. The Knatchbulls were an old Kentish family whose fine estate at Mersham-le-Hatch had been in their possession for three hundred years. Catherine was the daughter of a younger son of the family, Wadham Knatchbull, Rector of Chilham in Kent; at the time of the marriage she was twenty-six and her husband forty-five. In their 'pleasant mansion and situation', the couple enjoyed 'happiness, peace of mind and health',[5] but after four years of marriage there was no sign of a child to inherit the properties of Godmersham and Chawton.

In old age Henry Austen recalled from his childhood a conversation between his parents on the morning that they received a letter from Mr and Mrs Knight inviting Edward to spend his holidays with them. Fearful of the effects on the boy's studies of being many weeks away from Steventon, Mr Austen began to express his doubts, but his less unworldly wife 'used no arguments, and suggested no explanations' – in front of the children, at least – 'but merely said, "I think, my dear, you had better oblige your cousins, and let the child go".'[6]

Henceforth all Edward's holidays were spent with the Knights, who in course of time offered to adopt him as their heir. It was an admirable arrangement to all concerned. For the Austens, thanks to Cassandra's wisdom and foresight, this was not only one son well provided for but certain advantage to the whole family, for they were confident that Edward's generous heart and early ties of affection would prompt him to help his brothers and sisters whenever he could; whilst for the Knights it was the best way to see Godmersham pass after their own time into the right hands – to a person whose ideas they had helped to mould and who by nature they knew to be as equable and upright as themselves. Whether Edward had been selected on the basis of suitability of character or simply by his position in the family order – the eldest son James being tacitly regarded as heir to the Leigh Perrots, another wealthy childless couple – the Knights had obtained the best 'man of business' as his mother called Edward.

Meanwhile the two little girls of the family had been sent to school – twice – in a reversal of normal eighteenth-century practice, whereby money was spent on male education and daughters left to scramble themselves into a little learning at home. Perhaps George Austen felt less well qualified to teach girls, or perhaps their room was wanted for paying pupils. At any rate, when in 1783 Mrs Austen's sister Mrs Cooper decided to send her only daughter Jane to a school kept by her sister-in-law Mrs Cawley, widow to a former Principal of Brasenose College, it was agreed at Steventon that Cassandra and Jane should go too. Not yet eight, Jane was really rather young to go away, but she could not endure the idea of any separation from her beloved elder sister.

After a few months the little school moved from Oxford to Southampton, where it was soon struck by an epidemic of 'putrid sore throat', perhaps diphtheria. Both mothers rushed down to retrieve their suffering daughters; all the girls recovered, but tragically Mrs Cooper caught the infection and died.

Undaunted, the Austens next sent their daughters to the Abbey School at Reading kept by the old-fashioned Mrs La Tournelle, who had a cork leg, a kind heart, an assumed French name and very little in the way of intellectual attainment. Cassandra and Jane remained with her very happily for a couple of years, but since they could evidently educate themselves better by being given the run of their father's library, the benefit of his knowledge and taste, and the stimulation of their clever brothers' conversation, they were brought home, to read, write, sketch, sew and play in the place they loved best, Steventon Rectory.

For a student of character such as Jane, there was education of another kind in the observation of her brother James, who, at home in the vacations, was already showing signs of his lifelong propensity to fall in love. In 1785 the object of his admiration was Lady Catherine Powlett, a daughter of the sixth Duke of Bolton, of Hackwood Park, an aristocratic neighbour of the Austens. Twenty-year-old James wrote a sonnet[7] to her, and another, equally romantic, to the woman he fell in love with the following year, Charlotte Brydges. She was the sister of Anne Lefroy, whose husband was rector of Ashe, and of Egerton Brydges, a young man of literary pretensions who for a time rented the vacant rectory at Deane from George Austen in order to be near the Lefroys.

Of course James was not in a financial position to propose

Broadford House, Horsmonden, Kent, showing Georgian additions
to the Tudor house

Francis Austen, by Ozias Humphrey

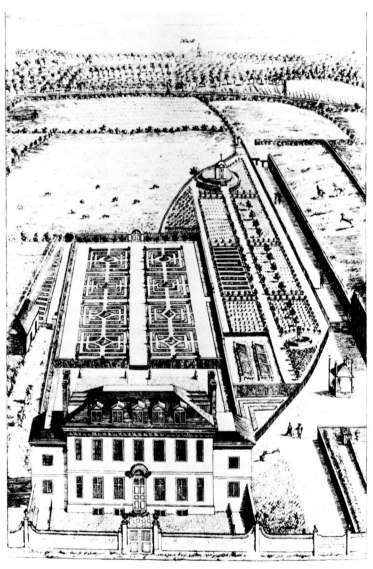

The Red House, Sevenoaks, in 1719, home of Francis Austen from
1743 to his death in 1791

Philadelphia Hancock, Jane
Austen's aunt, from a
miniature by Sharp

The Reverend George
Austen

Steventon Rectory, sketched by Anna Lefroy

Eliza Hancock, later Comtesse de Feuillide
and Mrs Henry Austen

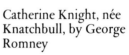

Thomas Knight the
younger, Edward Austen's
benefactor, by George
Romney

Catherine Knight, née
Knatchbull, by George
Romney

Godmersham Park,
Kent

Edward Austen, later
Knight, painted in
1789

Elizabeth Bridges, later Mrs
Edward Austen

The Reverend James Austen

Anne Mathew, later Mrs
James Austen

The frigate *Unicorn* with Charles Austen aboard in action against *La Tribune* 8th June 1796

Jane Leigh Perrot, Jane
Austen's aunt

Captain Francis Austen at
the time of his marriage in
1806

Stoneleigh Abbey, Warwickshire, seat of the Leigh family

marriage to either of his loves; relieving his feelings in poetry had to suffice.

When Eliza wrote to Philadelphia on 17 January 1786, she had important news to give:

> It is now in agitation whether I shall or shall not set out for England next June; my husband votes for the affirmative but I am not myself quite determined from some reasons which you will be a better judge of, when I have let you into a little piece of *family history*, namely my dear friend that it is now two months since I have had a prospect of giving you an additional relation; should a son be in *store* for M. de Feuillide, he greatly wishes him to be a native of England for he pays me the compliment of being very partial to my country, but I own I have some repugnance to undertaking so long a journey in a situation so unfit for travelling ...
>
> On my arrival in England I shall supplicate your aid for the brat I mean to introduce to you, and which I am sure I shall be much at a loss what to do with, as never was a being less qualified, nor one who had less taste for the cares of a nursery than your humble servant.

On 23 May, she wrote from Guyenne:

> My visit to England mentioned in my last is no longer a matter of doubt, and indeed notwithstanding my reluctance to quitting home in my present situation and my still greater regret at a separation from the Comte de Feuillide at a period when I could the most have wished for his presence, I purpose setting out on this long projected journey the 30th or 31st of this month; but in all probability I shall not reach England before the latter end of June or beginning of July since it will be impossible for me to avoid making some stay in Paris. I mean to spend a very few days in London, and if my health allows me, immediately paying a visit to Steventon, because my uncle informs us that Midsummer and Christmas are the only seasons when his mansion is sufficiently at liberty to admit of his receiving his friends.
>
> You will easily imagine how much my thoughts and time must be taken up at this moment since independent of the fatigue and bustle inseparable from the preparations of such an expedition as I am about to undertake, my spirits are constantly agitated and alternately raised and depressed by the idea of once more meeting friends that are very dear to me, and quitting the best of husbands whose extreme concern at parting with me in my present situation adds greatly to my feelings on this occasion. Had it been possible for him to have quitted the important works he is carrying on in this part of the world, he would

certainly have accompanied me, but he has promised to join me as soon as his affairs can permit him to do so. I must endeavour therefore to make myself easy *en attendant* and look forward only to the satisfaction I promise myself in being once again an inhabitant of a country which the presence of my friends and family must ever endear to me.

I feel however somewhat mortified at making what may be termed my first appearance amongst persons whose approbation I am so ambitious of, in a situation so thoroughly unfavourable to good looks as that I at present *labour under*; and my vanity is not a little hurt at the idea of presenting myself in my native land after so long an absence with a visage of a comfortable length at all times, but which my having grown extremely thin since I have aspired to the honour of being a mother, has added about an ell to, whilst my waist as you may suppose much more increased in circumference than even my face in length; add to all this a very tolerable share of tan with which I have contrived to heighten the native brown of my complexion, during a two year residence in the country.

Notwithstanding all these disadvantages I yet flatter myself my friends will receive me kindly, since after all the qualifications of the heart and not those of the exterior are what are most to be attended to.

George Austen must have had an abundance of pupils just then, if he could receive Eliza and her mother only during the scholastic holidays at Christmas and Midsummer. Of his own sons, only Charles was still a pupil.

Henry had completed his studies with a most satisfactory display of brilliance and was only waiting for another Founder's Kin fellowship to fall vacant before joining James, who was now studying for his MA at Oxford. Meanwhile Frank, three years Henry's junior, had already left home. Whilst Henry was intended for a clerical career like James, there was a limit to the number of livings that might be mustered in the family, and the younger sons had to consider other professions. Brave, enterprising, hardy and above all practical, Frank chose, or had chosen for him, the Navy.

Nobody in the family network had influence in naval circles, and in those days promotion depended as much on influence as on merit; but that could not be helped. The life ahead was a challenging prospect for the twelve-year-old boy who entered the recently established Royal Naval Academy at Portsmouth in April 1786. The inevitable hardships of a life at sea, aggravated by the brutality of the Navy as it was then, and the superadded dangers of war, would test his courage and endurance to the full.

Eliza's endurance must have been called for in the eight hundred or so mile journey, including a Channel crossing, which she made in an advanced state of pregnancy, in poorly sprung carriages on bad roads. Her husband must have had an extraordinarily strong desire for his heir to be born in England to justify his encouraging her to submit to such an ordeal, particularly as he could not escort her himself. She was, however, attended by her mother – these two were never separated – and the long journey was accomplished in safety, though surely not in comfort.

Almost immediately upon her arrival in London, Eliza gave birth to a son on 25 June, some month or six weeks prematurely. He survived, though he was always sickly. She called him Hastings – a difficult name, one would have thought, for his own father to pronounce.

At least the early birth saved her from appearing in front of her relations for the first time in nine years in the unflattering stage of late pregnancy. It is not known when she was reunited with the family at Steventon; perhaps as she had missed Midsummer she had to wait until Christmas (in which case her tan would have disappeared too!)

The following spring Henry was invited to spend a month in Orchard Street, where the Comtesse and Mrs Hancock had taken a house. Though he was not quite sixteen, this most handsome, extrovert and amusing of all her cousins had evidently already aroused Eliza's interest. Doubtless he made her laugh and, with his extraordinary precocity, had already at his command sufficent gallantry to express most agreeably the admiration such a sophisticated and fascinating woman inspired in him. Possibly he had for as long as he could remember felt attracted to the piquant little face in the miniature his father owned. Now, in their cousinly relationship, which allowed a certain amount of licence, there rapidly developed a pleasurable frisson of sexual awareness.

The meeting between Eliza and Philadelphia Walter did not take place until Eliza had been in England for more than a year, when they took a holiday together in Tunbridge Wells. Happily Philadelphia's first impressions are preserved in a letter which she wrote to her brother James on 19 September 1787:

I came home on Tuesday from Penshurst to which place my aunt and madame brought me the day before. I had spent ten days with them at the Wells. They came here and stayed one night when I returned with them and lived a gayer life than I ever before experienced, enjoyments for every hour; for a few first days I was miserable, and would have given anything to have got away to any retired corner, but their very great kindness, affection and attention to me soon reconciled me to the dissipated life they led and put me in mind that every woman is at heart a rake ...

You will expect my opinion of my friends. To begin with my Aunt, I do not know a fault she has – so strictly just and honourable in all her dealings, so kind and obliging to all her friends and acquaintance, so religious in all her actions, in short I do not know a person that has more the appearance of perfection.

The Countess has many amiable qualities, such as the highest duty, love and respect for her mother; for whom there is not any sacrifice she would not make, and certainly contributes entirely to her happiness: for her husband she professes a large share of respect, esteem and the highest opinion of his merits, but confesses that love is not of the number on her side, though still very violent on his: her principles are strictly just, making it a rule never to bespeak anything that she is not quite sure of being able to pay for directly, never contracting debts of any kind.

Her dissipated life she was brought up to – therefore it cannot be wondered at, but her religion is not changed. Her partiality to me was very great. I do not believe she has a thought she would wish to keep from me, though I took the liberty of differing in opinion on many subjects: we often kept up a dispute for some time. They were very desirous of keeping me longer with them, and as they had some thought of going for a week in Brighton wished me to be of the party, but I declined it upon my mother's account.

They go at Christmas to Steventon and mean to act a play *Which is the Man?* and *Bon Ton*. My uncle's barn is fitting up quite like a theatre, and all the young folks are to take their part. The Countess is Lady Bob Lardoon in the former and Miss Tittup in the latter. They wish me much of the party and offer to carry me, but I do not think of it. I should like to be a spectator, but am sure I should not have courage to act a part, nor do I wish to attain it: it's agreed I am to spend some time with them in Town after Christmas: they do not go abroad till the spring.

Eliza was determined that her Fanny Price-like cousin should have some fun despite herself, and wrote on 16 November in the most encouraging terms, refuting all possible objections and concluding:

Your accommodations at Steventon are the only thing my aunt Austen and myself are uneasy about, as the house being very full of company, she says she can only promise you 'a place to hide your head in' but I think you will not mind the inconvenience, I am sure I should not to be with you. Do not let your dress neither disturb you, as I think I can manage it so that the *Green Room* should provide you with what is necessary for acting.

We purpose setting out the 17th of December, so that if you can come to us in Orchard Street the day before, I shall be happy to have you go down with me, and when once the plays are over, if you are determined to quit us, we will consent however reluctantly to part with you. I assure you we shall have a most brilliant party and a great deal of amusement, the house full of company and frequent balls. You cannot possibly resist so many temptations, especially when I tell you your old friend James is returned from France and is to be of the acting party.

Philadelphia could resist, however, and Eliza was obliged to write again on 23 November, with a touch of impatience: 'I will only allow myself to take notice of the strong reluctance you express to what you call *appearing in public*. I assure you our performance is to be by no means a public one, since only a select party of friends will be present ... You wish to know the exact time which we should be *satisfied with* and therefore I proceed to acquaint you that a fortnight from New Year's Day *would do*, provided however you could bring yourself to act, for my aunt Austen declares "She has not room for any *idle young* people".'

Philadelphia Walter did not go to Steventon, but the others managed perfectly successfully without her. James Austen returned from his visit of pleasure in France to be ordained deacon at Oxford on 10 December, whence he repaired to Steventon and to his part in the theatricals. Besides acting, he wrote two prologues and an epilogue for performance on stage. To Georgian minds, there was nothing either incongruous or improper in the fact that James sandwiched a moment in his life of high seriousness and dedication between two episodes of leisurely amusement. Unlike the Victorians, the Georgians had the happy knack of wearing their religion lightly; it was no less fundamental to their lives for that.

On 14 July the following year James was appointed curate of Stoke Charity, a village a few miles to the south-west of Steventon; but he continued to reside largely in college, where Henry now joined him, his plans to accompany his beautiful cousin on her return to France thwarted, as Philadelphia Walter explained to her brother in the second of the following two letters. The first, written on 21 April 1788 at Orchard Street, refers to the trial of Warren Hastings, which lasted from 1787 to 1795 and which surely was a source of sorrow and distress to the Austen family:

I never experienced so thorough a racketing life and had no idea that it could be equal to what I now find it. This is the third week I have been in town. Our mornings are spent in a ridiculous sort of calls from one door to another without ever being let in, shopping and by way of a treat to me sometimes a walk in Kensington Gardens ... My dear friends are all affectionate kindness to me, and do everything for my pleasure. I have even the coach with a coronet always at my command, but when able to find my way I prefer walking ...

The opera we went in style to, as we sat in Mrs Hastings' box. I have had the pleasure of seeing a great deal of the Hastings ... I have drunk tea at her house in St James' Place – everything more elegant than I ever saw before. Mrs Hastings I admire exceedingly, very affable, lively and pleasing ...

I have once been to the trial which, because an uncommon sight, we fancied worth going to, and sat from 10 till 4 o'clock, completely tired, but I had the satisfaction of hearing all the celebrated orators, Sheridan, Burke and Fox. The first was so low we could not hear him, the second so hot and hasty we could not understand him, and the third was highly superior to either as we could distinguish every word, but not to our satisfaction as he is so much against Mr Hastings whom we all here wish so well.

In the summer Eliza with her mother and child paid a visit to Ramsgate in Kent. On 23 July Philadelphia Walter wrote to her brother:

Madame de F. and my aunt are returned to London. Poor little Hastings has had another fit; we all fear very much his faculties are hurt; many people say he has the appearance of a weak head: that his eyes are particular is very certain: our fears are of his being like poor George Austen. He has every symptom of good health, but cannot yet use his feet in the least, nor yet talk, though he makes a great noise continually ...

Henry Austen is sadly mortified at one of the Fellows of St John's choosing to marry or die, which vacancy he is obliged to fill up, and would totally prevent his accompanying his cousin to France, which was particularly harped upon both sides ...

Yesterday I began an acquaintance with my two female cousins, Austens. My uncle, aunt, Cassandra and Jane arrived at Mr F. Austen's the day before. We dined with them there. As it's pure nature to love ourselves I may be allowed to give preference to the eldest who is generally reckoned a most striking resemblance of me in features, complexion and manners. I never found myself so much disposed to be vain, as I can't help thinking her very pretty, but fancied I could discover *she* was not so well pleased with the comparison – which reflection abated a great deal of the vanity so likely to arise, and so proper to be suppressed.

The youngest (Jane) is very like her brother Henry, not at all pretty and very prim, unlike a girl of twelve: but it is a hasty judgment you will scold me for. My aunt has lost several fore-teeth which makes her look old: my uncle is quite white-haired, but looks vastly well: all in high spirits and disposed to be pleased with each other.

The letter was finished the following day:

I continue to admire my amiable likeness the best of the two in every respect: she keeps up conversation in a very sensible and pleasing manner. Yesterday they all spent the day with us, and the more I see of Cassandra the more I admire – Jane is whimsical and affected. They all say a violent deal about my visiting Steventon next Christmas ...

The visit of George Austen with his wife and daughters to Kent was the last occasion on which he was to see his kind uncle Francis, who was now ninety years of age. Did the two men indulge themselves in talking over old times? Francis could reflect with just pride on the long and steady advancement of the family during his lifetime, as it recovered from the blow of 1704 when he was an impressionable six-year-old.

He had seen his eldest son grow even richer than himself. Motley had married in 1772 Elizabeth, daughter and co-heiress of Sir Thomas Wilson, who brought with her a large dowry, and promise of more to come. The couple had acquired the first batch of their eleven children – including a daughter, Jane Austen, just four months younger than her second cousin of the same name – by 1777, when the death of Sir Thomas occurred. But his father-in-law's estate was not the only source from which Motley was enriched at this time.

He had christened his eldest son Francis Lucius, Lucius being the

name of the then Viscount Falkland, whose wife Sarah was
Motley's godmother. She was a connection on his mother's side of
the family and had been chosen for the honour of sponsoring
Motley by the astute Francis Austen, who knew that her fortune
was hers to dispose of as she pleased. It had come to her from her
father, Thomas Inwen MP, a hop merchant and member of the
Brewers' Company. Sarah had married firstly and most gloriously
Henry Howard, Earl of Suffolk, and secondly and most
disinterestedly the penniless Viscount Falkland, whom, we are told,
she had loved since she was a child.

In her will, proved on 22 June 1776, after specific bequests
amounting to more than £40,000, she left 'all and every of my
Manors Messuages Farms Rents and Real Estates ... in the Counties
of Kent, Essex, Middlesex, Bedfordshire, Cambridgeshire, Lin-
colnshire or elsewhere in the Kingdom of England unto Francis
Motley Austen Esquire, grandson to the late Thomas Motley
Esquire of Beckenham on trust to sell after the death of Viscount
Falkland'.[8]

Henry Austen was many years later to refer to this dryly as 'a
small legacy of £100,000' – guesswork on his part, surely, but a
goodly inheritance by anybody's standards.

As for Francis' younger sons, John had been 'rather a wild youth',
according to Philadelphia Walter. He had joined the army against
his father's wishes and had gone abroad leaving Francis Austen
'rather displeased, but his wrath is subsided by a long absence, and
his utmost wishes have lately been to live till his return.' The return
of John from the East Indies coincided with the George Austens'
visit to Kent and the bells of Sevenoaks were rung in celebration.
John had risen to the rank of Major and was now married with two
sons of his own.

Sackville, Francis' other son by his second marriage, had died
two years before this visit, leaving a wife but no children. He had
taken over the coveted living of West Wickham in 1780 from his
cousin the Reverend Henry Austen, who had suddenly become
converted to Unitarianism (it is said after talking to a labourer over
his garden hedge) and retired to spend the rest of his life in
Tonbridge.

After two years' absence from her home and husband, Eliza was preparing to return to them both – and to introduce her son to his father. Before she left England she had one last meeting with her two attractive Austen cousins. From Orchard Street she wrote to Philadelphia Walter on 22 August:

I am sure the meeting our Steventon friends gave you great pleasure, they talked much (for they dined with us on their way back to Hampshire) of the satisfaction their visit into Kent had afforded them. What did you think of my uncle's looks? I was much pleased with them, and if possible he appeared more amiable than ever to me. What an excellent and pleasing man he is; I love him most sincerely as indeed I do all the family. I believe it was your first acquaintance with Cassandra and Jane ...

I am but just returned from an excursion into Berkshire, during which we made some little stay at Oxford. My cousin James met us there, and as well as his brother was so good as to take the trouble of showing us the lions. We visited several of the colleges, the museum etc and were very elegantly entertained by our gallant relations at St John's, where I was mightily taken with the garden and longed to be a fellow that I might walk in it every day, besides I was delighted with the black gown and thought the square cap mighty becoming. I do not think you would know Henry with his hair powdered and dressed in a very *tonish* style, beside he is at present taller than his father ...

As Eliza returned to France, her young cousin Frank completed his course of studies at the Naval Academy, having outstripped most of the other pupils there. The Commissioner of the Dockyard wrote to the Admiralty desiring their Lordships to permit him to join the *Perseverance*, of thirty-six guns, which was being fitted up at Portsmouth to form part of the Squadron under the direction of Cornwallis, recently appointed Commander-in-Chief of India, and recommending him for promotion at soon as he had served his time as a Volunteer – the lowliest rank in the Navy.

A copy of the Commissioner's letter was read out to the other students as an incitement to emulate his 'diligence, exertion and orderly behaviour'.[9] Frank may have been unable to compete with the brilliant Henry and James in classical learning, but in his own field he was proving that he could excel.

As he prepared to put to sea in December 1788, he received from his father a letter couched in serious, even formal language, and yet thoroughly affectionate and sincere – the letter of a caring parent concerned to set his child on the right path for life. Frank was to keep and treasure it always.

From this 'memorandum', as he called it himself, and from all the other tributes to his exceptionably lovable nature, George Austen emerges as fulfilling his daughter Jane's idea of the perfect father – neither negligent of his children's morals like Mr Bennet nor repressive of their emergent personalities like Sir Thomas Bertram. No wonder they all turned out well.

My dear Francis, – While you were at the Royal Academy the opportunities of writing to you were so frequent that I gave you my opinion and advice as occasion arose, and it was sufficient to do so; but now you are going from us for so long a time, and to such a distance, that neither you can consult me or I reply but at long intervals, I think it necessary, therefore, before your departure, to give my sentiments on such general subjects as I conceive of the greatest importance to you, and must leave your conduct in particular cases to be directed by your own good sense and natural judgment of what is right ...

The little world, of which you are going to become an inhabitant, will occasionally have it in their power to contribute no little share to your pleasure or pain; to conciliate therefore their goodwill, by every honourable method, will be the part of a prudent man. Your commander and officers will be most likely to become your friends by a respectful behaviour to themselves, and by an active and ready obedience to orders. Good humour, an inclination to oblige and the carefully avoiding every appearance of selfishness, will infallibly secure you the regards of your own mess and of all your equals. With your inferiors perhaps you will have but little intercourse, but when it does occur there is a sort of kindness they have a claim on you for, and which, you may believe me, will not be thrown away on them.

Your conduct, as it respects yourself, chiefly comprehends sobriety and prudence. The former you know the importance of to your health, your morals and your fortune. I shall therefore say nothing more to enforce the observance of it. I thank God you have not at present the least disposition to deviate from it. Prudence extends to a variety of objects. Never any action of your life in which it will not be your interest to consider what she directs! She will teach you the proper disposal of your time and the careful management of your money, – two very important trusts for which you are accountable. She will teach you that the best chance of rising in life is to make yourself as useful as possible, by carefully studying everything that relates to your profession, and distinguishing yourself from those of your own rank by a superior proficiency in nautical acquirements.

As you have hitherto, my dear Francis, been extremely fortunate in making friends, I trust your future conduct will confirm their good opinion of you; and I have the more confidence of this expectation because the high character you acquired at the Academy for propriety of behaviour and diligence in your studies, when you were so much younger and had so much less experience, seems to promise that riper years and more knowledge of the world will strengthen your naturally good disposition. That this may be the case I sincerely pray, as you will readily believe when you are assured that your good mother, brothers, sisters and myself will all exult in your reputation and rejoice in your happiness ...

As you must be convinced it would be the highest satisfaction to us to hear as frequently as possible from you, you will of course neglect no opportunity of giving us that pleasure, and being very minute in what relates to yourself and your situation. On this account, and because unexpected occasions of writing to us may offer, 'twill be a good way always to have a letter in forwardness. You may depend on hearing from us at every opportunity ...

Keep an exact account of all the money you receive or spend, lend none but where you are sure of an early repayment, and on no account whatever be persuaded to risk it by gaming.

I have nothing to add but my blessing and best prayers for your health and prosperity, and to beg you would never forget you have not upon earth a more disinterested and warm friend than,

Your truly affectionate father,

Geo. Austen.

Aboard the *Perseverance*, 14½-year-old Frank began his practical training at sea to complement the theory learnt at the Academy. Without false modesty his memoir records:

Embarked in the *Perseverance* with Captain Isaac Smith, our youth was soon remarked as possessing a more than usual degree of theoretical knowledge of his profession and being, although rather small of stature, of a vigorous constitution and possessing great activity of body, was not long in acquiring a competent knowledge of the practical parts of seamanship to which he was urged by the natural energies of his mind and a general thirst for knowledge, he became in a very short time a very good practical observer which in those days was rather an uncommon thing. In this he was encouraged by his captain, himself an excellent nautical astronomer, having been two voyages round the world with the celebrated circumnavigator, Cook.

Of the voyage itself the memoir says:

Little worthy of remark occurred during the space of nearly three years that he continued on board the *Perseverance*. It was a period of profound peace, and the squadron in India was chiefly occupied in moving from one side of the peninsula to the other, according to the monsoons, and an occasional visit to numerous settlements in the vast extent of territory occupied by the English in the East. This afforded him an opportunity of seeing a great variety of places and through his captain's kindness (of whom as well as of the officers in general he was a decided favourite) he was on several occasions introduced to the notice of persons of the first consequence in India.

Edward too was abroad at this time, sent by his adoptive parents the Knights not to university but to do the Grand Tour of Europe – a further education thought particularly appropriate for a future landed gentleman. His reception at the Court of Dresden was among the highlights of his journey through Germany, France and Italy.

Eliza remained in France, whence she wrote rather wistfully to Philadelphia on 11 February 1789 of the Christmas festivities at the Rectory which she had had to miss: 'I suppose you have had frequent accounts from Steventon, and that they have informed you of their theatrical performances, *The Sultan* and *High Life Below Stairs*. Miss Cooper performed the part of Roxalana, and Henry The Sultan. I hear that Henry is taller than ever ...'

Returned to Oxford after the Christmas vacation, James and Henry collaborated on a literary venture. Jointly they founded, edited and largely wrote a weekly paper called *The Loiterer*, which appeared regularly between January 1789 and March 1790. Mostly it was in a humorous vein, and one of the contributions, a letter signed by 'Sophia Sentiment', is thought to be the work of their sister Jane – whose juvenile writings, produced at home for her own pleasure and for reading aloud in the evenings to entertain her clever, critical and fun-loving family, were already showing signs of superior intelligence, technical accomplishment and comic genius.

6

Our very good children
1791-96

Edward returned to England with nothing to do but to marry and live happily ever after in his allotted role of well-heeled country gentleman.

In the early part of 1791 he became engaged to Elizabeth, the 'very pretty',[1] seventeen-year-old daughter of Sir Brook Bridges of Goodnestone Park in Kent. Like Edward, Elizabeth came from a large and affectionate family, and she shared his taste for a simple country life. Her mother, Lady Bridges, thought Edward 'a very sensible, amiable young man', and Mr Knight 'in the handsomest manner declared his entire approbation' of the union, though in view of their youth he wished it not to take place immediately.[2] In any case, the death of Elizabeth's father during the course of that year made some delay seemly.

Eliza de Feuillide, back in London, gives a charming picture of Edward at this time. Writing to Philadelphia Walter on 23 June she says: 'On Sunday Edward Austen called ... He is now preparing to visit the Lakes with Mr and Mrs K. and a large party as I understand, no less than twelve in number, but his beloved alas! is not to bless him with her presence on this occasion. I asked him how he would be able to exist; which enquiry he answered with that calm smile of resignation which his sex generally wear under circumstances of this nature.' Of all the Austen brothers, placid Edward was the one least susceptible to Eliza's flirtatious teasing.

The wedding took place on 27 December, and the couple made their first home at Rowling, a medium-sized house that was part of the Bridges property. Having 'no high ideas',[3] they were content with the modest allowance made them by Mr Knight. Elizabeth's father had been succeeded by her brother, the fourth baronet, another Sir Brook; the Dowager Lady Bridges took her remaining unmarried daughters to live at Goodnestone Farm. Thus Edward found himself surrounded by a whole new set of relations, to whom he soon became warmly attached.

James Austen too was in love again, this time in circumstances more propitious. He had left Oxford in March 1790 to become curate of Overton, a village larger than Stoke Charity and situated like Ashe and Deane on the road between Basingstoke and Andover. The following year he increased both his duties and his income by becoming vicar of Sherborne St John, just north of Basingstoke. As this parish had also a rector, the appointment was, in effect, another curacy.

(James' connection with Sherborne St John may explain why it was in the neighbouring village of Monk Sherborne that the two defectives of the family came to be lodged: his brother George and his uncle Thomas Leigh. The latter was under the care of some people named Culham until his death in 1821;[4] the former, who may or may not have lived in the same household, died of dropsy at Monk Sherborne in 1838[5] – the only known facts about any but his infant years.)

Settled in this very agreeable circle of rural Hampshire parishes and occupying the tiny vicarage of Overton, James became acquainted with Miss Anne Mathew of nearby Laverstoke House. She was five years older than himself, and socially more elevated, being the grand-daughter of the Duke of Ancaster; her parents were General and Lady Jane Mathew. An idea of her appearance may be gathered from Jane Austen's later description of Anne's nieces: 'Both prettyish; very like Anne; with brown skins, large dark eyes and a good deal of nose.'[6] A weakness for dark eyes was to be a recurrent theme with the Austens. The other word-picture we have of Anne is her daughter's memory of 'a tall and slender lady dressed in white'.[7] It was a fine match for James, and Anne, nearing thirty, must have found it impossible to resist the courtship of so ardent and personable a young man.

They were married on 27 March 1792 and, rejecting Overton vicarage as too small, took the lease of Court House in the same parish.[8] But within months they moved to the parsonage at Deane, where James became his father's curate, resigning his other clerical posts with the exception of Sherborne St John, which he retained all his life.

Vacating Deane parsonage to make way for James and Anne was a little family by the name of Lloyd (pronounced Floyd⁹), with whom the Austens had become quite intimate during the period of their tenancy and with whom their history was to be connected at several points. But this was for the future: meanwhile Mrs Lloyd, a clergyman's widow, and her two unmarried daughters good-naturedly moved to another rented house, at Ibthorp in the parish of Hurstbourne Tarrant. Separated now by nearly twenty miles, Martha and Mary Lloyd and Cassandra and Jane Austen sustained their friendship by means of visits and letters.

While George Austen thus provided the newly married couple with a home and an income, General Mathew proved himself equally dutiful and generous as a father by making them an allowance of £100 a year. It is recorded that, on the strength of this, James kept a carriage for his wife's ease, and a pack of harriers for his own recreation. Compared with his lucky younger brother, James may not have been rich, but his way of life was by no means without its elegancies. There seems always to have been a certain materialistic streak in James, along with the idealistic.

By now George Austen had seen all his sons successfully launched into the world. In 1791 twelve-year-old Charles, like Frank before him, enrolled at Portsmouth Naval Academy. Less serious than Frank, he was equally fitted by enthusiasm and courage to be a sailor. If he was following in Frank's footsteps, that was a pattern he was to pursue to some extent all his life; inevitably, perhaps, in the same profession, and five years behind him. Where Frank was doggedly ambitious, Charles was fresh and eager, with a boyish charm which never left him, and a capacity to inspire affection reminiscent of his father. Possessing a cheerful and contented frame of mind, Charles was the sort to derive enjoyment from whatever path in life was marked out for him – but the more active, the better.

Indeed, George Austen might have felt himself justified in hoping that all five healthy sons, endowed by nature with excellent abilities and provided by him with a sound education and fine moral training, might turn their individual opportunities to good account and, in creating satisfying lives for themselves, prove useful members of society.

1791 was a year of wretchedness for Eliza, as she had to watch her mother dying slowly and painfully of breast cancer. Mother and daughter were almost everything to each other; their relationship went deeper than with their respective husbands and was much more selfless. In two sentences Philadelphia Walter, writing to her brother James on 4 September, summed up the anguish on both sides: 'Poor Eliza is completely miserable and has the hard task of being forced to appear cheerful when her heart is ready to burst with grief and vexation.' But Mrs Hancock was not deceived. 'My aunt privately expressed to me how much she felt for her, and that she endeavoured to stifle her pains to avoid her the concern of seeing her mother's sufferings.'

The year began for Eliza at Margate, where, incredibly, little Hastings was subjected to a regiment of sea-bathing in January. Eliza had been advised 'that one month's bathing at this time of the year was more efficacious than six at any other', and she assured Philadelphia, 'Hastings grows much and begins to lisp English tolerably well, his education is likewise begun, his grandmamma having succeeded in teaching him his letters. The sea has strengthened him wonderfully and I think has likewise been of great service of myself. I still continue bathing notwithstanding the severity of the weather and frost and snow, which I think somewhat courageous.'

But as the year wore on, concern for her mother's health superseded that for her son's. In June she was 'endeavouring to amuse my mother, and if possible render her present situation less irksome'. And on 1 August she wrote: 'Her courage and resignation are wonderful and a fresh proof of the happy disposition and excellent way of thinking which all who know her must long since have been convinced she was endowed with.'

The same letter continues: 'M. de F. has promised me the favour of a visit in September, and should it take place and Mamma's health admit we shall then go to Bath, a journey from which I promise myself much pleasure, as I have a notion it is a place quite after my own heart; however, the accomplishment of this plan is very uncertain, as from the present appearance of things France will probably be engaged in a war which will not admit of an officer, whose service will certainly be required, quitting the country at such a period.'

Poor Mrs Hancock suffered a momentary disappointment, to which the weak nerves of ill health rendered her vulnerable, on finding that she had not been mentioned in the will of her uncle Francis, who died that summer aged ninety-three. Eliza, feeling it all the more on her mother's account, called such neglect 'extremely unkind'; but of course there were many who felt they had a claim on the old man's remembrance. The bulk of his fortune went to Motley, who used it, and the proceeds from the Red House, which he sold, to purchase the very fine estate of Kippington, near Sevenoaks. Despite having two surviving sons and numerous grandchildren of his own, however, Francis did not forget his favourite nephew. George Austen received a bequest of £500 and was very grateful for it.[10]

As the year drew to its close, it became obvious that Mrs Hancock would not recover. On 9 October Philadelphia sent her brother a letter which reveals her an unworthy recipient of her affectionate half-cousin's confidences: 'Poor Eliza must be left at last friendless and alone. The gay and dissipated life she has long had so plentiful a share of has not ensured her friends among the worthy: on the contrary many who otherwise have regarded her have blamed her conduct and pitied her thoughtlessness. I have frequently looked forward to the approaching awful period, and regretted the manner of her life, and the mistaken results of my poor aunt's intended, well-meant kindness: she will soon feel the loss and her want of domestic knowledge. I have just wrote to assure her she may command my services.'

In fact Philadelphia Hancock lingered on until 26 February 1792. At last the Comte de Feuillide managed to obtain compassionate leave of absence from the army and came to England to comfort his wife, taking her on the promised visit to Bath, from which in her dejected spirits she derived little amusement. The Comte wanted to remain in London but a letter came from France admonishing him for outstaying his leave and informing him that if he did not return immediately he would be considered an emigrant, and the whole of his property forfeited to the nation. Return therefore he did; he was already heavily in debt and could not risk losing all he had. It was judged safer for Eliza and her son to remain in England.

During the spring and summer she paid visits to various friends in the country, but from August until the end of the year she was at Steventon, her spirits soothed by the society of her fond relations and the tranquillity of their way of life.

From Steventon Rectory she wrote on 26 October to Philadelphia:

> I will endeavour to answer all your enquiries as well as I can. In the first place then I have the real pleasure of informing you that our dear uncle and aunt are both in perfect health. The former looks uncommonly well, and in my opinion his likeness to my beloved mother is stronger than ever. Often do I sit and trace her features in his, till my heart overflows at my eyes. I always tenderly loved my uncle, but I think he is now dearer to me than ever, as being the nearest and best beloved relative of the never to be sufficiently regretted parent I have lost.
>
> Cassandra and Jane are both very much grown (the latter is now taller than myself) and greatly improved as well in manners as in person, both of which are now much more formed than when you saw them. They are I think equally sensible, and both so to a degree seldom met with, but still my heart gives the preference to Jane, whose kind partiality to me indeed requires a return of the same nature. Henry is now rather more than six foot high, I believe. He also is much improved, and is certainly endowed with uncommon abilities, which indeed seem to have been bestowed, though in a different way upon each member of this family – As to the coolness which you know had taken place between H. and myself, it has now ceased, in consequence of due acknowledgments on his part, and we are at present on very proper relation-like terms; you know that his family design him for the Church.
>
> Cassandra was from home when I arrived: she was then on a visit to Rowling, the abode of her brother Edward from which she returned however some time since, but is now once more absent as well as her sister on a visit to the Miss Floyds who live at a place called Ibthorp about eighteen miles I believe from hence. They both return on Monday next.
>
> I suppose you have heard long since of the death of Dr Cooper; his daughter came immediately here, I know not whether you are personally acquainted with her, but I think you must recollect my

having mentioned her (she was one of the theatrical troop). At the time of her father's death she was at the very brink of wedlock, the day being fixed, but the above mentioned melancholy event necessarily occasioned a delay of the nuptials which are now fixed for some time in December and are to be celebrated in this place so that I suppose we are to be mighty gay. Indeed, I am delighted with the thoughts of it, for I never was but at one wedding in my life and that appeared a very stupid business to me. I hope I shall be better amused at this; all this while I have not told you who the happy man is: be it therefore known unto you, he is Captain Williams of the Royal Navy (I am sure you will now be much more interested about him). His present fortune is but small, but he has expectation of future preferment. The happy pair are to inhabit the Isle of Wight, to which they have kindly given me a pressing invitation; and which if I am alive next summer I may possibly accept ...

I suppose you know that both Mrs James and Mrs Edward Austen are in the increasing way. The latter I have only had a peep at, and the former I have not seen a great deal more of, I think them both pleasant as far as I can judge ...

I can readily believe that the share of sensibility I know you to be possessed of would not suffer you to learn the tragical events of which France has of late been the theatre without being much affected. My private letters confirm the intelligence afforded by the public prints and assure me that nothing we there read is exaggerated. M. de F. is at present in Paris. He had determined on coming to England, but finds it imposssible to get away ...

I know you will kindly wish for some account of Hastings. He has I think gained much health and strength from his residence here. He is the plaything of the whole family.

As Eliza said, the next generation of Austens was about to appear. 'Mrs Edward' gave birth to Fanny Catherine on 23 January 1793, and 'Mrs James' to Jane Anna Elizabeth on 15 April. Both little girls took their first names from their maternal grandmothers – although the child at Deane was always known as Anna.

In 1792 Frank was promoted Lieutenant, before many who were older or more experienced in the service than he. At the age of eighteen he was now, as his log-books show, able to give the order for flogging. It was a system ripe for abuse, and consequently mutiny; but Frank himself, though a strict disciplinarian, was to behave with the utmost propriety and humanity throughout his long career as an officer. Uncouth and potentially violent though the majority of men on board must have been, and taxing on the nerves though conditions at sea often were, it is recorded that Frank kept control without ever once uttering an oath.

He came home in 1793 after an absence of five years, in which he had grown up more than five years' worth. Mixed with the family's joy and pride must have been wonder at the enormous change between the fourteen-year-old lad they had said goodbye to and the experienced, self-reliant, much-travelled officer of nineteen whom they now warmly welcomed back to a civilized and gentle home environment. As he so stiffly wrote, 'It will not be deemed extraordinary or unreasonable that he should have been desirous of enjoying a few weeks of his family's society disengaged from professional duties, although the War in which England was then recently involved with France equally fitted him to expect no respite from active service.'

But events in France touched the family more horrifically than the mere curtailment of Frank's holiday. On 22 February 1794 the Comte de Feuillide fell victim to the guillotine. He had foolishly, if gallantly, tried to bribe one of the Secretaries of the Committee of Safety to secure the liberty of the widow of an army colleague, Jacques Marboeuf, Marquis and *Maréchal-de-camp*. The fifty-five-year-old Marquise stood accused of laying down certain arable lands on her estate to fodder crops, with the idea of producing a famine in an effort to undermine the Republic.

De Feuillide was double-crossed by the Secretary and arrested at his lodging in the rue Grenelle et St Honoré, where incriminating documents and sums of money parcelled up for the bribery were seized. The Marquise, the Comte and the Marquise's man of business who had acted as a go-between in the attempt, all were sentenced to death.[11]

1794 saw the birth of Edward's first son, another Edward, on 10 May, and the death of his adoptive father, Thomas Knight, on 23 October, during a visit to his Chawton property. He left the whole of his estates in Kent and Hampshire to his widow for life, after which they were to pass to Edward Austen.

Edward's family continued its annual increase with the birth of George on 22 November 1795, but the year brought loss rather than gain to James Austen, for his wife died on 3 May, leaving him with a bewildered little Anna calling for her Mamma. Unable to endure it, James sent his two-year-old daughter to Steventon to be comforted and cared for by her grandmother and aunts.

Anna arrived during the first joyous burst of Jane's creativity, just as her juvenile writings were maturing into the sustained and polished productions of her early adult years, and while the suspicion of her own powers was still bewitchingly new. *Elinor and Marianne* was already written, *First Impressions* now in progress: first versions of two of the greatest novels in the language. Anna was therefore witness to, and retained a vivid memory of, the laughing and talking that went on in her aunts' dressing-room – for all their brothers being gone, Cassandra and Jane had now the luxury of a room to themselves besides the one they slept in – as chapters were read aloud and characters discussed.

At about this time, Cassandra became quietly engaged. The attachment between herself and the Reverend Thomas Fowle dated from childhood, when, seven years her senior, he had been a pupil at the Rectory, as had his elder brother, Fulwar Craven Fowle, a particular friend of James Austen. The boys' mother was sister to Mrs Lloyd, which was how that lady came to be George Austen's tenant at Deane; and Fulwar was now married to his own first cousin Eliza, the sister of Martha and Mary.

In their respective families, the engagement gave a great deal of satisfaction, but it was not announced publicly. For one thing, Cassandra disliked to be the centre of attention, and for another, it was no means certain when the marriage might take place.

Although he was twenty-nine at the time of the engagement and, if he had loved Cassandra since boyhood, had already waited long, Tom was still not in a position to marry. His luckier elder brother was curate to their father at Kintbury in Berkshire, and destined to step into that living; as a younger son, Tom had to accept second best. Since 1793 he had been rector of Allington, in Wiltshire, but the stipend was insufficient to support a family. He had the promise of a more comfortable living in Shropshire, which was in the gift of the same patron, his twenty-five-year-old kinsman Lord Craven; but it was not acceptable to Tom's feelings just to be waiting for the death of the incumbent there and doing nothing to help himself, so when his lordship in a fit of 'military furor', according to his own mother, purchased a colonelcy in the Third Regiment of the Line about to go as part of a nineteen-thousand strong force to the West Indies, and invited his impoverished and deserving cousin to accompany the expedition as chaplain, Tom accepted.

Respecting Cassandra's wishes, he made no mention of the engagement to Lord Craven and sailed out at the beginning of 1796, hoping to return in twelve or eighteen months a richer man. It was an unpropitious passage. The large fleet was struck by exceptionally violent storms in mid-Atlantic, dozens of ships were sunk, and hundreds of men drowned. Those that escaped the worse effects of the tempests, among them Lord Craven's regiment including Tom, were dispersed across the ocean and reached the West Indies only after a protracted, perilous and uncomfortable voyage, to begin their campaigning weeks behind schedule and with much depleted forces.[12]

Danger at sea was also experienced by Charles that year.[13] Since leaving the Academy he had served on board the *Unicorn*, commanded by Captain Thomas Williams, the husband of his cousin Jane, née Cooper. Cruising off the Scilly Isles together on 8 June 1796, the *Unicorn* and the *Santa Margarita* sighted and gave chase to three unidentified vessels, which as they closed turned out to be *La Tribune*, *La Tamise* and *La Legère* of the French fleet. The *Unicorn* pursued *La Tribune* in a running fight lasting ten hours, eventually getting alongside in order to take the wind out of her sails. For a little over half an hour they engaged in heavy gunfire, and when, in a lull, the smoke cleared away, *La Tribune* was seen attempting to get to the windward – in which manoeuvre she was promptly thwarted by the *Unicorn*. A few more broadsides brought down the French ship's masts, and she surrendered.

Lives had been lost on board *La Tribune*, but there was not so much as an injury amongst the British crew. In the course of the day's action, which was to result in a knighthood for Thomas Williams, a distance of 210 miles had been covered by the *Unicorn*. Charles thus early in his career gained first-hand experience of the hazards and excitements of battle, and of the rewards which could ensue.

The same summer saw a long shore leave for Frank, who had

spent the last three years in a succession of frigates on the home station and who was becoming increasingly impatient for further promotion. It was almost two years since his father had tried the only influential friend he had, writing in November 1794 to thank Warren Hastings

… for the friendly manner in which you have undertaken our cause and the application you have made on behalf of my son. As to the event of it I am not very sanguine, convinced as I am that all patronage in the Navy rest with Lord Chatham; however as it may be of material service to have a warm friend at the Board I am very thankful you have procured us one in Admiral Affleck … Should we not succeed in our first object of getting him promoted it might forward his views to have him removed to a flag ship on a more probable station; and this is a circumstance you might if you have no objection suggest to the Admiral when you meet him in town … I shall not trouble you with anything further on the subject than to assure you I should not have introduced my son to your notice had I not been convinced that his merits as a man and a sailor will justify my recommendations.[14]

Promotion was slower to come than Frank wished, but at least his next ship was satisfactory in his eyes. News of the appointment reached him during a visit he and Jane were making to their brother Edward in September 1796. All the pleasures of a holiday at Rowling – shooting with Edward, country walking with Jane, making a wooden butter-churn for little Fanny, and dancing with Elizabeth's relations at Goodnestone – had suddenly to be left as Frank was required to report for duty within three days. 'The *Triton* is a new 32 Frigate, just launched at Deptford,' Jane informed Cassandra.[15] 'Frank is much pleased with the prospect of having Captain Gore under his command.'

If the two sailor brothers were too young or too busy with their careers to think of romance, it was very much the preoccupation of the rest of the family during the middle nineties. Cassandra was waiting patiently for her lover's return; Jane was enjoying a light-hearted flirtation with a visiting Irish nephew of their neighbours at Ashe Rectory, called Tom Lefroy; and both Henry and James were showing a romantic interest in their widowed cousin.

Never lacking in self-confidence, Henry made a proposal of

marriage in 1795, but it was declined by Eliza, who was enjoying her independence and who had besides a marked dislike for his intended profession of the Church. In this, however, Henry was wavering, and in fact since 1793 he had been toying with an alternative occupation. He still spent much of his time at St John's College, where he obtained his master's degree in 1796, but he also undertook the spasmodic duties of lieutenant in the Oxfordshire militia.

Created to defend the country from invasion, the militia was a largely amateur body organized on a county basis.[16] It differed from the regular army not only in its deployment at home rather than abroad, in defence rather than in attack, but in the important particular that its commissions could not be purchased. The idea was that landowners (or their heirs) in the county concerned would come forward to serve in the militia in the protection of their own territory, thus preserving their independence from Crown or government and ensuring that their power was not unconstitutionally used. Specific qualifications were laid down for each rank – the holder of a lieutenancy, for example, was supposed to own property worth £50 a year in rents. These stipulations, which derived from the aftermath of the Civil War, were more readily overlooked in more stable times, especially as fewer and fewer landowners could be bothered to take up arms. Thus officers tended to be recruited from the class of young men who wanted to be soldiers, who could not afford a commission in the regular army but who had friends to vouch for a spurious land 'qualification'. One such was Henry, who found he had a taste for military life. Eliza thoroughly approved.

He even made some efforts to join the regular army but by the end of the year had settled for a captaincy in the Oxfordshire militia. As the war with France intensified, the role of the militia was taking on a new significance. Henry now regarded himself as a full-time soldier and, almost certainly to the regret of his father, decided against taking holy orders.

Yet still Eliza continued to resist Henry's courtship. Perhaps in a fit of pique, he became engaged to another woman – to Mary, elder daughter of Sir Richard Pearson, an officer of Greenwich Hospital. The engagement was entered into in the late summer of 1796.

The lady's portrait was proudly shown at Steventon, and the lady herself introduced to Edward at Rowling, and to Jane in London on her way thither. George Austen, perhaps alarmed at this second example of his sons's volatility in the important decisions of his life, invited her to the Rectory. Jane wrote to Cassandra from Rowling: 'If Miss Pearson should return with me, pray be careful not to expect too much beauty. I will not pretend to say that on a *first view*, she quite answered the opinion I had formed of her. – My mother I am sure will be disappointed, if she does not take great care. From what I remember of her picture, it is no great resemblance.'

However, the hastily formed engagement was of brief duration and was, with unavoidable awkwardness, broken off. On 7 November Eliza wrote to Philadelphia: 'Our cousin Henry Austen has been in town: he looks thin and ill. I hear his late intended is a most intolerable flirt, and reckoned to give herself great airs. The person who mentioned this to me says she is a pretty wicked looking girl with bright black eyes which pierce through and through. No wonder this poor young man's heart could not withstand them.' Evidently Eliza did not notice the resemblance to herself, mental as well as physical, in this description.

Meanwhile James, not unnaturally supposing that Henry had given up his pursuit of Eliza, began to imagine that he was in love with her himself. James was a person, like Captain Benwick of *Persuasion*, who 'must love somebody'; his eagerness to remarry was no slight to Anne's memory but a compliment to the happiness marriage had brought him.

The two cleverest brothers could not have been more different in temperament. James was serious, contemplative, emotional, capable of deep attachment; Henry uniformly cheerful, charming and buoyant, less demanding in personal relationships, but with an ability to infuse life and spirit into any gathering of people. There was no doubt which personality was better suited to Eliza's own. However, for a time, while under her spell, James may well have felt that he had reason as well as passion on his side. He was, after all, only four years Eliza's junior as opposed to Henry's ten; he could offer her a comfortable home and an assured income, which Henry could not; and finally, their both having being widowed and left with one child to bring up endowed the projected union with a particular suitability. As for her horror of burying herself in a country parsonage – he could hardly take that as a serious obstacle, when he considered with what evident enjoyment her visits to Steventon were always passed.

For some time he persevered in his courtship – but not perhaps for as long as Eliza, in London, complacently believed. Writing on 13 December, she told Philadelphia:

> I am glad to find that you have made up your mind to visiting the Rectory, but at the same time, and in spite of all your conjectures and belief, I do assert that preliminaries are so far from settled that I do not believe the parties will ever come together, not however that they have quarrelled, but one of them cannot bring her mind to give up dear liberty, and yet dearer flirtation – After a few months stay in the country she sometimes thinks it possible to undertake sober matrimony, but a few weeks stay in London convinces her how little the state is to her taste. – Lord S———'s card has this moment been brought me which I think very ominous considering I was talking of matrimony, but it does not signify, I shall certainly escape both peer and parson.

However, James was not a man to persist in a hopeless suit, and if Eliza would not have him, he turned to somebody who would, somebody more homely and grateful for what he could offer her. On 30 December Eliza enquired of Philadelphia: 'Has Cassandra informed you of the wedding which is soon to take place in the family? James has chosen a second wife in the person of Miss Mary Floyd, who is not either rich or handsome, but very sensible and good humoured. – You have perhaps heard of the family, for they occupied my uncle's house at Deane six or seven years since, and the eldest sister is married to Mr Fulwar Fowle who is brother to Cassandra's intended: Jane seems much pleased with the match, and it is natural she should be having long known and liked the lady.'

It was not jealousy that led Eliza to say Mary was neither rich nor handsome, but the simple truth, for she had no fortune, and her face had been scarred by smallpox. On her father's side the family was obscure, but her mother had a very colourful history.[17]

Mrs Martha Lloyd had been born one of the five daughters of the Honourable Charles Craven and his wife Elizabeth, a society lady whose neglect of and cruelty towards the five girls (while her husband was absent carrying out his duties as Governor of Carolina) resulted in some of them running away, and all of them making marriages more lowly than their real rank in life warranted. Mary Craven, in her desperation to escape, married a horse-dealer and repented all her life. Jane and Martha Craven fared less badly, both becoming wives of clergymen – but not before Martha had been obliged to earn her own living, under an assumed name, as a sempstress at a school. Jane married the Reverend Thomas Fowle, vicar of Kintbury, and Martha the Reverend Noyes Lloyd, vicar of Bishopstoke in Wiltshire.

In both families money was in short supply. The Fowles had four sons, of whom the two eldest, designed for the church, were sent to be pupils of George Austen.

The four Lloyd children, Martha, Eliza, Charles and Mary, were all born at Bishopstoke, and then their father gained preferment to Enborne, near Newbury. It was here, four years after the arrival of the family, that they were attacked by smallpox, brought into the rectory by a coachman who concealed the fact that it was in his own cottage.

Mr Lloyd prudently, though no doubt in anguish, kept away so as not to carry the infection to church; but the rest of the household – mother, servants and children together – contracted the disease. Seven-year-old Charles died, and the others bore the marks of it all their lives.

The education of the three daughters proceeded upon homely and practical lines, suitable to their station in life. A master came to Enborne Rectory to teach writing and arithmetic; thereafter the girls were left to acquire what knowledge they might. From their mother they learnt to spin, to make lace and to knit all their own everyday stockings. So that they might have at least one personal attraction, that of moving gracefully, they were sent to Newbury for dancing lessons once a week for seven years. Such was the success of this measure that Jane Austen more than once praised Martha's elegant figure.

Even more than Jane, Mrs Austen was delighted with the match made now between Mary and James. Free from worldly ambition and possessing an abundance of common sense and warmth of heart, Mrs Austen knew that to satisfy James' nature his wife must be devoted, and to make his home comfortable on a moderate income she must be useful: Eliza was neither of these things. Her foibles had never been regarded as indulgently by her clear-sighted aunt as by her fond uncle. Mrs Austen's relief in the knowledge that her sensitive eldest son had put himself out of the power of his cousin to torment him any longer found expression in the letter she wrote to Mary on 30 November:

> Mr Austen and myself desire you will accept our best love, and that you will believe us truly sincere when we assure you that we feel the most heartfelt satisfaction at the prospect we have of adding you to the number of our very good children. Had the election been mine, you, my dear Mary, are the person I should have chosen for *James's wife*, *Anna's mother* and *my daughter*; being as certain, as I can be of anything in this uncertain world, that you will greatly increase and promote the happiness of each of the three. Pray give our love to Mrs Lloyd and Martha and say we hope they are well pleased with, and as much approve of, their future son and brother, as we with, and of our daughter. I look forward to you as a real comfort to me in my old age, when Cassandra is gone into Shropshire, and Jane – the Lord knows where. Tell Martha, she too shall be my daughter, she does me honour in the request – and Mr W. shall be my son if he pleases – don't be alarmed my dear Martha, I have kept and will keep your secret as close as if I had been entrusted with it; which I do assure you I never was, but found it out by my own sprack wit – but as we are now all of one family, there is no occasion I should keep it any longer a secret from herself. Farewell my dear Mary for the present, and believe me yours most affectionately, C. Austen.

Was ever a prospective daughter-in-law welcomed more warmly than this?

7

Sober matrimony

1797-1800

James and Mary were married on 17 January 1797 at Hurstbourne Tarrant. Mary had then the strange experience of returning as mistress to her own former home, which she had vacated five years before to make way for her predecessor.

We catch a glimpse of her at this time through the eyes of a neighbour, Mrs Chute, of 'The Vyne', who wrote on 29 January to her sister Miss Augusta Smith: 'This morning was absolutely devoted to receiving company ... first Mr and Mrs James Austen, a bridal visit; she is perfectly unaffected, and very pleasant; I like her. Was it not for the small-pox which has scarred and seamed her face dreadfully, her countenance would be pleasing.'[1]

Within the family, however, Mary was not quite to fulfil the high expectations she had aroused – particularly with regard to Anna, who was now removed from the delightful company of her aunts and, uprooted for the second time in her young life, returned to Deane. A forward, intelligent, stubborn child, she made life difficult for her stepmother, who had not the tact or forbearance to cope with a trying situation. Mary's own shortcomings, as they manifested themselves over the years, were a brusqueness of manner, a tendency to indulge in criticism and complaint, and a lack of consideration for the feelings of others.

These were faults quite foreign to the Austen nature. Contentment with one's lot, forbearance, mildness, unselfishness, pleasant manners and attention to the comfort of all those with whom one's life overlapped – these were the qualities the Austens valued and upon which they built their remarkable family unity. Not everybody could be as clever as themselves, not everybody was

109

blessed with the sunshiny disposition which was one of their inherited traits – but everybody could make the attempt to suppress self in the interests of social and family harmony.

'Excellence in every relation of life' was the highest praise Jane could bestow on another sister-in-law, Elizabeth; even Eliza, despite some deficiency of principle, was too well mannered to make anybody feel uncomfortable. (Besides, again and again, it can be seen that association with the Austens brought out all that was best in her.) As for Jane and Cassandra themselves, it was said by others in the family that the latter had the merit of having her temper always under command, and the former had the happiness of a temper that never needed to be commanded.

Mary only, of all the women who married into this generation of the Austen family, was, over a period of time, judged and found wanting by her sisters-in-law. Nevertheless, they recognized that she had many good qualities, and she sometimes surprised them by a really kind deed. With her mother-in-law she remained on excellent terms; there was a downrightness about *her*, too, which chimed well with Mary.

Above all, Mary proved a good wife to James: steady, loyal and supportive. That she made him happy seems likely from the many affectionate verses which he addressed to her over the years,[2] but that he gradually grew a little like her, becoming irritable and petty, cannot be denied.

As James was settling into his second marriage, Cassandra's hopes of her first were suddenly dashed. In February her fiancé died in the West Indies, of yellow fever. The shattering news took three months to reach her, and to heighten the tragedy, Lord Craven, who returned to England abashed by the whole experience, was understood to have said that, had he known Tom Fowle was an engaged man, he would not have encouraged him to risk his life in such a climate. But he was speaking with the benefit of hindsight. The expedition had been a disaster from start to finish, and his lordship never went soldiering again.

A glimpse of Cassandra's fortitude in suffering comes to us via Jane and Eliza. The latter wrote to Philadelphia on 3 May:

I have just received a letter from Steventon where they are all in great affliction (as I suppose you have heard) for the death of Mr Fowle, the gentleman to whom our cousin Cassandra was engaged. He was expected home this month from St Domingo where he had accompanied Lord Craven, but alas instead of his arrival news were received of his death. This is a very severe stroke to the whole family, and particularly to poor Cassandra for whom I feel more than I can express. Indeed I am most sincerely grieved at this event and the pain which it must occasion our worthy relations. Jane says that her sister behaves with a degree of resolution and propriety which no common mind could evince in so trying a situation ...

I have been under some uneasiness on Hastings' account for he has had some fainting fits which were not however either preceded or followed by any illness, so that I endeavour to flatter myself they were only the result of the relaxation which the sudden setting in of the mild weather has occasioned him. His spirits are extremely good, and he both sleeps and eats well. I believe it is since I last wrote to you that I have had accounts of my property in France. The national convention have laid their clutches on it as I expected, but it seems they are so kind ·as to keep up the farms etc and I am assured that a decree has passed which secures its restoration to me whenever I can claim it in a proper manner, to do this I am urged to go to France or to send Hastings, but I do not feel inclined to do either one or the other while the war lasts ...

Captain Austen has just spent a few days in town. I suppose you know that our cousin Henry is now Captain, Paymaster, and Adjutant. He is a very lucky young man and bids fair to possess a considerable share of riches and honours. I believe he has now given up all thoughts of the Church, and he is right for he certainly is not so fit for a parson as a soldier ...

With a French invasion now a serious fear, Henry's regiment was posted to East Anglia. By adding the responsibilities of adjutancy and paymastership to those of captaincy, he had raised himself to a position where he could earn considerable sums. Officers were rewarded not only by regular pay but by dividing between them the surplus after equipping and paying the expenses of their men out of the funds provided. Every arrangement to do with the militia seems to have been open to abuse – as indeed was so much of life in that under-legislated era – but Henry was undoubtedly one of those who made the sytem work to his advantage *within the bounds of total honesty*.

From about this time dated Eliza's relenting towards Henry's renewed courtship. In her letters to Philadelphia she continued to express reluctance to marry, but it was perhaps because she did have marriage in mind that she sought to gain control of her own financial affairs. The trustees of Warren Hastings' gift to her, George Austen and John Woodman, agreed to the cessation of the trust and the vesting of the fortune in her own name following legal advice which she took in June. The next month she wrote to Philadelphia from Manchester Street:

> I had the pleasure of seeing our Uncle Austen some little time since when himself and his youngest son Charles dined with me. This latter is really a fine youth and I think his father looks as young and as well as he did ten years since. Have you heard that Cassandra's intended has left her a thousand pounds – I was extremely glad to learn it and thought you would be equally so, but as it is perhaps a secret do not mention it when you write to Steventon.
>
> I do not hear that Mrs James is breeding but I conclude it is so for a parson cannot fail of having a numerous progeny. Henry is at Norwich … I believe his match with a certain friend of ours, which I know you looked upon as fixed, will never take place. For my own part, I think this young man ill-used but the lady is so well pleased with her present situation that she cannot find it in her heart to change it, and says in her giddy way that independence and the homage of half a dozen are preferable to subjection and the attachment of a single individual. I am more and more convinced that she is not at all calculated for sober matrimony.

On the pretext of the benefit of sea bathing to Hastings, Eliza now paid a visit to Lowestoft, protesting to Philadelphia on 22 September: 'Indeed it is wonderful how the child's health improved in the course of a very few days after his arrival … Thus my dear friend you see that the continguity of Suffolk and Norfolk was not my motive for visiting this place, and indeed had you known that Lowestoft is no less than 28 miles from Norwich, you would probably have dismissed all your wicked surmises for you must allow that a person who cannot absent himself from his corps for more than a few hours at a time, cannot very conveniently travel 56 miles to pay a visit.'

Presumably Henry *did* find time to make the fifty-six mile journey, and Eliza *did* find it in her heart to accept his long-standing proposal of marriage – for the wedding ceremony took place on the last day of 1797. Charges of changeability have been laid at Henry's door, but he had loved and pursued Eliza pretty steadily since he was a boy of sixteen – even, one feels, through his ill-judged engagement to another woman. As for Eliza, no admirer but Henry had been able to touch her feelings or arouse in her anything more positive than complacency in their admiration. Agreeable though her independence was to her, her feelings for Henry could no longer be withstood.

She wrote to her godfather three days before the wedding:

As I flatter myself you still take an interest in my welfare, I think it incumbent upon me to acquaint you with a circumstance by which it must be materially influenced. I have consented to a union with my cousin Captain Austen who has the honour of being known to you. He has been for some time in possession of a comfortable income, and the excellence of his heart, temper and understanding, together with steady attachment to me, his affection for my little boy, and disinterested concurrence in the disposal of my property in favour of this latter, have at length induced me to an acquiescence which I have withheld for more than two years. Need I say, my dear Sir, that I most earnestly wish for your approbation on this occasion, and that it is with the sincerest attachment I shall ever remain, Your much obliged and affectionate god-daughter, Elizabeth de Feuillide.

On 11 December (and making no mention of her imminent wedding) Eliza had written to Philadelphia: 'I have heard very lately from my cousin Jane who is still at Bath with her mother and sister. Mr Hampson whom I saw yesterday and who enquired after yourself and family, told me he had heard Cassandra was going to be married but Jane says not a word of it.' There was no truth in the rumour. For the rest of her life Cassandra remained faithful to the memory of her beloved fiancé, and this devotion it was, I believe, not any brief romance of Jane's own, which inspired Anne Elliot's impassioned speech in *Persuasion* about woman's capacity to go on loving 'even after hope or existence is gone'. Whilst no one in Jane Austen's fiction is taken directly from life – she was too creative an artist for that – surely the character of Anne, whom she described as 'almost too good for me', is to some extent an immortalization of the elder sister whom she always insisted was better and wiser than herself. By the time Jane came to write *Persuasion*, she had lived with Cassandra's unmawkish, unostentatious devotion to Tom's memory for nearly twenty years.

1797 brought tragedy to Cassandra, and disappointment to Jane – disappointment not of a romantic but of a literary nature. Her father, whose taste and judgement she respected, deemed *First Impressions* worthy of publication and even offered to pay the costs if that were the only way publication could be secured. This was a very generous offer from a man whose moderate income had to stretch to many family commitments – proof of his enthusiasm for his daughter's work and of the sexual equality of his thinking. He had started all his sons off on their respective careers and would do no less for his talented younger daughter.

But the firm of Cadell, to whom he applied on 1 November, declined even to read the manuscript – and so ended Jane's modest hopes and any attempt to seek publication for another six years. The rebuff made no difference to her will to write – she began on *Susan* (later called *Northanger Abbey*) almost immediately afterwards – but it did confirm her instinctive priorities: family obligations before public ambition; family approval before public acclaim.

Henry's duties continued to keep him on the east coast. From Ipswich, Eliza wrote to Philadelphia on 16 February 1798:

Matrimony is generally accused of spoiling correspondents but I was so bad a one before I entered the holy estate that it could not well make me a worse, and therefore I trust my dear friend that you do not put down my late silence to its account. Indeed the fact is that in addition to my accustomed dislike to writing, my time has been constantly taken up, for on my arrival here most of the families in the place were civil enough to visit me, and my brother officers and brother officers' wives of course did likewise. To all these visitations succeeded invitations to parties which are as thick in this country as hops in yours, and besides these parties there is at least one ball every week – so that what with my morning avocations and walks and drives for I am sometimes so gracious or so imprudent as to trust my neck to Henry's coachmanship, I find it difficult to make a leisure hour.

And now having accounted for if not justifed my late omission let me return you my sincere acknowledgement for your good wishes and kind congratulations on an event by which I have hitherto had every reason to hope that my happiness will be greatly forwarded. Unmixed felicity is certainly not the produce of this world, and like other people I shall probably meet with many unpleasant and untoward circumstances but all the comfort which can result from the tender affection and society of a being who is possessed of an excellent heart, understanding and temper, I have at least ensured – to say nothing of the pleasure of having my own way in everything, for Henry well knows that I have not been much accustomed to control and should probably behave rather awkwardly under it, and therefore like a wise man he has no will but mine, which to be sure some people would call spoiling me, but I know it is the best way of managing me ...

Perhaps I may never be mistress of a rectory but as soon as I have done campaigning I shall look out for some settled residence where you will ever be a most welcome guest. I have some thoughts of going to London for a few days in the course of the next month, and proceeding from thence into Hampshire. It will be a comical sort of an expedition, for I mean to send my servants etc by the stage, and let Henry drive me, because it will save post-horses, for you must know that I am become excessively stingy and am scraping up all I can against the arrival of the French who will of course deprive me of everything but the few guineas which I may have contrived to hoard.

I suppose you have seen a print of the rafts on which they mean to reach us. It seems these rafts are to be worked with wheels which have the effect of oars, that they are to be bordered with cannon and support a tower filled with soldiers. I can hardly believe that they seriously mean to trust to such a contrivance, which I should suppose a rough sea would soon render ineffectual – however I do believe that they will make an attempt on this country, and Government appears convinced of it, for *we* have received orders to add one hundred and fifty men to *our* regiment, and hold *ourselves* in readiness to march at the shortest notice so that I am going to be drilled and to bespeak my regimentals without further delay.

I have not yet given you any account of my brother officers of whom I wish you could judge in person for there are some with whom I think you would not dislike a flirtation. I have of course entirely left off *trade* but I can however discover that Captain Tilson is remarkably handsome and that Messrs Perrott and Edwardes may be chatted with very satisfactorily, but as to my Colonel Lord Charles Spencer, if I was married to my third husband instead of my second I should still be in love with him. He is a most charming creature, so mild, so well bred, so good, but alas! he is married as well as myself and what is worse he is absent and will not return to us in less than a month.

The inhabitants of this place are much more fashionable people than I expected and are exceedingly kind to us strangers. As everything is known in such small circles they are acquainted with my having been a

Comtesse, and politely give me the precedence which courtesy grants to
that title in England ...

Adieu my dear Phillida I don't tease you with soft things from my
cousin (I have an aversion to the word *husband* and never make use of it)
because they are all implied for I trust you do not doubt the very
sincere regard which I assure you he often expresses for you and yours.
Once more adieu, say everything that is kind for me to your good
mother and poor father whenever he shows any recollection of me.

Philadelphia's 'poor father', William Walter, died that April after
a long and distressing illness.

While Henry hoped to make his fortune in the militia, Frank and
Charles also looked to the war to advance them in their profession.
Frank had followed eighteen months on the *Triton* with six on the
Seahorse and was now serving with the *London*, blockading the
Spanish fleet of Cadiz and still awaiting promotion. Indeed, by the
end of 1798 both sailor brothers were agitating for improvement in
their lot. It was true that in December 1797 Charles had been made
very joyful by promotion to lieutenant, but he was appointed to
serve on board the *Scorpion*, which was only a brig, offering limited
opportunities for action and glory. The only notable event of
Charles' year with this small vessel was the capture of a Dutch ship
carrying six guns. He was becoming impatient for a transfer.

On 18 December 1798 the Reverend George Austen wrote to
Admiral Gambier in an effort to forward the careers of his two naval
sons. His acquaintance with the Admiral must have been very slight,
but when personal influence counted for so much, any such contact
was worth trying. Reporting her father's letter to Cassandra, Jane
wrote of the Admiral: 'He must already have received so much
satisfaction from his acquaintance and patronage of Frank, that he
will be delighted I dare say to have another of the family introduced
to him.'

Less than a week later, on 24 December, she was able to pass on
the Admiral's speedy and satisfactory reply:

Admiral Gambier, in reply to my father's application, writes as follows:
– 'As it is usual to keep young officers in small vessels, it being most
proper on account of their inexperience, and it being also a situation
where they are more in the way of learning their duty, your son has
been continued in the *Scorpion*; but I have mentioned to the Board of

Admiralty his wish to be in a frigate, and when a proper opportunity offers and it is judged that he was taken his turn in a small ship, I hope he will be removed. With regard to your son now in the *London*, I am glad I can give you the assurance that his promotion is likely to take place very soon, as Lord Spencer has been so good as to say he would include him in an arrangement that he proposes making in a short time relative to some promotions in that quarter.' ...

I have sent the same extract of sweets of Gambier to Charles, who, poor fellow, though he sinks into nothing but an humble attendant on the hero of the piece, will, I hope, be contented with the prospect held out to him. By what the Admiral says, it appears as if he had been designedly kept in the *Scorpion*. But I will not torment myself with conjectures and suppositions; facts shall satisfy me.

Frank had not heard from any of us for ten weeks when he wrote to me on November 12 in consequence of Lord St Vincent being removed to Gibraltar. When his commission is sent, however, it will not be so long on its road as our letters, because all the Government despatches are forwarded by land to his lordship from Lisbon with great regularity.

In this letter she also wrote affectionately of another brother: 'Poor Edward! It is very hard that he, who has everything else in the world that he can wish for, should not have good health too ... I know no one more deserving of happiness without alloy than Edward is.'

On 27 December Frank was raised to the rank of Commander and appointed to the *Peterel* sloop, stationed at Gibraltar, whilst Charles was appointed to the *Tamar* frigate. He was allowed a month's home leave before joining her, and on 21 January, Jane wrote to Cassandra:

Charles leaves us tonight. The *Tamar* is in the Downs, and Mr Daysh advises him to join her there directly, as there is no chance of her going to the westward. Charles does not approve of this at all, and will not be much grieved if he should be too late for her before she sails, as he may then hope to get into a better station. He attempted to go to town last night, and got as far on his road thither as Deane Gate; but both the coaches were full, and we had the pleasure of seeing him back again. He will call on Daysh tomorrow to know whether the *Tamar* has sailed or not, and if she is still at the Downs he will proceed in one of the night coaches to Deal.

The youngest son, Charles was the first in the family to adopt the new male fashion for short, unpowdered hair. Jane added: 'Martha writes me word that Charles was very much admired at Kintbury, and Mrs Lefroy never saw anyone so much improved in her life, and thinks him handsomer than Henry. He appears to far more advantage here than he did at Godmersham, not surrounded by strangers and neither oppressed by a pain in his face or powder in his hair.'

This letter was written in instalments, and the next day, on receipt of one from Cassandra, she added on the same subject: 'I thought Edward would not approve of Charles being a crop, and rather wished you to conceal it from him at present, lest it might fall on his spirits and retard his recovery.' She was also able to report: 'Our own particular little brother got a place in the coach last night, and is now, I suppose, in town,' which she followed up the day afterwards with, 'I have just heard from Charles, who is by this time at Deal. He is to be Second Lieutenant, which pleased him very well. The *Endymion* is come into the Downs, which pleases him likewise. He expects to be ordered to Sheerness shortly, as the *Tamar* has never been refitted.'

The frigate *Endymion*, on which Charles had already served as a midshipman, was under the command of his old friend and captain Sir Thomas Williams, newly widowed by the tragic death in a carriage accident of Charles' cousin Jane in August 1798. Strange and sad it was that the wife, enjoying an uneventful and apparently safe existence in the peaceful English countryside, was the one to meet violent and premature death, whilst the husband, risking his life almost daily at war and at sea, survived.

Apart from the pleasure of serving again with this good friend, Charles evidently reckoned that his chances of seeing action would be greater under a captain of such proven bravery and enterprise. Within three weeks of his arrival at the Downs, with the typical Austen mixture of luck, charm and persistence, Charles had got his own way and secured a transfer from the *Tamar* to the *Endymion*.

If Charles was well satisfied for the present, Frank had reason to be more content. At the age of twenty-four he had command of a ship, with all the glittering prospects of prize-money which that entailed. In time of war the opportunities for enterprising captains to amass quite considerable sums were highly favourable. That

April the *Peterel* assisted two other British vessels in the capture of a Spanish ship which happened to be carrying not only a brigadier-general and a lieutenant-colonel but treasure to the value of 9,000 Spanish dollars. Of this, 1,469 dollars fell to *Peterel*'s share, Frank personally receiving 750 dollars, a little over half this sum. The next officer was awarded less than a tenth of Frank's prize, and so on down the line, ending with the seamen who got just 2 dollars each.

Frank took part in the capture of many French and Spanish ships over the next three years, serving first in the western Mediterranean and then with Sir Sydney Smith's squadron at Alexandria, Cyprus, Jaffa and Rhodes. It was a period of intense activity as British naval supremacy was gradually established under the brilliant leadership of Nelson.

On land and on sea the Austen brothers were busy upholding the honour of their nation in the last years of the century. The threat of a French invasion of the shores of Ireland was taken seriously enough by Parliament to authorize the shipping out of twelve thousand troops of the English militia to defend them. Never before had the militiamen been required to serve away from home, but in their country's hour of need many of them responded enthusiastically.

The Oxfordshires, under their commander Lord Charles Spencer, were among those who made the crossing in the early part of 1799. However, the mood among the men changed as they endured several months' garrison duty in a country still largely hostile to British rule, unalleviated by a sense of purpose – for the French failed to appear. Representations were made to Lord Charles Spencer of a general unwillingness to remain. By a combination of threats and promises, the men were induced to stay until Christmas, after which, they were promised, they would be stationed again near their homes and families.[3]

Eliza Austen had been among those wives left behind, writing dismally from her temporary lodgings in Dorking to Philadelphia Walter on 29 October 1799:

Austen who has now been absent near seven months gives me hopes of his return some time in December; he is now in Dublin but is kind enough to say that he would prefer my hermitage, although the Irish metropolis is rendered particularly pleasant to him by the attentions which he experiences from the Lord Lieutenant in consequence of having been introduced to him by his very good friend Lord Charles Spencer – he (I mean Austen) has been so fortunate as to enjoy uninterrupted health but I cannot say as much for myself, having been far from well these last two years.

I had hoped much from country air, early hours, and a very quiet life, but I have been disappointed. Hastings too suffers much from frequent and very violent returns of fits which I believe to be epileptic and which have hitherto baffled all the aid of medicine; their effects on his mental powers, if his life should not be destroyed by them, must be of the most melancholy nature, and are a constant source of grief to me.

Compared with his brothers, who all had their fortunes to strive for, Edward's life was uneventful. The almost annual addition to the number of his children has been all we have had to record of him since his marriage in 1791. But in November 1797 a significant change took place.

Mrs Knight had occupied Godmersham in solitary splendour now for three years. She was only forty-one when she was widowed, and still an attractive woman, her looks unravaged either by child-bearing or by shortage of money. She enjoyed excellent health and spirits and possessed a lively, decisive turn of mind. She was outward-looking, interested in other people and their affairs.

In 1796 there was some rumour that she was considering remarrying, but nothing came of it, and towards the end of the following year she reached an important decision. She would relinquish Godmersham in favour of Edward and his growing family (a third son, Henry, was born that May), reserving for herself the comfortable annuity of £2,000 out of the estate, plus sufficient to purchase a small but elegant house. The one she chose was called Grey Friars, in Canterbury. Here she would be well placed to enjoy all the civilized pleasures of the county town, and still within easy reach of her adopted son, whose residence at Godmersham, she had concluded, would be beneficial not only to himself, wife and children but to the tenantry and neighbourhood in general. Having thus arranged everything mentally to her own satisfaction, she wrote to her man of business and family connection, Mr Deedes.

Edward's reaction to this piece of generosity, and Mrs Knight's reply,[4] which silenced all further protest, show both in a pleasing light. Their relationship seems to have been sincerely affectionate and disinterested.

Edward wrote on 23 November from Rowling:

My dearest Madam – I went to bed last night fully determined on paying you an early visit this morning in consequence of two letters of yours to Mr Deedes, which he yesterday gave me to peruse, but the more I have thought of it the less I find myself capable of conversing with you on so extraordinary and important a subject. I have therefore determined to make use of my pen, though I am confident I shall even then fall very short of expressing half what I feel at the moment I am writing. It is impossible, my dearest Madam, for anyone to have a higher sense of your unlimited bounty and kindness to me than both Elizabeth and myself; were we not truly sensible of it we should indeed be most the ungrateful of beings, but I trust and indeed know you are convinced of the sincerity of our gratitude and affection.

Believe me, therefore, my dear Madam, equally sincere when I say it is impossible for us in this instance to accede to your plan. I am confident we should never be happy at Godmersham whilst you were living at a smaller and less comfortable house – or in reflecting that you had quitted your own favourite mansion, where I have so often heard you say your whole happiness was centered, and had retired to a residence and style of living to which you have been ever unaccustomed, and this to enrich us.

We are, believe me, thanks to your continued bounties, comfortable and happy: nor do I know how that happiness can be better continued than by seeing you in a situation where I know you must be more comfortable than any alteration can possibly make you. You will, therefore, my dear Madam, not think us ungrateful if I again repeat my wishes that you abandon your present plan – the remembrance of it will be cordially engraved on our minds: our feelings I will not endeavour to express. – I shall now take an early opportunity of seeing you; till then, adieu!'

Mrs Knight replied the next day from Godmersham Park:

If anything were wanted, my dearest Edward, to confirm my resolution concerning the plan I propose executing, your letter would have that effect; it is impossible for any person to express their gratitude and affection in terms more pleasing and gratifying than you have chosen, and from the bottom of my heart I believe you to be perfectly sincere when you assure me that your happiness is best secured by seeing me in the full enjoyment of every thing that can contribute to my ease and comfort, and that happiness, my dear Edward, will be yours by acceding to my wishes.

From the time that my partiality for you induced Mr Knight to treat you as our adopted child I have felt for you the tenderness of a mother, and never have you appeared more deserving of affection than at this time; to reward your merit, therefore, and to place you in a situation where your many excellent qualities will be called forth and rendered useful to the neighbourhood, is the fondest wish of my heart. Many circumstances attached to large landed possessions, highly gratifying to a man, are entirely lost on me at present; but when I see you in the enjoyment of them, I shall, if possible, feel my gratitude to my beloved husband redoubled, for having placed in my hands the power of bestowing happiness on one so very dear to me.

If my income had not been sufficient to enable both of us to live in affluence, I never should have proposed this plan, for nothing would have given me more pain than to have seen a rigid economy take place of that liberality which the poor have always experienced from this family; but with the income I have assigned you, I trust, my dear Edward, you will feel yourself rich. You must be satisfied however on that head; and I hope you will very soon come over, when you shall inspect every account I have, and form your own judgment ...

I am desirous of making the Deed irrevocable, during your life; for your being kept in a state of dependence on my wish, perhaps caprice, would not be less painful to you, than disagreeable to myself ...

You will observe, my dear Edward, that I depend on your obedience to my wish, and assure yourself and my dear Lizzie, that the sacrifice I make is far from being so great as you imagine; the emolument of a great income is no object to me, for reasons I have already stated to Mr Deedes, and even the pain I shall feel in quitting this dear place will no longer be remembered when I see you in possession of it. My attachment to it can, I think, only cease with my life; but if I am near enough to be your frequent daily visitor, and within reach of the side of you and your boys, and Lizzie and her girls, I trust I shall be as happy, perhaps happier than I am now.

The following August Mr and Mrs Austen and their daughters began a two-month visit to Edward, now luxuriously ensconced at Godmersham. Whilst they were there, Elizabeth gave birth to her fourth son, William, on 10 October. A fortnight later the Austens returned home, leaving Cassandra behind to help with the little ones.

At Deane, too, there was a new child. On Sunday 18 November Jane wrote to Cassandra, 'I have just received a note from James to say that Mary was brought to bed last night, at eleven o'clock, of a fine little boy, and that everything is going on very well.'

A week later she was able to report that the baby's eyes were 'large, dark and handsome'. The christening ceremony was performed on 30 December, one of the godfathers being his uncle Edward, and the other General Mathew, with whom James had maintained a respectful friendship, though Mary never learnt to overcome her fear of her predecessor's father, whose word was undisputed law in his own family.

The child was given the names James Edward but always known as Edward. Bypassing the rather difficult temperaments of his own parents, he was fortunate to inherit the happy and lovable disposition of his paternal grandfather – as well as the fine intellect and literary taste that both George and James Austen possessed. He was to grow into the nephew with the closest affinity to Jane, and to be her first biographer.

At Godmersham Edward's health continued to trouble him and he decided to take the cure at Bath in the early summer of 1799. With his wife, daughter Fanny and son Edward, he travelled via Steventon, collecting his mother and sister Jane and taking them on to Bath. They took a house in Queen Square and spent a very pleasant month there. On Sunday 2 June Jane wrote that Edward 'drinks at the Hetling Pump, is to bathe tomorrow, and try electricity on Tuesday', none of which appeared to have much effect, but his symptoms eventually passed and for the remainder of his long life he enjoyed excellent health.

This was not Jane's first visit to Bath by any means, but formerly she had always stayed with her uncle and aunt Leigh Perrot, who owned a house in the Paragon, on the London road, a part of the town she found particularly disagreeable. Not altogether agreeable either was the character of her aunt. Jane Leigh Perrot was a difficult, capricious, stern and unbending sort of woman, whom all the world respected but nobody but her husband much liked; he was devoted to her, and she to him. A childless couple, their lives centred upon one another and upon their two homes, 1 Paragon and Scarlets in Berkshire.

Their devotion was tested to the full, and not found wanting, when, shortly after the six Austens had left Bath, an experience of nightmarish proportions befell them.

In August 1799 Mrs Leigh Perrot was accused by a Bath shopkeeper of stealing a card of lace worth £1. The charge was ludicrous, of course; she was the wife of a very wealthy man, and her integrity was beyond reproach. In fact the near-bankrupt shopkeeper had parcelled up two cards of lace, where only one had been requested and paid for, with the idea of blackmailing the couple to prevent the case going any further.

The Leigh Perrots, however, were united in desiring to clear their name of such base imputations and to expose the villainy of their accuser. They could not be perfectly certain that a verdict of guilty might not be brought in; had it been, the penalty for this petty crime was death, although transportation for fourteen years would probably have been imposed instead. In case there was such a miscarriage of justice, Mr Leigh Perrot made arrangements to sell Scarlets if necessary so that he could accompany his wife to Australia.

He *did* accompany her to Ilchester jail (bail being refused) or rather to the house of the jailor, Mr Scadding, where the couple were permitted to lodge, and where they endured 'vulgarity, dirt, noise from morning to night'.[5] Not surprisingly, such conditions made them both ill; Mr Leigh Perrot was already suffering from gout, but his wife hesitated to send for the only medical man of Ilchester as he combined the trades of apothecary and surgeon with those of coal-dealer and brick- and tile-maker!

For the fastidious couple whose lives had hitherto been so elegant and orderly, the sudden change was a terrible shock. Had she known what horrors were in store for her, Mrs Leigh Perrot wrote, she would have chosen death instead. However, she bore up remarkably well; misfortune enabled her to reveal the best side of her character. She wrote to her cousin Montague Cholmeley: 'My dearest Perrot with his sweet composure adds to my philosophy; to be sure he bids fair to have his patience tried in every way he can. Cleanliness has ever been his greatest delight and yet he sees the greasy toast laid by the dirty children on his knees, and feels the small beer trickle down his sleeves on its way across the table unmoved ... Mrs Scadding's knife well licked to clean it from fried onions helps me now and then – you may believe how the mess I am helped to is disposed of – here are two dogs and three cats always full as hungry as myself.'

Mrs Austen offered to send one or both her daughters to keep their aunt company in her confinement; luckily for them, she unselfishly declined, as she could not let 'those elegant young women' suffer as she was suffering. The whole of the winter was spent by the Leigh Perrots in the cold and discomfort of the Scaddings' home, the trial not being set until the end of March. As the date approached, Mrs Austen made further offers. Jane Leigh Perrot wrote to Montague Cholmeley:

My dear affectionate sister Austen, though in a state of health not equal to *trials* of any kind, has been with the greatest difficulty kept from me. In a letter from her a few days ago I had the pain to hear of her valuable son James having had his horse fall with him by which a leg was broken. This is a loss indeed because he had been a perfect son to me in affection and his firm friendship all through this trying business had taught me to look to him and his wife (a relation of Lord Craven's, well bred and sensible) to have come to us at the assizes. *Now* I can neither ask mother or wife to leave him nor could I accept the offer of my nieces – to have two young creatures gazed at in a public court would cut one to the very heart.

At Taunton Assizes on 29 March 1800 Mrs Leigh Perrot was 'most honourably acquitted'. Restored to the peace and comfort of her home in Bath after an ordeal of seven months, she wrote to Montague Cholmeley: 'That these wretches had marked me for somebody timid enough to be scared, and rich enough to pay handsomely rather than go through the terrible proceedings of a public trial nobody doubts; and by timing it when I had only my husband with me they were sure I could have no evidence against them. Surely our boasted laws are strangely defective.'

For the honour of clearing themselves, and the pleasure of languishing in a miserable and unhealthy confinement for seven months, the Leigh Perrots were faced with expenses totalling nearly £2,000.

During his cousin's imprisonment, Montague Cholmeley had

written to advise against the Leigh Perrots' ever resuming residence in 'that infernal Bath, a place I always hated, and shall now never think of without horror, being now more than ever convinced that it is neither more nor less than a den of villains, and a harbour for all sorts of swindlers'. Mrs Leigh Perrot, however, chose to return 'principally because I know the waters are more than ever necessary to my dear husband, and because I thought it right on every account to return to Bath.'

Nor did her terrible experiences give her brother and sister-in-law any distaste for the city they had married in, it seems. Suddenly, towards the end of the year 1800, Mr and Mrs Austen decided to leave Steventon and retire to Bath.

We know that their decision *was* a sudden one because as late as November furniture was being bought for the Rectory, and improvements being made to the garden at Steventon. 'Hacker has been here today, putting in the fruit trees. – A new plan has been suggested concerning the plantation of the new inclosure on the right hand side of the Elm Walk – the doubt is whether it would be better to make a little orchard of it, by planting apples, pears and cherries, or whether it should be larch, mountain-ash and acacia . – What is your opinion?' Jane asked Cassandra, who was again on a visit to Godmersham, on the 20th of that month; and on the 8th she had written of two new tables that had been delivered, and of a chiffonier ordered – all of which had to be left behind when they went to Bath. It was uneconomic to transport furniture such a distance; their own beds were the only items considered indispensable to take.

Cassandra was still at Godmersham, and Jane on a brief visit to Ibthorp, when their parents made the decision at the beginning of December. There is a family tradition that when Jane, accompanied by Martha Lloyd, arrived back at Steventon to be greeted cheerily by her mother, almost on the doorstep, with the words, 'Well girls! it is all settled. We have decided to leave Steventon and to go Bath,' she fainted with the shock.

She was soon, characteristically, trying to reconcile herself to the change – but it was not one at all to her taste. Bath was all very well for a holiday, but neither Jane nor Cassandra liked the idea of permanent residence in a city. They were deeply attached to

Steventon and to the rural way of life. But, at twenty-five and twenty-eight respectively, these two young women had no say in where they were to live, no alternative but to accompany their parents wherever they chose to go.

8

The best of fathers, and men

1801-06

When the Reverend George Austen left Steventon in the spring of 1801, he was seventy and had been in possession of the living for forty years. Frank's memoir describes his father at this period 'being incapacitated from age and increasing infirmities to discharge his parochial duties in a manner satisfactory to himself'.

Nevertheless, he was still a strikingly handsome man, for, as his grand-daughter Anna testified, the good looks for which he had always been remarkable stood by him all his life. Even in old age, she recalled, 'his hair in its milk-whiteness ... was very beautiful, with short curls about the ears. His eyes were not large, but of a peculiar and bright hazel.'[1] And to these attractions was added 'the sweet, benevolent smile which always distinguished him', according to his daughter Jane.

The first four months of 1801 were occupied making the many arrangements attendant on the great change in the Austens' lives. Cassandra was still at Godmersham. 'There is something interesting in the bustle of going away,' Jane wrote to her, forcing herself to look on the bright side.

A letter from Charles, written at sea on 7 February, furnished some news: 'Charles spent three pleasant days in Lisbon ... He received my letter, communicating our plans, before he left England, was much surprised of course, but is quite reconciled to them, and means to come to Steventon once more while Steventon is ours.' That Charles was 'much surprised' confirms how unpremeditated was his parents' decision to retire to Bath, for he had been home as recently as 22 November.

Though the Rectory and the 'parochial duties' were to devolve upon James, George Austen was to continue Rector in name and salary. Jane wrote of her father's efforts to increase the tithes, and their hopes of having £600 a year to live upon in Bath. £50 a year was to be spared for a curate to help James, who evidently did not share his father's taste for farming, as a neighbour, Mr Holder of Ashe Park, agreed to take over the lease of the farm and the employment of George Austen's faithful bailiff.

The question of servants generally had to be settled; Jane wrote to Cassandra: 'My mother looks forward with as much certainty as you can do, to our keeping two maids – my father is the only one not in the secret. We plan having a steady cook, and a young giddy housemaid, with a sedate, middle aged man, who is to undertake the double office of husband to the former and sweetheart to the latter. – No children of course to be allowed on either side.'

Then there were the books: 'My father has got above 500 volumes to dispose of; I want James to take them at a venture at half a guinea a volume,' and the horses: 'the brown mare, which as well as the black was to devolve on James on our removal, has not had patience to wait for that, and has settled herself even now at Deane.'

Cassandra left Godmersham in February and stayed three weeks in London at the new home of Henry and Eliza. He had left the militia a considerably richer man than when he had entered it. The custom of paying officers gratuities on demobilization had recently been established, and with the interest from Eliza's fortune, the couple were wealthy enough to take a good house in Upper Berkeley Street, and to keep their own carriage.

Cassandra was home in time to participate in the final packing and farewells. So was Frank, who happened to be on leave, awaiting his next appointment. The many and varied exploits of the *Peterel* under his command, especially the single-handed capture of five French vessels attempting to take supplies to Napoleon's stranded army in Egypt in the summer of 1800, had gained him promotion to the rank of Flag Captain. Too elevated now for the *Peterel*, Frank had been relieved of his duties while cruising in the eastern Mediterranean and had been obliged to make his own way home on any ship that was going. He was now considered fit to command the flagship of an admiral; in the event he was appointed to the

Neptune, with Admiral Gambier on board.

Meanwhile, at the beginning of May, the departure from Steventon was made. Frank accompanied his father first to Godmersham and then to London, Cassandra visited Ibthorp and Kintbury, while Mrs Austen and Jane travelled straight to Bath, where they stayed with the Leigh Perrots and began the business of house-hunting.

Jane's first letter from Bath gives a pleasing picture of her uncle, James Leigh Perrot: 'I had not been two minutes in the dining room before he questioned me with all his accustomary eager interest about Frank and Charles, their views and intentions.'

On 27 May she was able to give some delightful news of Charles himself:

> He has received £30 for his share of the privateer and expects £10 more – but of what avail is it to take prizes if he lays out the produce in presents to his sisters. He has been buying gold chains and topaze crosses for us; – he must be well scolded. The *Endymion* has already received orders for taking troops to Egypt – which I should not like at all if I did not trust to Charles' being removed from her somehow or other before she sails. He knows nothing of his destination he says, – but desires me to write directly as the *Endymion* will probably sail in 3 or 4 days. – He will receive my yesterday's letter today, and I shall write again by this post to thank and reproach him, – We shall be unbearably fine.

Meanwhile there had been news of the sale of the livestock, furniture and effects left behind at Steventon. 'Sixty one guineas and a half for the three cows gives one some support under the blow of only eleven guineas for the tables. Eight for my pianoforte is about what I expected to get; I am more anxious to know the amount of my books, especially as they are said to have sold well.' It must have been hard to give up not only their home but virtually all their possessions. Jane rented a pianoforte while she lived in Bath.

Mr Austen collected Cassandra from Kintbury, and they joined the other half of the family in house-hunting from the Paragon at the beginning of June. After rejecting many houses on the grounds of size, expense, aspect or fear of dampness, they settled on 4 Sydney Place.

This was a part of Bath they had once thought they could not afford, but presumably it was decided that the extremely favourable location made the extra cost worthwhile. On the newly laid out Bathwick estate, one of the few level areas in Bath, their chosen home was approached via the magnificent Great Pulteney Street and was directly opposite the very pleasant Sydney Gardens.

Bath at this time was no longer so fashionable as it had been in the middle of the preceding century; by the upper classes it had been deserted in favour of the new seaside resorts, leaving it the home of retired clergymen, generals and admirals, or the winter quarters of the conservative gentry – middling people like themselves, to whom it offered an agreeable and not too expensive way of life.

But the Austens had caught the new enthusiasm for the sea themselves. Intrinsic in the plan of settling in Bath had been the refinement of escaping from it every summer. Enclosed by hills, full of people, animals, sewage and decomposing food, the city could be an airless, enervating and unhealthy spot during the hottest months of the year.

'The prospect of spending future summers by the sea or in Wales is very delightful,' Jane had written in January, whilst still trying to reconcile herself to leaving Steventon. There is no evidence to suggest that the Austens ever actually ventured into Wales, but the next few summers were spent by them in the pretty little south Devon coastal resorts of Sidmouth, Dawlish and Teignmouth.

On one of these holidays, it is believed, yet without any of the details being known, Jane met and fell in love with a young man whom even Cassandra considered worthy of her sister and who returned her feelings; but before the romance could blossom into a positive engagement, the Austens received the melancholy news of his death. Such was Jane's only real entanglement of the heart, and it was as ill-fated as Cassandra's. Her romance being shorter-lived, however, there is reason to suppose she was able the more quickly to shake off her dejection – especially as hers was 'not a mind for affliction', as she herself was to say of her brother Henry, whom she resembled in so many ways.

Nevertheless, the experience went deep. In December 1802 Jane accepted, one evening, a highly eligible proposal of marriage from Harris Bigg-Wither, whose father owned Manydown Park in

Hampshire and whose sisters were among her dearest and earliest
friends. It was a match with everything to recommend it, but
overnight she realized her mistake and the following morning, in
great distress, withdrew her word. Having known love, she could
not now marry without it. Henceforward both Austen sisters
thought of themselves as spinsters – as dutiful daughters, sisters and
aunts – as everything but potential wives.

On 9 October 1801 Hastings Capot de Feuillide died, aged fifteen.
His physical and mental state of health had ever been a source of
worry to Eliza, who replied, twenty days after her son's death, to
Philadelphia's letter of condolence:

> I am much obliged by your kind participation in an event which
> though, as you rightly consider it, a desirable release has greatly affected
> my spirits. So awful a dissolution of a near and tender tie must ever be a
> severe shock, and my mind was already weakened by witnessing the sad
> variety and long series of pain which the dear sufferer underwent – but
> deeply impressed as I am with the heart-rending scenes I have beheld I
> am most thankful for their termination, and the exchange which I
> humbly hope my dear child has made of a most painful existence for a
> blissful immortality.
>
> In addition to my affliction on poor Hastings' account, I have
> undergone much anxiety concerning Henry, who for five months never
> enjoyed an hour's health. His complaints were a cough, hectic pain in
> the side and in short everything which denotes a galloping
> consumption in which I believe all his acquaintance thought him. At
> length a prescription of Dr Baillie's (who had already tried a variety of
> medicines to no purpose) removed some of the above symptoms, and
> from that time he has mended so fast that he is now nearly as well as I
> had always known him to be previous to this attack.
>
> I conclude that you know of our uncle and aunt Austen and their
> daughters having spent the summer in Devonshire. They are now
> returned to Bath where they are superintending the fitting up of their
> new house. Their eldest son James is in possession of Steventon where
> he has made such alterations and embellishments that it is almost a
> pretty place – not however that I have seen it, for you know that I am
> not given to visiting and have taken near four years to accomplish a
> journey to Godmersham Park, for which place I purpose setting out
> tomorrow morning. Mrs E.A. produced her seventh child about six or
> seven weeks since.

Elizabeth Austen's latest babies were girls: her namesake, always known as Lizzy, born on 27 January 1800, and Marianne born on 15 September 1801. In the year of Marianne's birth, her father became High Sheriff of Kent. But that was as far as Edward's ambition for public life went, and he declined standing for Parliament, though encouraged by many to do so.

After the Peace of Amiens the following year, Eliza and Henry crossed to France in an unsuccessful attempt to recover her property there. They were still in France when hostilities were resumed, and escaped internment only through Eliza's perfect command of the French language.

Like many other officers at the Peace of Amiens, Frank went on half pay, but the renewal of war in 1803 brought him an entirely new set of responsibilities. In order to defend the coast from possible French attack, a new body known as the 'Sea Fencibles' was instituted. It was composed of local fishermen who were paid one shilling a day plus a food allowance whenever they were required for duty, each stretch of coast being under the command of a naval officer. Frank was appointed to take charge of the section between North Foreland and Sandown, with headquarters at Ramsgate. His job was to raise and organize his corps, to exercise them once a week and to ensure the beaches were watched whenever the weather favoured an enemy attack.

This seems rather a feeble occupation for an able-bodied man of twenty-nine who had proved himself highly courageous and enterprising at sea, and who must have been longing to have a share of the action now that fighting had recommenced. His scorn for the system he was part of found expression many years later when he wrote, 'The Sea Fencibles in the author's opinion if they had ever been called upon to service would have been a non-descript half-sailor half-soldier and efficient at neither.'

At the time, however, Frank approached his new duties with his customary diligence and zeal, beginning by preparing a meticulously detailed document investigating the most likely landing-places and concluding that a successful invasion was possible if the enemy chose their weather carefully and could evade the British warships lying in wait for them offshore.

Frank's adherence to correct behaviour, regardless of what other people were doing or saying, caused him to be remarked as '*the officer who knelt in church*' at Ramsgate. One of the residents of the little town was Miss Mary Gibson, whom Frank came to know and love. After a year's acquaintance he became engaged to her in February 1804, during a visit to the theatre at Covent Garden. 'Do you happen to recollect anything of the evening? I think you do, and that you will not readily forget it,'[2] he teased her gently eighteen months later, for the engagement was perforce a long one.

Napoleon's flotilla of flat-bottomed troop-carrying barges, which had been assembling at Boulogne since the resumption of hostilities, had by 1804 assumed such seriously threatening proportions that a permanent blockade on the port by British warships was necessary. Frank moved a step closer to the action when he became part of this blockading force on his appointment in May of that year to the *Leopard*, flagship of Rear-Admiral Louis.

Indulging in theatricals, Napoleon paraded through his maritime provinces with the Bayeux tapestry on display, attempting to whip up invasion fever. The English certainly feared the large army of veteran soldiers they believed were encamped along the French coastline waiting the right moment to embark. However, one of the ingenious measures they adopted in an effort to protect themselves met with some misgivings from Frank. His memoir records:

> Captain Austen was present at the attempt made to destroy the enemy's flotilla at Boulogne by means of vessels loaded with combustibles which were to be exploded by clockwork machinery and which totally failed from the impossibility of directing the vessels with any tolerable precision to the object intended to be assailed. This horrible mode of warfare seems scarcely justifiable in principle (amongst civilised nations) short of self-preservation and perhaps its entire want of success may have been a fortunate circumstance for England who could not have expected to be the only power to use such machines and whose shipping would be constantly liable to similar attack with much greater facility from the exposed situations of the anchorages then used.

Notwithstanding this failure on the part of the British, Napoleon was sufficiently deterred by the presence of warships in the Channel from making his invasion bid. He realized that this stood little chance of success unless the French had supremacy of the seas – and the next year saw the culmination of his struggle to achieve just that.

As this decisive period in naval history approached, the other sailor in the family, Charles, was suddenly wholly removed from the main theatre of conflict by an appointment which seemed to be promotion at the time but which turned out to have a detrimental long-term effect on his fortunes. In October 1804 he was sent out to the East Indies to take up command of the sloop *Indian*, which shortly afterwards was directed to the North American station. Here both captain and ship were to remain for the next six years, engaged in the unprofitable, tedious and unsung work of searching for deserters and intercepting such American trade as Britain deemed illicit. Thus prevented from gaining either distinction or prizes in the imminent great battle with the French, Charles was also exiled from his family for longer than either he or they could like.

Elizabeth Austen had recently produced two more children – Charles Bridges on 11 March 1803 and Louisa on 13 November 1804 – but for her sister-in-law Jane these were unproductive years. She made a start on a new novel but abandoned it. Her genius seemed to require a settled rural home to flourish properly.

In 1803 another attempt at publication was made on her behalf, this time by Henry, who as a man of affairs in London was better placed than her now frail and never very business-like father to act for her. The manuscript of *Susan* was sold for the sum of £10 to the publishing house of Crosbie who actually advertised it as one of their forthcoming novels – but then, evidently deciding not to risk any more of their money, never set it up in type.

Parents and daughters spent the summer of 1803 at Lyme in Dorset, and liked it so much that they returned the following year, joined by Henry and Eliza. After three years in their house at Sydney Place, the lease was given up, and when they returned to Bath in the autumn of 1804, it was to a slightly less desirable and presumably cheaper part of the town, Green Park Buildings, on the low-lying area by the river.

Fully alert still in mind, George Austen was growing increasingly, but not alarmingly, infirm; he had walked about at Lyme with the aid of a stick and a servant. His death on 21 January 1805, after a feverish illness of only forty-eight hours, was quite unexpected. 'He was mercifully spared from knowing that he was about to quit the objects so beloved, so fondly cherished as his wife and children ever were. – His tenderness as a father, who can do justice to?' wrote Jane in a letter breaking the news to Frank at sea.

Since it was the custom for male mourners only to accompany a funeral, just James and Henry saw their father buried at Walcot church, where forty years before he had been married. The following day Henry wrote to Frank:[3]

Yours reached me yesterday soon after my return from Walcot Church when in company with James I saw deposited the remains of the best of fathers, and men. Language is so inadequate to what we all feel on such a subject, that you will know why I prefer silence to imperfect praise. The surviving are now what we must all think of. My mother and sisters derive their best present consolation from the exertions of their own minds, and a long habitual resignation to the decrees of heaven. Whilst however our dear parent continues to inhabit this world I think measures are already taken to ensure her a continuance of every necessary, I hope of every comfort. James behaves like a man of feeling and a true son on the occasion. He has appropriated fifty pounds a year to our dear trio; I shall do as much as long as my present precarious income remains. Edward has been very properly written to on the occasion – I shall be more than surprised if he does not pledge himself to as much as James and I together. In this case my mother will have a good 400 pounds per annum, and I know she feels herself thoroughly satisfied therewith. You see therefore my dear brother that you need not abridge yourself to any part of your own modicum – I know of what you are capable – And when you have taken a galleon, you shall keep a carriage for my mother if you choose –

Your letter perfectly satisfied us for your absence. We know enough of your situation not to indulge unreasonable demands. We shall be very glad to hear as soon as possible of your ultimate destination. *I* rather think you *will* go to the Mediterranean – Douglass is mentioned as to command at Dungeness –

James and I return to Steventon together on Wednesday, and I shall be at home on Friday. My uncle and aunt have both shown much feeling and real affection during the whole of our severe trial. My aunt *herself* could not help loving such a being as the one whom we lament. – I believe that my mother will remain in this house till Lady Day, and then probably reduce her establishment to one female domestic and take furnished lodgings. She does not like to leave Bath altogether so long as Mr Perrot continues here and seems to derive comfort from her society.

Just at this time Frank learned that Rear-Admiral Louis had been promoted to the *Canopus*, and he with him. The *Canopus*, which had been captured from the French at the Battle of the Nile, was one of the finest fighting ships in the British Navy. With such enhanced prospects Frank generously offered to contribute £100 annually to his mother's income, despite his own plans for marriage. Henry replied on 28 January:

Your letter received this morning has given us all the sincerest pleasure in the intelligence which it conveys of the improvement of your present situation and approaching prospects. – We all heartily wish you joy of the *Canopus*, which I see is an 80 guns ship, and which I calculate will nett you £500 per annum. It was so absolutely necessary that your noble offer towards my mother should be made more public than you seemed to desire, that I really cannot apologise for a partial breach of your request. With the proudest exultations of maternal tenderness the excellent parent has exclaimed that never were children so good as hers. – She feels the magnificence of your offer, and accepts of half. I shall therefore honour her demands for 50 pounds annually on your account. James had the day before yesterday communicated to me and her his desire to be her banker for the same annual assistance, and I as long as I am *an agent* shall do as he does. If Edward does the least he ought, he will certainly insist on her receiving a £100 from him. So you see my dear F. that with her own assured property and Cassandra's both producing about £210 per annum, she will be in receipt of a clear 450 pounds per annum. – She will be very comfortable, and as a smaller establishment will be as agreeable to them, as it cannot but be feasible, I really think that my mother and sisters will be full as rich as ever. They will not only suffer no personal deprivation but will be able to pay occasional visits of health and pleasure to their friends. My mother had a good night yesterday and is proportionably refreshed this day. Everything is now so far settled that James and I set out on our return tomorrow. I accompany James to Steventon, but shall be home on Thursday evening. I shall now not quit London for some time. – All your commissions shall be attended to, and Mary shall receive my earliest visit.

And finally in this little group of letters evidently cherished by Frank came one from James, written on 30 January:

The date of this will inform you that I am returned home and you will be pleased to learn that *we* (for Henry accompanied me) left our mother and sisters at least as well as we had right or reason to expect. My mother's two last nights were good ones and their good effects were visible both in her looks and spirits. – She is always composed and at times cheerful. Her future plans are not quite settled, but I believe her summers will be spent in the country amongst her relations and chiefly I trust among her children – the winters she will pass in comfortable lodgings in Bath. It is a just satisfaction to know that her circumstances will be easy, and that she will enjoy all those comforts which her declining years and precarious health call for.

You will I am sure forgive Henry for not having entirely complied with your request of secrecy upon one very important subject in your letter. I would not upon any account have lost the pleasure I derived from such a proof of your feelings of delicacy – I will not pay you so bad a compliment as to say I was in the least surprised at it – for in honest truth your behaviour was just what I expected. I knew your heart and your wishes; and I rejoiced to find that your means and your prospects are such as enable you to indulge them. You would indeed have had a high gratification could you have witnessed the pleasure which our dear mother experienced when your intention was communicated to her ...

Henry desires me to say that he will attend to your commissions and that you may expect to hear from him soon. He goes to London tomorrow.

Mary and the young ones are well; they desire to add their love and good wishes to mine – Adieu my dear brother. May health, success and honour attend you during your absence; and may you have a speedy return and reap the reward which your principles and exertions deserve in the enjoyment of domestic comforts and the society of her who can best make your home comfortable to you.

By the death of his father James became Rector of Steventon. His 'young ones' received an addition later that year when on 18 June Mary gave birth to a daughter, named Caroline Mary Craven.

On the expiration of the Green Park Buildings lease, Mrs Austen and her daughters moved to Gay Street, an extremely agreeable part of the town between Queen Square and the Circus. Here they were joined by Martha Lloyd, who came to make her home with them on the death of her mother that April.

The annual visit to the sea was by no means given up, perhaps thanks to the generosity of Edward – for he and Elizabeth, Henry and Eliza, and the party from Bath joined forces for a holiday to Worthing that year. Whilst this scheme was in agitation, Jane told Cassandra: 'I wrote to Henry because I had a letter from him, in which he desired to hear from me very soon. His to me was most affectionate and kind, as well as entertaining; there is no merit to him in *that*, he cannot help being amusing ... He offers to meet us on the sea-coast if the plan, of which Edward gave him some hint, takes place. Will this not be making the execution of such a plan, more desirable and delightful than ever. – He talks of the rambles we took together last summer with pleasing affection.'

Frank was becoming impatient to marry, but his personal life had to wait for a lull in the great events then attendant upon his profession. The early summer had been spent by him chasing across the Atlantic and back. In order to prevent the various elements of Napoleon's fleet from combining – and so overpowering the British in the Channel and embarking the long-encamped troops – ten ships, headed by Nelson's *Victory* with the *Canopus* second in line sailed on 11 May to search for Villeneuve with the orders from Nelson, 'Rendezvous Barbadoes'. The distance of 3,200 miles was accomplished by 4 June, but they had missed finding the French fleet and began the long voyage back eleven days later, the winds now against them. They combined at Ushant with Admiral Collingwood's fleet, making thirty-five ships in all.

Throughout September the British blockaded the French and Spanish at Cadiz. Having been in a state of high anticipation all year, both sides were now geared for battle.

To maintain the British fleet at sea, there had to be a constant detachment of ships making the passage to Gibraltar in order to take on supplies, and at the beginning of October it was the turn of the *Canopus*, among others, to perform that duty. Thus by the unluckiest of chances Frank narrowly missed the most glorious action of all, Trafalgar. A long diary letter written to his fiancée during the month of October describes his feelings of frustration as he first suspected, and then had confirmed, this wretched mischance. No element of relief as the escape of personal danger seems to have alleviated his disappointment.

October 21. – We have just bid adieu to the convoy, without attending them quite so far as was originally intended, having this day received intelligence, by a vessel despatched in pursuit of us, that on Saturday, 19th, the enemy's fleet was actually under way, and coming out of Cadiz.

Our situation is peculiarly unpleasant and distressing, for if they escape Lord Nelson's vigilance and get into the Mediterranean, which is not very likely, we shall be obliged, with our small force, to keep out of their way; and on the other hand, should an action take place, it must be decided long before we could possibly get down even were the wind fair, which at present it is not. As I have no doubt but the event would be highly honourable to our arms, and be at the same time productive of some good prizes, I shall have to lament our absence on such an occasion on a double account, the loss of pecuniary advantage as well as of professional credit. And after having been so many months in a state of constant and unremitting fag, to be at last cut out by a parcel of folk just come from their homes, where some of them were sitting at their ease the greater part of last war, and the whole of this, till just now, is particularly hard and annoying.

You, perhaps, may not feel this so forcibly as I do, and in your satisfaction at my having avoided the danger of battle may not much regret my losing the credit of having contributed to gain a victory; not so myself!

I do not profess to like fighting for its own sake, but if there has been an action with the combined fleets I shall ever consider the day on which I sailed from the squadron as the most inauspicious one of my life.

October 27, off Tetuan. – Alas! my dearest Mary, all my fears are but too fully justified. The fleets have met, and, after a very severe contest, a most decisive victory has been gained by the English twenty-seven over the enemy's thirty-three. Seventeen of the ships are taken and one is burnt; but I am truly sorry to add that this splendid affair has cost us many lives, and amongst them the most invaluable one to the nation, that of our gallant, and ever-to-be-regretted, Commander-in-Chief, Lord Nelson, who was mortally wounded by a musket shot, and only lived long enough to know his fleet successful. In a public point of view, I consider his loss as the greatest which could have occurred; nor do I hesitate to say there is not an Admiral on the list so eminently calculated for the command of a fleet as he was. I never heard of his equal, nor do I expect again to see such a man. To the soundest judgment he united prompt decision and speedy execution of his plans; and he possessed in a superior degree the happy talent of making every class of persons pleased with their situation and eager to exert themselves in forwarding the public service. As a national benefit I cannot but rejoice that our arms have been once again successful, but at the same time I cannot help feeling how very unfortunate we have been to be away at such a moment, and, by a fatal combination of unfortunate though unavoidable events, to lose all share in the glory of a day which surpasses all which ever went before, is what I cannot think of with any degree of patience; but, as I cannot write upon that subject without complaining, I will drop it for the present, till time and reflection reconcile me a little more to what I know is now inevitable.

Frank would have been gratified to know that his good opinion of the heroic Admiral was returned. On 30 March that year Nelson had written to the Earl of Moira: 'Captain Austin [*sic*] delivered to me your Lordship's letter of February 11th. A frigate would have been better calculated to have given Captain Austin a fortune out of the Mediterranean than coming under my command where nothing is to be got, except the French fleet should put to sea ... Captain Austin I knew a little before; he is an excellent young man.'

On 31 October, having rejoined the victorious fleet, Frank was able to send fuller particulars of the battle and the state of the ships on both sides, summing up: 'The action appears in general to have been obstinately contested, and has doubtless been unusually bloody; but it has also been so decisive as to make it improbable the Spaniards or French will again risk a meeting with a British fleet.'

His own prospects, however, did not give equal cause for rejoicing: 'By the death of Lord Nelson I have again lost all chance of a frigate. I had asked his lordship to appoint me to one when he had the opportunity, and, though I had no positive promise from him, I have reason to believe he would have attended to my wishes. Of Admiral Collingwood I do not know enough to allow of my making a similar request: and not having been in the action I have no claims of service to urge in support of my wishes.'

As he had feared, Frank was not transferred to a frigate but remained with the *Canopus*, which was not fulfilling the high expectations he had formed of her but was proving distressingly slow. However, some consolation for all these trials to his sailor's heart lay ahead for Frank when, for the second time in a year, he crossed the Atlantic and found himself participating in the highly successful action of St Domingo, on 6 February 1806.

The following day Frank snatched a few moments from his

duties to write Mary a short letter which would go off with the Admiral's despatches. After describing the battle, he wrote: 'I am in hopes this action will be the means of our speedy quitting this country, and perhaps to return to Old England. Oh, how my heart throbs at the idea! The *Canopus* sails so bad that we were nearly the last ship in action; when we did get up, however, we had our share of it. Our people behaved admirably well, and displayed astonishing coolness during the whole time ... We have not suffered much in masts and rigging, and I fancy not an officer is killed in the whole squadron.'

Accompanied by their three prizes, one of which was so badly damaged as to require towing, the British squadron came triumphantly into Portsmouth on 29 April 1806. On 24 July, at Ramsgate, Frank married Mary Gibson, 'happy in the possession of one of the most amiable of her sex, to whom he had long been tenderly affected and who fully deserved his warmest affections by her unwearied endeavours to promote his comfort and happiness'.

Henceforward there were two Mary Austens in the family. To avoid confusion they were often referred to as Mrs James and Mrs Frank, or Mrs J.A. and Mrs F.A.

It was to Mrs James that Mrs Austen wrote on 10 April 1806, dating her letter 'Trim Street still'; having stayed only briefly in Gay Street, Henry's 'dear trio' were again contemplating a move, for Mrs Austen stated: 'We are disappointed of the lodgings in St James' Square; a person is in treaty for the whole house, so of course he will be preferred to us who want only a part. We have looked at some others since, but don't quite like the situation – hope a few days hence we shall have more choice, as it is supposed many will be quitting Bath when this gay week is over.'

Their plans were given quite a different direction, however, by Frank's return and the discussions which evidently ensued; for whether for reasons for economy or to provide company and support for Frank's wife while he was at sea, it was agreed by all concerned that the two households should amalgamate.

Southampton was the chosen spot for this shared home. Frank would be the only man in an establishment of five females: his new wife, his mother, his two maiden sisters and their friend Martha Lloyd. It was an extraordinary arrangement but not one likely to

have been embarked on by the sensible Austens unless they had felt
pretty confident it would work, contribute to the happiness of all
parties and produce no ill feeling between them.

As a family, after all, they had brought to perfection the art of
living in harmony together. One of the younger generation,
Caroline Austen, recalled in old age their 'spirit of forbearance and
generosity' and how their conversation was 'never troubled by
disagreements as it was not their habit to argue with each other'.

Before settling in Southampton that autumn, Mrs Austen and her
daughters embarked on a series of summer visits, this time travelling
gradually northward until reaching the Staffordshire home of
Edward Cooper, who had invited his aunt to his rectory at Hamstall
Ridware in a letter written that spring to congratulate her on
'Frank's victory and safety'.

The departure from Bath was made on 2 July – 'with what happy
feelings of escape!' remembered Jane, surprisingly fervently, two
years later. Jane and Cassandra must surely have taken care to
conceal from their mother their unabated dislike of the city whilst
she chose to remain there; it is hardly likely that she would have
done so against their expressed wishes, their known distaste: a
remarkably unselfish concealment sustained for a period of five
years.

The little party went first to Clifton – another elegant resort of
fashion and fine buildings not dissimilar from Bath but enjoying an
airy cliff-top situation and much preferred by Cassandra and Jane –
and then on to Adlestrop rectory in Gloucestershire. This was the
home of three of Mrs Austen's first cousins: the Reverend Thomas
Leigh, younger son of her uncle William, his unmarried sister
Elizabeth and his wife Mary, daughter of her uncle Theophilus.

The Austen ladies arrived at a time of great excitement and
confusion, for Thomas Leigh had just come into a magnificent but
somewhat uncertain inheritance. On the very day that they had left
Bath for ever, a mutual relation, the Honourable Mary Leigh of
Stoneleigh Abbey in Warwickshire, had died in her Kensington
town house. Usually referred to by the courtesy a title of 'Mrs
Leigh', she was the surviving unmarried sister of the fifth and last
Lord Leigh, who had died insane in 1786.

Stoneleigh Abbey had been left to her by her brother only for life, but some ambiguity in his will concerning who should succeed her – the phrase 'the first and nearest of my kindred being male and of my name and blood' tending to set the natural heir, James Leigh, behind his uncle Thomas Leigh, and Thomas Leigh's cousin James Leigh Perrot (although both of these rather elderly men were childless, and the property must eventually devolve on James Leigh) – persuaded Mary to specify in her own will that the three gentlemen concerned should inherit in the order her brother had seemed to wish.

From the first James Leigh Perrot, deeply attached to his own home, Scarlets, and probably feeling that there were not many years ahead of him anyway, was prepared to relinquish his place in the succession for financial compensation. Thomas Leigh, who might have felt the same and let his nephew take on Stoneleigh straight away, had no such intention and to make quite sure of the inheritance went immediately to the Abbey.

His nephew and cousin, together with the Honourable Mary Leigh's man of business, Mr Hill, had meanwhile gathered in London to sort everything out and were not best pleased. James Leigh Perrot wrote to his wife on 5 July:[4] 'I am to dine again at Mr Hill's today, that we may have some leisure to talk over the whole business. Mr Hill tells me the uncle and nephew must and will act very handsomely towards me. When Mr Thomas Leigh thinks proper to make his appearance, same proposals and steps must be made and taken towards an accommodation; I hope and flatter myself they will be satisfactory to you and me. To the uncle and nephew any accommodation must be highly advantageous. I cannot imagine it possible you will receive any other letter from me. How glad shall I be to tell you how dearly I love and value you, instead of employing my pen for that purpose!'

Eventually Thomas Leigh joined the others, and 'an accommodation' was reached (though not ratified for another two years, the period of delay being attended by the usual confusions and uncertainties). The uncle and nephew did indeed 'act very handsomely', for the final settlement was that James Leigh Perrot should receive a sum of £20,000 raised by mortgage on Stoneleigh, a further £4,000 from the personal property of James Leigh, and an annuity of £2,000 payable to himself or his widow for life. Jane

Leigh Perrot lived to be over ninety; she and her husband thus gained something like £80,000 from the agreement which Jane Austen, unable to foresee her aunt's longevity, called in one of her letters a 'vile compromise'.

Thomas Leigh was back at Adlestrop in time to receive his guests, but almost immediately another visit to Stoneleigh became necessary. He therefore took his visiting relations with him, and Mrs Austen, Cassandra and Jane were able to explore the huge mansion, which boasted forty-five windows at the front, and the garden extending to 5½ acres.

After visiting Edward Cooper in Staffordshire, Mrs Austen and Jane moved into Southampton lodgings and began to look about for a suitable house to rent with Frank and his now pregnant wife. Cassandra was once again required at Godmersham, where Elizabeth gave birth to her tenth child on 16 November – a daughter christened Cassandra Jane.

At about this time there was something of a dilemma being experienced at Steventon for James had been offered the opportunity to augment his income, but upon terms that his conscience found difficult to accept.[5] The acquisitive and the ethical, two very powerful forces in James' nature, were thus in conflict. Mary's feelings were presumably all on one side, for she loved a good income as much as anybody, and could not be expected to participate in the high-flown principles that even James' clerical friends thought over-nice. But this was one of those cases where the wife, knowing she has no influence, wisely seeks none, leaving the husband's conscience to wrestle with itself.

The offer came by way of Mary's connections with the families of Fowle and Craven. The Reverend Thomas Fowle, her uncle, had resigned the living of Kintbury in favour of his son Fulwar but had retained for himself the adjacent smaller living of Hamstead Marshall, which was worth about £200 a year. In 1806 old Mr Fowle died, and the patron of the living, the same Lord Craven who had tried to help Tom Fowle, asked Fulwar to recommend 'an honest man' who would agree to hold the living for a few years until the youth for whom it was eventually designed should be of an age to take it. Why Fulwar himself could not fulfil this function is not clear, but he had no hesitation in recommending James Austen. The arrangement from the first seems to have been that these two brothers-in-law would divide the stipend equally between them; perhaps Fulwar was to do duty at Hamstead, or to supervise the curate James might install there, while James himself, of course, would be the nominal vicar.

This £100 was therefore James' for the accepting, and at no cost in labour or inconvenience to himself. He hesitated, however, not because he would be an absentee incumbent or because he felt he might be tempted to retain the living dishonestly after it was wanted (as another clergyman Lord Craven had once installed on the same understanding had once cheated him by doing) but solely on account of the words which must be used in the acceptance.

As his daughter Caroline many years after his death wrote, 'He did not think the arrangement simoniacal in spirit; but there stood the ugly word; and he doubted whether a promise to give up at a certain period, did not go against the *letter* of the declaration which he would have to make.'

None of those few in his immediate circle he felt qualified to advise him shared his scruples, and he went to the trouble of travelling to London on purpose to consult someone of higher authority in ecclesiastic affairs, but in vain was he told that such livings had been held before by very good men. His conscience would not be satisfied; he gave himself another week to be sure of his own mind, and then declined the living.

Caroline concludes her account: 'If Lord Craven ever knew the reason of the refusal, he must have despaired of ever getting the right man for his purpose – having found one with too little conscience and another with too much.'

9

The house by the pond

1807-10

For nearly eighty years, Broadford, the original home of the Austens, had been inhabited by the John Austen whose father of the same name had been that fortunate elder brother singled out from the widow Elizabeth's brood to enjoy the whole inheritance of his grandfather. This John Austen, sixth of his line and name, had succeeded his father in 1728 at the age of twelve, had married Joanna Weeks of Sevenoaks in 1759 and had raised but one child, Mary, who died unmarried in 1803. When, therefore, the old man himself came to die, at the age of ninety-one, on 26 January 1807, and to be buried with his ancestors in the little church of Horsmonden, it was the end of an era. The question of who would inherit Broadford now occupied the family.

On 20 February Jane was able to write to Cassandra (still in Kent herself – but there was little connection now between the east and west Kent divisions of the family, and the news travelled via Hampshire): 'We have at last heard something of Mr Austen's will. It is believed at Tonbridge that he has left everything after the death of his widow to Mr Motley Austen's third son John; and as the said John was the only one of the family who attended the funeral, it seems likely to be true.' It was, and this lucky John Austen came into the property after Joanna Austen's death in 1811. Why the third of Motley's sons was chosen cannot be known: perhaps because he had sons himself – Francis Lucius had only daughters, and the next brother, Colonel Thomas Austen, no children at all – or perhaps for the continuity of the name; what is certain is that this branch of the family was already extremely rich indeed. No wonder Jane added the exclamation, 'Such ill-gotten wealth can never prosper!' It must have been exasperating to watch these great fortunes being handed down on both sides of the family, and to remain so pressed for every pound themselves.

Not that Mrs Austen was discontented; when she closed her accounts at the turn of the year, she was pleasantly surprised by the 'comfortable state of her own finances', wrote Jane on 7 January: 'she began 1806 with £68, she begins 1807 with £99, and this after £32 purchase of stock. Frank too has been settling his accounts and making calculations, and each party feels quite equal to our present expenses; but much increase of house-rent would not do for either.'

A house had been found to rent in Castle Square. It was the property of Lord Lansdown, was situated right next to the Southampton ramparts which would afford them agreeable walks and, best of all, had its own garden, the want of which had been one of the drawbacks of their Bath homes. 'We hear that we are envied our house by many people, and that the garden is the best in town,' wrote Jane, whose letters of January and February are full of the preparations to both house and garden needful before taking occupation in March.

Since his triumphant return from St Domingo, Frank had been without a ship, content to be so for a while and to enjoy a little domesticity with his new wife. Skilful with his hands and never idle, he gladly contributed to the furbishment of their new home: 'Frank has got a very bad cough, for an Austen: – but it does not disable him from making very nice fringe for the drawing-room curtains.' Among his outdoor pursuits was skating on the frozen water-meadows. His own memoir speaks of this newly married period being passed in such 'tranquil enjoyment' that he 'ceased to regret and almost to wish for professional employment'.

While the family were still in their temporary Southampton lodgings, they were visited by Mrs James Austen and her little daughter Caroline. It was an Austen custom to pass many of the long winter evenings reading aloud in the family circle round the fire, a constant supply of books being borrowed from the lending library. The current novel was *The Female Quixote* by Charlotte Lennox, which, wrote Jane, 'now makes our evening amusement; to me a very high one, as I find the work quite equal to what I remembered it. Mrs F.A., to whom it is new, enjoys it as one could wish; the other Mary, I believe, has little pleasure from that or any other book.'

There was even worse to say of James, who joined his wife and family in Southampton between clerical duties. 'I am sorry and angry that his visits should not give one more pleasure; the company of so good and so clever a man ought to be gratifying in itself; – but his chat seems all forced, his opinions on many points too much copied from his wife's, and his time here is spent I think in walking about the house and banging the doors, or ringing the bell for a glass of water.' This must rank as the harshest remark one Austen ever made of another – the harshest to survive, at any rate. In general, their mutual admiration was as strong as their affection and their loyalty.

Much was happening in the family that year. Henry took an important step in his second career. After leaving the militia he had involved himself in the world of banking and now, with two officer-friends, he established the firm of Austen, Maunde & Tilson, with offices at 10 Henrietta Street, Covent Garden. For the past two years he and Eliza had been living at 16 Michael's Place, Brompton.

Of even greater moment was the marriage of Charles, which took place in Bermuda on 1 May. His bride was Frances Fitzwilliam Palmer – known as Fanny – the eighteen-year-old daughter of John Grove Palmer, Attorney-General of that island, who kept also a London residence in Keppel Street. The shore leave of Charles' youth had been passed in Hampshire, where he had danced and flirted with the young ladies of that neighbourhood; but the age for falling seriously in love came upon him during his long exile from England, so his bride was unknown to the family. The Palmers did, however, have connections with the Fowles of Kintbury. Fanny was gentle and affectionate, while Charles himself must have been an irresistible lover for so young a girl: handsome, sweet-tempered, enthusiastic and brave, with a boyish charm. His eagerness to introduce his wife to his family, and theirs to meet her, may be imagined; but still he was obliged to languish on the North American station.

During the spring Edward's eldest son reached the age of thirteen and became a commoner at Winchester – to which august school he was followed in due course by all his brothers. A governess was kept for Fanny and her little sisters. Edward Austen thus reversed the educational practice of his own father.

In April Frank received notice of his appointment to command the *St Albans*, which he joined at Sheerness harbour, 'leaving his wife in an advanced state of pregnancy at home', as his memoir noted. Mary Jane Austen was born on 27 April: a sixth female for the household at Castle Square. In June the *St Albans* sailed on convoy duty to the Cape of Good Hope, returning on 1 January 1808. The following month she sailed again, this time under sealed orders, which upon opening Frank found to contain directions to accompany yet another convoy to St Helena.

The island was not yet, of course, associated with Napoleon but was under the rule of the East India Company. This was a lucrative assignment for Frank. As well as the 200 guineas he was paid for the convoy duty, the Board of East Indian directors voted him another 400 guineas, and, according to his memoir, 'The captains of the eight ships he convoyed, in a letter expressive of their sense of his gentleman-like conduct to themselves as well as his attention to the safety of the convoy requested his acceptance of a piece of plate as a testimony of their satisfaction and best wishes.'

With reciprocal generosity Frank wrote to the directors of the company to commend the skill of the captains in their employ, particularly 'the cheerfulness and alacrity with which they repeatedly towed for many successive days some heavy sailing ships of the convoy, a service always disagreeable, and often dangerous'. He added, 'I cannot conclude without observing that the indefatigable attention of Captain Hay of the *Retreat*, in availing himself of every opportunity to get ahead, and his uncommon exertions in carrying a great press of sail both night and day, which the wretched sailing of his ship, when not in tow, rendered necessary, was highly meritorious, and I think it my duty to recommend him to the notice of the Court of Directors as an officer deserving a better command.'

It was Frank's habit to learn as much as he could about every region of the world in which he found himself, and he made detailed notes not only about nautical matters but concerning the geography, vegetation, commerce, government and population of every port of call. His remarks on the inhabitants are the most interesting. Off Boulogne, a rare gleam of humour had crept in: 'The inhabitants are French, subjects to Napoleon the First, lately exalted to the imperial dignity by the unanimous suffrages of himself and his creatures.'

His entry for St Helena was more serious:

The inhabitants are chiefly English, or of English descent, although there is a considerable number of Negroes on the island, which with very few exceptions are the property of individuals or of the Company, slavery being tolerated here. It does not however appear that the slaves are or can be treated with that harshness and despotism which has been so justly attributed to the conduct of the land-holders or their managers in the West India Islands, the laws of the Colony not giving any other power to the master than the right to the labour of his slave. He must, to enforce that right, in case a slave prove refractory, apply to the civil power, he having no right to inflict chastisement at his own discretion. This a wholesome regulation as far as it goes, but slavery however it may be modified is still slavery, and it is much to be regretted that any trace of it should be found to exist in countries dependent on England, or colonised by her subjects.

Frank had hardly put in to an English port when he was off again, with a Brigadier-General and staff on board, together with a convoy of troopships, to Portugal, where all were landed in time to support Wellington hold the heights of Vimiera. On 21 August Frank recorded in the log that he observed the battle from the sea, and the following day his entry read: 'Sent all the boats on shore to assist in taking off the wounded of our army to the hospital ships. Boats also employed embarking French prisoners on board some of the transports.' He returned to the anchorage at Spithead on 2 September.

The *St Albans* remained in British waters for the next half year, chiefly at Spithead, and now the domestic arrangements between Frank and his mother came to an amicable end. It was more convenient for Frank and Mary to make their home at Yarmouth. 'Our Yarmouth division seem to have got nice lodgings,' wrote Jane to Cassandra on 1 October, 'and with fish almost for nothing, and plenty of engagements and plenty of each other, must be very happy.'

As for Mrs Austen, she was undecided for the present whether to remain in Southampton – albeit in a smaller house – or remove to Alton. In this lively little Hampshire town not far from Edward's Chawton estate, Henry had established a branch of his bank, known as Austen, Grey & Vincent. 'I depended upon Henry's liking the Alton plan,' wrote Jane in the same letter, 'and expect to hear of something perfectly unexceptionable there, through him.' Her mother, she reported, was now thinking much more of Alton than of another house in Southampton, and 'really expects to move there'. Though both daughters were now in their middle thirties, it was evidently still Mrs Austen who made the major decisions.

A taste for Alton had perhaps been acquired the previous summer when the three Austen ladies accompanied Edward, Elizabeth and their two eldest children on a visit to Chawton House, recently vacated. Edward took this opportunity to inspect his property and prepare it for the arrival of a new tenant, Mr Middleton, the following year.

When Jane wrote of their possible removal to Alton, Cassandra was at Godmersham yet again in her customary role as nurse to Elizabeth. Jane herself had visited there earlier that summer, along with James, Mary, Edward and Caroline. Her report to Cassandra on the welcome she was given and on the changes she saw in Edward's family makes agreeable reading.

Fanny and Lizzy met us in the hall with a great deal of pleasant joy … Fanny is grown both in height and size since last year, but not immoderately, looks very well, and seems as to conduct and manner just what she was and what one could wish her to continue.

Elizabeth, who was dressing when we arrived, came to me for a minute attended by Marianne, Charles and Louisa, and, you will not doubt, gave me a very affectionate welcome. That I had received such from Edward also I need not mention; but I do, you see, because it is a pleasure. I never saw him look in better health, and Fanny says he is perfectly well. I cannot praise Elizabeth's looks, but they are probably affected by a cold. Her little namesake has gained in beauty in the last three years, though not all that Marianne has lost. Charles is not quite so lovely as he was. Louisa is much as I expected, and Cassandra I find handsomer than I expected, though at present disguised by such a violent breaking-out that she does not come down after dinner. She has charming eyes and a nice open countenance, and seems likely to be very lovable. Her size is magnificent.

The house by the pond

James' son Edward, who must have been rather a lonesome child (for one of his sociable disposition), his two sisters being respectively five years older and seven years younger than himself, immensely enjoyed the companionship of his cousins. On arrival 'he was almost too happy, his happiness at least made him too talkative.' Later in the visit Jane reported, 'he has nice playfellows in Lizzy and Charles,' and 'his Uncle Edward talks nonsense to him delightfully – more than he can always understand.' Three-year-old Caroline, however, was rather overwhelmed: 'I believe the little girl will be glad to go home; her cousins are too much for her.'

Whilst her half-brother and -sister were visiting Godmersham, Anna had been sent to stay with her grandmother and aunt at Southampton. Unlike her contemporary Fanny, who gave no cause for concern, Anna was both wayward and brilliant – cutting off her hair, to her family's horror, yet showing a taste for literature that made Jane rejoice. Nevertheless Fanny was the favourite with Jane; when it was Cassandra's turn to report from Godmersham, in October, Jane replied, 'I am greatly pleased with your account of Fanny; I found her in the summer just what you describe, almost another sister – and could not have supposed that a niece would ever have been so much to me. She is quite after one's own heart; give her my best love, and tell her that I always think of her with pleasure.'

Cassandra had reached Godmersham just after the birth, on 28 September, of Brook John. At first, she was able to send good accounts of the mother, but on 10 October Elizabeth suddenly died.

Shock and sorrow reverberated round the family. Jane wrote on 13 October:

We have felt, we do feel, for you all – as you will not need to be told – for you, for Fanny, for Henry, for Lady Bridges, and for dearest Edward, whose loss and whose sufferings seem to make those of every other person nothing. – God be praised! that you can say what you do of him – that he has a religious mind to bear him up, and a disposition that will gradually lead him to comfort. – My dear, dear Fanny! – I am so thankful that she has you with her ... With what true sympathy our feelings are shared by Martha, you need not be told; – she is the friend and sister under every circumstance. We need not enter into a panegyric on the departed – but it is sweet to think of her great worth – of her solid principles, her true devotion, her excellence in every relation of life.

Elizabeth had enjoyed just thirty-five years of existence and had brought eleven children into the world – of whom the eldest, Fanny, at 15½, now had to take the place of mother to the rest. Of Lizzy in particular Jane wrote two days later: 'Poor child! ... one's heart aches for a dejected mind of eight years old.' She added, 'We are heartily rejoiced that the poor baby gives you no particular anxiety.'

The two eldest boys, now both at Winchester, were immediately collected by their uncle James and spent some time recovering from their grief first at Steventon and then at Southampton, whence Jane reported on 24 October: 'They behave extremely well in every respect, showing quite as much feeling as one wishes to see, and on every occasion speaking of their father with the liveliest affection. His letter was read over by each of them yesterday, and with many tears; George sobbed aloud, Edward's tears do not flow so easily; but as far as I can judge they are both very properly impressed by what has happened ... George is almost a new acquaintance to me, and I find him in a different way as engaging as Edward.'

She devised various entertainments to distract them, including a trip up the River Itchen. 'Both the boys rowed great part of the way, and their questions and remarks, as well as their enjoyment, were very amusing; George's enquiries were endless, and his eagerness in everything reminds me often of his Uncle Henry.'

Frank obtained compassionate leave to pay a consolatory visit to his brother; letters of sympathy poured in from all the family connections, many of them sent to Southampton to avoid giving Edward the distress of having to reply. Last to hear the news was Charles, whose own wife was safely delivered of a daughter, rather inharmoniously named Cassandra Esten Austen, on 22 December 1808.

Two days after this birth Charles wrote to his sister Cassandra from Bermuda:

I wrote to Jane about a fortnight ago acquainting her with my arrival at this place and of my having captured a little Frenchman, which I am truly sorry to add, has never reached this port, and, unless she has run to the West Indies, I have lost her – and, what is a real misfortune, the lives of twelve of my people, two of them mids. I confess I have but little hopes of ever hearing of her again. The weather has been so very severe since we captured her. I wish you a merry and happy Christmas, in which Fan joins me, as well as in bespeaking the love of her dear grandmother and aunts for our little Cassandra. The October and November mails have not yet reached us, so that I know nothing of you of late. I hope you have been more fortunate in hearing of me. I expect to sail on Tuesday with a small convoy for the island of St Domingo, and, after seeing them in safety, open sealed orders, which I conclude will direct me to cruise as long as my provisions, etc will allow, which is generally a couple of months.

Cassandra stayed on at Godmersham and Jane wrote: 'I am glad you are to have Henry with you again; with him, and the boys, you cannot but have a cheerful, and at times even a merry Christmas.'

In the same letter in which she expressed these hopes, Jane also reported:

… a communication of some weight – no less than that my uncle and aunt are going to allow James £100 a year. We hear of it through Steventon; – Mary sent us the other day an extract from my aunt's letter on the subject – in which the donation is made with the greatest kindness, and intended as a compensation for his loss in the conscientious refusal of Hamstead living – £100 a year being all that he had at the time called its worth – as I find it was always intended at Steventon to divide the real income with Kintbury. – Nothing can be more affectionate than my aunt's language in making the present, and likewise in expressing her hope of their being much more to-gether in future, than to her great regret, they have of late years been. – My expectations for my mother do not rise with this event … The hundred a year begins next Ladyday.

And on 27 December Jane informed Cassandra: 'James means to keep three horses on this increase of income; at present he has but one. Mary wishes the other two to be fit to carry women, and in the purchase of one Edward will probably be called upon to fulfil his promise to his godson. We have now pretty well ascertained James's income to be eleven hundred pounds, curate paid, which makes us very happy – the ascertainment as well as the income.'

In February Cassandra returned to Southampton, and two months later the Austens left the city for good. Edward had not been too preoccupied with his own grief to give some thought as to where his mother might live; and the offer of one of his own properties in the village of Chawton was thankfully and joyfully accepted.

The dwelling, which with equal justice could be described as a large cottage or a small house, was to be vacated at Midsummer by Edward's steward and his wife. The Austen ladies felt no need to inspect it before giving their acceptance. It was in the part of the world they loved best, and where they might hope to be surrounded by relations. They knew that village life, and especially Hampshire village life, was going to suit them, and they were confident that Edward would do all in his power to make their home comfortable and pleasant.

In her old age Caroline Austen wrote a description of Chawton cottage as it had been in her girlhood when her grandmother and three aunts lived there:[1]

I have been told I know not how truthfully, that it had been originally a roadside inn – and it was well placed for such a purpose – just where the road from Winchester comes into the London and Gosport line – The fork between the two being partly occupied by a large shallow pond – which pond I believe has long since become dry ground.

The front door opened on the road, a very narrow enclosure of each side protected the house from the possible shock of any runaway vehicle – A good sized entrance, and two parlours called dining and drawing room, made the length of the house; all intended originally to look on the road – but the large drawing room window was blocked-up and turned into a bookcase when Mrs Austen took possession and another was opened at the side, which gave to view only turf and trees – a high wooden fence shut out the road (the Winchester road as it was) all the length of the little domain, and trees were planted inside to form a shrubbery walk – which carried round the enclosure, gave a very sufficient space for exercise – you did not feel cramped for room; and there was a pleasant irregular mixture of hedgerow, and grass, and gravel walk and long grass for mowing, and orchard – which I imagine arose from two or three little enclosures having been thrown together, and arranged as best might be, for ladies' occupation – There was besides a good kitchen garden, large court and many out-buildings, not much occupied – and all this affluence of space was very delightful to children, and I have no doubt added considerably to the pleasure of a visit.

Everything indoors and out was well kept – the house was well furnished, and it was altogether a comfortable and ladylike establishment, though I believe the means which supported it, were but small.

The house was quite as good as the generality of parsonage houses then – and much in the same old style – the ceilings low and roughly finished – *some* bedrooms very small – *none* very large but in number sufficient to accommodate the inmates, and several guests.

The dining room could not be made to look anywhere but on the road – and there my grandmother often sat for an hour or two in the morning, with her work or her writing – cheered by its sunny aspect and by the stirring scene it afforded her.

I believe the close vicinity of the road was really no more of an evil to her than it was to her grandchildren. Collyer's daily coach with six horses was a sight to see! and most delightful was it to a child to have the awful stillness of night so frequently broken by the noise of passing carriages, which seemed sometimes, even to shake the bed.

The village of Chawton has, of course, long since been tranquillised – it is no more a great thoroughfare, and *other* and *many* changes have past over it – and if any of its visitants should fail to recognise from my description, the house by the pond – I must beg them not hastily to accuse me of having exaggerated its former pleasantness.

It was as if Jane knew that her art would prosper in such an environment, for before leaving Southampton she took a step which showed that novel-writing *for publication* was now her object. She wrote to the publishers who had paid £10 for *Susan*, threatening to offer the book elsewhere if they did not proceed with publication. Their reply was one of counter-threat, and she dropped the matter for the time being; but nothing could shake her now, and her other manuscripts were taken out again for further revision, whilst new plots and people began to crowd her brain.

After paying some family vists, the Austen ladies and Martha Lloyd took possession of their new home on 7 July 1809. Five days later, at Alton, where Frank had taken the lease on a small house, his wife gave birth to a son, who was given the same two Christian names as his father. Frank himself had been at sea since April, and when, on 26 July, Jane wrote to congratulate him, her high spirits broke out in rhyme. Playfully expressing the hope that the new Francis William would be a replica of his father, the verse gives a delightful picture of Frank's personality as others saw it to set against the somewhat rigid account he was apt to give of himself:

Thy infant days may he inherit,
Thy warmth, nay insolence of spirit; –
We would not with one fault dispense
To weaken the resemblance
  May he revive thy Nursery sin,
Peeping as daringly within,
His curly Locks but just descried,
With, 'Bet, my be not come to bide.' –
  Fearless of danger, braving pain,
And threatened very oft in vain,
Still may one Terror daunt his soul,
One needful engine of Control
Be found in this sublime array,
A neighbouring Donkey's awful Bray.
So may his equal faults as Child,
Produce Maturity as mild!
His saucy words and fiery ways
In early Childhood's pettish days,
In Manhood, show his Father's mind
Like him, considerate and kind;
All gentleness to those around,
And eager only not to wound.

Another facet of Frank's character, his extraordinary professional calm, is illustrated by an incident which occurred during the *St Albans'* voyage to China, on East India Company convoy duty. An army officer named Pakenham was given passage down the Malay coast and on one occasion was enjoying a swim, while Frank, in the words of his grandson John Hubback,[2] 'watched the sea surface as sharks were many thereabouts. Presently he spoke to the swimmer, quietly so as to avoid panic. "Mr Pakenham, there is a shark approaching, a shark of the blue species. I advise you to leave the water immediately." Pakenham could not believe the Captain to be serious as he spoke so quietly and deliberately. "Surely, Captain Austen, you are joking." "I am not in the habit of joking, Mr Pakenham; there is a need for hurry." ' This incident resulted in the lifelong friendship of the two men.

The *St Albans* anchored in the Canton river on 18 September and was detained there on various matters until 2 March 1810. She arrived back in England that July, having called at St Helena on the way. These had been lucrative voyages for Frank, who now felt justified in taking a holiday to enjoy the society of his wife, his daughter and the son whose first year of life he had missed entirely. He relinquished command of the *St Albans* in September and by his own wish remained unemployed until December, when he was appointed Flag Captain to his old friend Lord Gambier on board the *Caledonia*, stationed off the coast of France.

In the same month that Frank quitted the *St Albans*, his brother Charles took command of the *Cleopatra*, and shortly afterwards, with his wife and two daughters – Harriet Jane had been born on 19 February that year – he at last set sail for England.

10

Brotherly vanity and love

1811-14

Now that she was about to become a published author, Jane was fortunate to have at her disposal Henry's business acumen and London home. The firm of Thomas Egerton had agreed to publish the revised and newly named *Sense and Sensibility* at her own risk, and by April 1811 she was staying with the Henry Austens at their house in Sloane Street in order to correct the proofs.

Eliza, now approaching fifty, was Eliza still: a fashionable party-giver and socialite, though her health was unreliable and she had trouble sleeping. Jane was caught up in a whirl of engagements, but, 'No, indeed, I am never too busy to think of S & S. I can no more forget it, than a mother can forget her sucking child,' she replied to Cassandra's enquiry. The novel was to be published anonymously in June.

'I give you joy of our new nephew,' the same letter declared. This was Frank's second son, Henry Edgar, born in Portsmouth lodgings on 21 April.

It was at one of Eliza's parties, that the first news of Charles reached them. 'Captain Simpson told us, on the authority of some other Captain just arrived from Halifax, that Charles was bringing the *Cleopatra* home, and that she was probably by this time in the Channel – but as Captain S. was certainly in liquor, we must not quite depend on it. – It must give one a sort of expectation however, and will prevent my writing to him any more.'

Mrs Austen had visitors at Chawton Cottage while both her daughters were away, and Jane added, 'I would rather he should not reach England till I am at home, and the Steventon party gone. My mother and Martha both write with great satisfaction of Anna's behaviour. She is quite an Anna with variations – but she cannot have reached her last, for that is always the most flourishing and showy – she is at about her 3rd or 4th which are generally simple and pretty.'

The previous 'variation' had been a rebellious one, for Anna, 'being dull when her brother went to school got engaged to Michael Terry, a good looking neighbour – to the displeasure of her parents. Later she broke it off – also to their displeasure.'[1]

A change of admirals had resulted in Frank's being superseded on the *Caledonia*, and so with his young family he took lodgings for the early part of the summer at Cowes, Isle of Wight. In July they visited Steventon, and on the 18th of that month Frank accepted command of the *Elephant*, which had been Nelson's flagship at Copenhagen in 1801, and took her into the North Sea.

Charles and his wife also visited Steventon as part of a round of family visits which followed their arrival in England. His niece Caroline recalled: 'I thought they both looked very young for an uncle and aunt. She was fair and pink with very light hair and I admired her greatly.'[2]

Indeed, Fanny appears to have given general satisfaction in the family. Cassandra's good opinion is preserved in a letter[3] written on 18 August to her cousin Philadelphia on the occasion of that lady's marriage, at the age of fifty, to George Whitaker of Pembury near Tonbridge:

> My brother Charles and his family spent one week with us during Eliza's visit and they all left us together last Thursday. After an absence from England of almost seven years you may guess the pleasure which having him amongst us again occasioned. He is grown a little older in all that time, but we had the pleasure of seeing him return in good health and unchanged in mind. His Bermudan wife is a very pleasing little woman, she is gentle and amiable in her manners and appears to make him very happy. They have two pretty little girls. There must be always something to wish for, and for Charles we have to wish for rather more money. So expensive as everything in England is now, even the necessaries of life, I am afraid they will find themselves very, very poor.

In November Charles was appointed to the *Namur* as Flag Captain to his friend of long standing and relation by marriage Sir

Thomas Williams, who was now Commander-in-Chief at the Nore. Having spent such a long period on an unprofitable station, Charles had realized no fortune, and economy obliged his wife and infants to live with him on board. This arrangement, of doubtful comfort, and the contrasting luxury of the style in which Edward's children were brought up are both mentioned by Cassandra in another letter to Philadelphia Whitaker written on 20 March 1812:

> We had short visits from Edward and from Charles and his pretty little wife early in the winter, and Henry spent two days with us in January. Charles and his Fanny came to us for a few days previous to their taking possession of their aquatic abode, he is Captain of the *Namur* at Sheerness and she and his children are actually living with him on board. We had doubted whether such a scheme would prove practicable during the winter, but they have found their residence very tolerably comfortable and it is so much the cheapest home she could have that they are very right to put up with little inconveniences.
>
> My brother Edward was prevented coming to us for many weeks by poor Mrs Knight's ill health; he was however so much pressed by business that he did at length venture to leave her and had the satisfaction of receiving good accounts of her during the whole of his absence. She is not now in the immediate danger in which we at one time considered her and she has wonderful strength of constitution that we retain hopes of her struggling through her complaints, but she is still very far from well ...
>
> You are beforehand with me in your nephews and nieces, mine are not yet thinking of husbands and wives, not that I know of at least. My eldest nephew has just kept his first term at St John's College, Oxford and is now returning to all the liberty and enjoyment of his happy home. I hope those young people will not have so much happiness in their youth as to unfit them for the rubs which they must meet with afterwards, but with so indulgent a father and so liberal a style of living I am aware there must be some danger of it.

Cassandra's reference to Edward's business visits corroborates Caroline's reminiscences that it was his habit to come to Chawton and Steventon generally twice a year in order to look after his affairs. Caroline paints an agreeable picture of Edward's personality:

> He must have been more his own 'man of business' than is usual with people of large property, for I think it was his greatest interest to attend to his estates. In my recollection, he never hunted or shot. He liked riding and made his horse the means of getting about, sometimes

coming to us in this manner from Chawton – if alone; a little roll behind his saddle bringing necessaries enough for a night or two ... Of the five brothers he, who had always unlimited means for such indulgencies was the only one without a strong taste for field sports, and *he* cared not for them at all. He was very cheerful and pleasant, and had some of my Aunt Jane's power and good nature, of telling amusing stories to his nephews and nieces.

Caroline's own father, James, loved horse-riding above all other recreations, and his son shared this taste. During 1812 James felt sufficiently in funds to buy Edward a new pony, named Sutton, and to rebuild the stables and smarten up the approach to the Rectory.

In June 1812 Mrs Austen and Jane stayed a fortnight at Steventon. Aged seventy-three, Mrs Austen was beginning to feel unequal to travelling and, with old-fashioned notions of propriety, determined that her last visit from home should be paid to her eldest son. She kept her resolution and never again slept a night away from Chawton cottage. The housekeeping there she had already relinquished into Cassandra's care, occupying herself with needlework, letter-writing and, whenever the weather allowed, her favourite pastime, gardening.

After her illness of that spring, Mrs Knight never fully recovered her health, and on 14 October 1812 she died. The terms of her husband's will now came into effect, and Edward, with all his children, adopted the surname Knight. On 29 November Jane wrote to Martha: 'We have reason to believe the change of name has taken place, as we have to forward a letter to Edward Knight Esquire from the lawyer who has the management of the business. I must learn to make a better K.'

Jane's letter also gave news of *Pride and Prejudice*, which had been remade from *First Impressions* and brought to its final state of highly polished perfection. *Sense and Sensibility* had sold sufficiently well for Jane not to be required to finance the publication of her second novel. She informed Martha: 'P & P is sold. – Egerton gives £110 for it. – I would rather have had £150, but we could not both be pleased, and I am not at all surprised that he should not choose to hazard so much. – Its being sold will I hope be a great saving of trouble to Henry, and therefore must be welcome to me. – The money is to be paid at the end of the twelvemonth.' To be earning by her own labour even modest sums after a lifetime of dependence on father and brothers must have been highly gratifying to Jane.

The close of the year brought two more births in the family — that of Frank's third son, George, on 20 October in lodgings at Deal; and that of Charles' third daughter, Frances Palmer, on 1 December in London, where Fanny was staying with her own relations for the confinement.

Jane's own 'darling child' arrived the following month. On Wednesday 27 January 1813 the three volumes of *Pride and Prejudice* reached Chawton, and the other free sets to which the author was entitled were despatched by Henry to his brothers. Cassandra happened to be staying at Steventon, where the reading circle included James' two literary-minded offspring, Anna and Edward. They had already enjoyed *Sense and Sensibility* with no idea of its authorship. Now Cassandra was given permission to reveal the secret to them; and clever, amusing Edward, only fourteen years of age, was inspired to comic verse:

To Miss J. Austen

No words can express, my dear Aunt, my surprise
Or make you conceive how I opened my eyes,
Like a pig Butcher Pile has just struck with a knife
When I heard for the very first time in my life
That I had the honour to have a relation
Whose Works were dispersed through the whole of the nation.
I assure you, however, I'm terribly glad;
Oh dear, just to think (and the thought drives me mad)
That dear Mrs Jennings's good-natured strain
Was really the produce of your witty brain,
That you made the Middletons, Dashwoods and all,
And that you (not young Ferrars) found out that a ball
May be given in cottages never so small.
And though Mr Collins so grateful for all
Will Lady de Bourgh his dear patroness call,
'Tis to your ingenuity really he owed
His living, his wife, and his humble abode.
Now if you will take your poor nephew's advice,
Your works to Sir William pray send in a trice;
If he'll undertake to some grandees to show it
By whose means at last the Prince Regent might know it,
For I'm sure if he did, in reward for your tale,

He'd make you a countess at least without fail,
And indeed, if the princess should lose her dear life,
You might have a good chance of becoming his wife.

Shortly after this was composed, Edward, who had previously
been a pupil at a preparatory school in Ramsbury, set off with his
father on horseback to catch the stage-coach which would take
them to Eton, but James happened to tear his coat on a bramble,
and they returned home. Before they set out again, James changed
his mind and decided to send Edward to Winchester College
instead.[4]

Eliza Austen died on 25 April 1813 and was buried beside her
mother and son at St John's parish church, Hampstead Heath.
Henry decided to leave Sloane Street and occupy quarters above his
bank at 10 Henrietta Street.

Jane was able to give a comfortable report of the new widower's
health and spirits when she wrote to Frank, stationed off the coast
of Sweden, on 3 July. Henry had just been appointed to the post of
Receiver-General of Taxes for Oxfordshire, having been Deputy
Receiver for some years. To secure the promotion he had required
surety to the value of £30,000; Edward stood for two-thirds of this
figure and Mr Leigh Perrot for the remaining third. The Knights
were spending the summer at Chawton House, now tenantless,
while Godmersham received a new coat of paint. At Chawton they
played host in turn to Henry and to the Steventon division, whilst
Charles' Cassy and Harriet, with their maid Betsy, had spent some
time at the cottage as a relief from shipboard life. Altogether then,
this was very much a family summer, and Jane's letter to Frank is
worth quoting at length for the family news it contains.

July begins unpleasantly with us, cold and showery, but it is often a
baddish month. We had some fine dry weather preceding it, which was
very acceptable to the holders of hay and the masters of meadows. – In
general it must have been a good haymaking season. Edward has got in
all his, in excellent order; I speak only of Chawton; but here he has had
better luck than Mr Middleton ever had in the five years he was tenant.
Good encouragement for him to come again; and I really hope he will
do so another year. – The pleasure to us of having them here is so great,
that if we were not the best creatures in the world we should not
deserve it.

We go on in the most comfortable way, very frequently dining together, and always meeting in some part of every day. – Edward is very well and enjoys himself as thoroughly as any Hampshire born Austen can desire. Chawton is not thrown away upon him. – He talks of making a new garden; the present is a bad one and ill situated, near Mr Papillon's; – he means to have the new, at the top of the lawn behind his own house. – We like to have him proving and strengthening his attachment to the place by making it better.

He will soon have all his children about him, Edward, George and Charles are collected already, and another week brings Henry and William ... We are in hopes of another visit from our own true, lawful Henry very soon, he is to be *our* guest this time. – He is quite well I am happy to say, and does not leave it to *my* pen I am sure to communicate to you the joyful news of his being Deputy Receiver no longer. – It is a promotion which he thoroughly enjoys; as well he may; the work of his own mind. – He sends you all his own plans of course.

Henry was planning a Scottish holiday with young Edward Knight. Jane continued:

The scheme for Scotland we think an excellent one both for himself and his nephew. Upon the whole his spirits are very much recovered. – If I may so express myself, his mind is not a mind for affliction. He is too busy, too active, too sanguine. Sincerely as he was attached to poor Eliza, moreover, and excellently as he behaved to her, he was always so used to be away from her at times, that her loss is not felt as that of many a beloved wife might be, especially when all the circumstances of her long and dreadful illness are taken into account. – He very long knew that she must die, and it was indeed a release at last.

Our mourning for her is not over, or we should now be putting it on again for Mr Thomas Leigh – the respectable, worthy, clever, agreeable Mr Thomas Leigh, who has just closed a good life at the age of 79, and must have died the possessor of one of the finest estates in England and of more worthless nephews and nieces than any other private man in the United Kingdoms. – We are very anxious to know who will have the living of Adlestrop, and where his excellent sister will find a home for the remainder of her days. As yet she bears his loss with fortitude, but she has always seemed so wrapped up in him, that I fear she must feel it very dreadfully when the fever of business is over.

There is another female sufferer on the occasion to be pitied. Poor Mrs. L.P. – who would now have been mistress of Stoneleigh had there been none of that vile compromise, which in good truth has never been allowed to be of much use to them. It will be a hard trial.

Charles's little girls were with us about a month, and had so endeared themselves that we were quite sorry to have them go. We have the pleasure however of hearing that they are thought very much improved at home – Harriet in health, Cassy in manners. – The latter *ought* to be a very nice child – nature has done enough for her – but method has been wanting: we thought her very much improved ourselves, but to have Papa and Mama think her so too, was very essential to our contentment. She will really be a very pleasing child, if they will only exert themselves a little. – Harriet is a truly sweet-tempered little darling. They are now all at Southend together. – Why do I mention *that*? As if Charles did not write himself ...

You will be glad to hear that every copy of S & S is sold and that it has brought me £140 besides the copyright, if that should ever be of any value. I have now therefore written myself into £250 – which only makes me long for more – I have something in hand – which I hope on the credit of P & P will sell well, though not half so entertaining ...

July 6. – Now my dearest Frank I will finish my letter. I have kept it open on the chance of what a Tuesday's post might furnish in addition, and it furnishes the likelihood of our keeping our neighbours at the Great House some weeks longer than we expected. Mr Scudamore, to whom my brother referred, is very decided as to Godmersham not being fit to be inhabited at present; – he talks even of two months more being necessary to sweeten it, but if we have warm weather I dare say less will do. My brother will probably go down and sniff at it himself and receive his rents. The rent-day has been postponed already ...

Our Cousins Colonel Thomas Austen and Margaretta are going aide-de-camps to Ireland and Lord Whitworth goes in their train as Lord Lieutenant; good appointments for each. – God bless you. – I hope you continue beautiful and brush your hair, but not all off. – We join in an infinity of love.

Taking Jane with them, the Knights and their servants left Chawton in the middle of September. From Godmersham Jane wrote again to Frank:

We left Chawton on the 14th, spent two entire days in town and arrived here on the 17th. My Brother, Fanny, Lizzy, Marianne and I composed this division of the family, and filled his carriage, inside and out. Two post-chaises under the escort of George conveyed eight more across the country, the chair brought two, two others came on horseback and the rest by coach. – And so by one means or another we are all removed ...

We were accommodated in Henrietta Street. Henry was so good as to find room for his three nieces and myself in his house. Edward slept at an hotel in the next street. – No. 10 is made very comfortable with cleaning and painting and the Sloane Street furniture. The front room upstairs is an excellent dining and common sitting parlour – and the smaller one behind will sufficiently answer his purpose as a drawing room. He has no intention of giving large parties of any kind. His plans are all for the comfort of his friends and himself ...

Henry has probably sent you his own account of his visit in Scotland. I wish he had had more time and could have gone further north, and deviated to the Lakes in his way back, but what he was able to do seems to have afforded him great enjoyment and he met with scenes of higher beauty in Roxburghshire than I had supposed the South of Scotland possessed. – Our nephew's gratification was less keen than our brother's. Edward is no enthusiast for the beauties of nature. His enthusiasm is for the sports of the field only. He is a very promising and pleasing young man however upon the whole, behaves with great propriety to his father and great kindness to his brothers and sisters – and we must forgive his thinking more of grouse and partridges than lakes and mountains. He and George are out every morning either shooting or with the harriers ...

I hope Edward's family-visit to Chawton will be yearly, he certainly means it now, but we must not expect it to exceed *two* months in future. I do not think, however, that *he* found *five* too long this summer. – He was very happy there. The new paint improves this house much, and we find no evil from the smell.

Henry had heard *Pride and Prejudice* praised in Scotland, and 'in the warmth of his brotherly vanity and love' had allowed the secret of the authorship to escape him. As Jane told Frank, 'A thing once set going in that way – one knows how it spreads! – and he, dear creature, has set it going so much more than once. I know it is all done from affection and partiality – but at the same time, let me here again express you to and Mary my sense of the *superior* kindness which you have shown on the occasion, in doing what I wished.'

One person to whom Jane had no objection knowing her identity was Warren Hastings, who had praised the novel in a letter to Henry. 'I am quite delighted with what such a man writes about it,' and, 'I long to have you hear Mr H.'s opinion of P and P. His admiring my Elizabeth so much is particularly welcome to me,' Jane had written to Cassandra from Henrietta Street.

The detour to London had been made partly so that Edward's daughters could visit a dentist. Lizzy's teeth were 'filed and lamented over', Marianne had two removed (with 'two sharp hasty screams') to make space for the remainder, and Fanny's were cleaned and some gold put in. 'It was a disagreeable hour,' reported Jane. However, the visit to London incorporated pleasure as well as pain, with shopping for finery. 'We must have been three quarters of an hour at Grafton House, Edward sitting by all the time with wonderful patience. There Fanny bought the net for Anna's gown, and a beautiful square veil for herself.'

There was more serious mention of Anna in Jane's letter to Frank. Anna had become engaged again – this time to Benjamin Lefroy, youngest son of the Reverend Isaac Lefroy of Ashe and his wife Anne, old friends and neighbours of the George Austens during their Steventon days. Mrs Lefroy, intelligent and sweet-natured, had particularly befriended and encouraged Jane, who had deeply mourned her death in a riding accident in 1804. Ben's eldest brother John had stepped into the living of Ashe on his father's death in 1806; twenty-two-year-old Ben was similarly designed for the Church, but not yet ordained or settled in life.

Jane wrote:

I take it for granted that Mary has told you of Anna's engagement to Ben Lefroy. It came upon us without much preparation; – at the same time, there was *that* about her which kept us in a constant preparation for something. – We are anxious to have it go on well, there being quite as much in his favour as the chances are likely to give her in any matrimonial connection. I believe he is sensible, certainly very religious, well connected and with some independence. – There is an unfortunate dissimilarity of taste between them in one respect which gives us some apprehensions, he hates company and she is very fond of it; – this, with some queerness of temper on his side and much unsteadiness on hers, is untoward.

Appearances continued unfavourable. About a month later Jane wrote from Godmersham to Cassandra who was now in London: 'I have had a late account from Steventon, and a baddish one, as far as Ben is concerned. He has declined a curacy (apparently highly eligible), which he might have secured against his taking orders; and, upon its being made rather a serious question, says he has not made up his mind as to taking orders so early, and that, if her father makes a point of it, he must give Anna up rather than do what he does not approve. He must be maddish. They are going on again at present as before – but it cannot last.'

Whilst Jane was still at Godmersham, Charles brought his family for a week's visit. A charmingly domesticated picture emerged of him at this period of his life, from the anticipation: 'I shall be most happy to see dear Charles, and he will be as happy as he can with a cross child or some such care pressing on him at the time,' to the arrival: 'Here they are safe and well, just like their own nice selves, Fanny looking as neat and white this morning as possible, and dear Charles all affectionate, placid, quiet, cheerful good humour,' and the progress of the visit itself: 'I think I have just done a good deed – extracted Charles from his wife and children upstairs, and made him get ready to go out shooting, and not keep Mr Moore waiting any longer.'

Little Cassy looked thin and ill when the family arrived, and it was felt that life on ship did not agree with her; in rough weather she suffered dreadfully from sea-sickness. She had been offered a home by her aunts and grandmother at Chawton cottage for the winter months but was reluctant to leave her parents. For the sake of her health, Fanny rather wished her to go; 'Charles is less inclined to part with her.'

He was persuaded to do so, however, and Cassy spent the winter under the particular care of her namesake aunt, who had a talent for teaching and who combined kindness with firmness – a more formidable and less delightful aunt than Jane, perhaps, but a very wise and worthy one.

Whilst Cassy was at Chawton, yet another Cassandra of her generation was added to the family. Frank's second daughter, born at Portsmouth on 8 January 1814, was christened Cassandra Eliza.

At the cottage Cassandra took care to shield Jane from the work involved in the child, for Jane was busy with *Mansfield Park*, which Henry read in manuscript form during a visit Jane paid him that March. This was the first novel to be wholly conceived and written at Chawton, and thus was quite new to Henry. His reactions, as mentioned by Jane during a series of letters, are interesting: 'Henry's approbation hitherto is even equal to my wishes. He says it is very different from the other two, but does not appear to think it is at all inferior. He has only married Mrs R. I am afraid he has gone through the most entertaining part. He took to Lady B. and Mrs N. most kindly, and gives great praise to the drawing of the characters. He understands them all, likes Fanny, and, I think, foresees how it will all be.' 'Henry is going on with *Mansfield Park*. He admires H. Crawford: I mean properly, as a clever, pleasant man.' 'Henry has this moment said that he likes my M.P. better and better; he is in the 3rd volume. I believe *now* he has changed his mind as to foreseeing the end; he said yesterday at least, that he defied anybody to say whether H.C. would be reformed, or would forget Fanny in a fortnight.' 'Henry has finished *Mansfield Park*, and his approbation has not lessened. He found the last half of the last volume *extremely interesting*.' The novel was published that May.

In London Henry and Jane were joined by Edward and Fanny Knight on their way back from Bath, where they had been visiting Edward's mother-in-law, Lady Bridges, who was there for her health. A young Kentish neighbour, John Plumtre, happened also to be staying in London; he dined at Henrietta Street and secured the whole party a box at the theatre. Henry saw 'decided attachment' between Fanny and this young man.

Fanny's exact contemporary, Anna, was still stubbornly continuing her engagement; and perhaps to distract herself from the long and uncertain period of waiting, or from an atmosphere of disapproval at home, she began to write a novel, which kept her occupied all summer.

Jane was back in London at the end of August, visiting Henry in yet another new home, 23 Hans Place, Kensington. 'It is a delightful place – more than answers my expectation,' she wrote to Cassandra. 'I find more space and comfort in the rooms than I had supposed, and the garden is quite a love.'

It was certainly useful to the family to have such a London base at their disposal. During Jane's visit they were joined for a few days by James and his son Edward. 'Their business is about teeth and wigs.'

Henry had not only a new house but new matrimonial ideas. A Miss Burdett had been mentioned in this connection in June, but now: 'Henry wants me to see more of his Hanwell favourite, and has written to invite her to spend a day or two here with me. His scheme is to fetch her on Saturday. I am more and more convinced that he will marry again soon, and like the idea of *her* better than of anybody else at hand.' The Hanwell favourite was one of the two Miss Moores, Harriet and Eliza. Perhaps one of the other possibilities 'at hand' was a widow, for on 2 September Jane wrote to Martha, who was staying in Bath: 'Henry takes me home tomorrow ... we shall lengthen the journey by going round by Sunning Hill; his favourite Mrs Crutchley lives there, and he wants to introduce me to her.' She added, 'He is in very comfortable health; – he has not been so well, he says, for a twelvemonth.'

There was a postscript to this letter. 'We have just learned that Mrs C. Austen is safe in bed with a girl. – It happened on board, a fortnight before it was expected.'

But this satisfaction proved as premature as the inconvenient birth itself. Poor Fanny survived her labour only to die six days later, on 6 September, at the age of twenty-four. The baby, Elizabeth, lived for just twenty days. Charles' feelings were much to be pitied. In addition to the normal grief of losing a beloved young wife, he had to reflect that he had never been able to provide her with a proper home and that shipboard life had possibly killed her and certainly made his eldest daughter ill. He sent the three motherless little girls now to the Palmers in Keppel Street, where Fanny's sister Harriet assumed care of them, particularly of the two youngest, Cassy still remaining the pupil of Cassandra for the greater part of each year.

At Chawton Cassy found a playmate and lasting friend in her cousin Mary Jane, a year her senior. From 1814 Frank, Mary and their five children became Edward's tenants at Chawton Manor – an arrangement productive of much satisfaction to their neighbours at the cottage, and a great deal of space and comfort to themselves. Now, when Edward and his family paid a summer visit to Chawton, they were guests in their own house.

Whether it would remain their own house much longer was suddenly called into question that year when Edward was threatened with the loss of all his Hampshire property by lawsuit. His opponents were the Baverstocks of Alton and the Hintons of Chawton, who alleged that they had discovered some irregularity in a disentailing deed executed in 1755. If this was so, it meant that the instrument remained good as long as the May line (for it was Thomas May, later Knight, who had executed it) survived but that, on its failing, the heirs-at-law of Elizabeth Knight came in. She had entailed the property first on Thomas May and, failing his line, on John Hinton.

The irregularity alleged was that the deed had been executed out of term time and therefore did not stand. It was not a very strong case, and at first Edward was inclined to give it little credence; not all the heirs-at-law of John Hinton were disposed to pursue the claim, but those that did persisted with it rather successfully for a couple of years, and in the end he was obliged to compromise. He paid £15,000 to clear his property of this claim on it – most of which went to the lawyers. The rest was divided unequally amongst the claimants. 'Baverstock was a clever and rather scampish brewer of Alton, whose father had maried Mr Hinton's daughter by his first wife, and as he chiefly promoted the suit, and bore the risk, he came in for a large share of the spoil.'⁵ To raise this amount of capital, Edward had to cut down a large swathe of timber at Chawton Park; for the next thirty years the resultant gap testified to the anxieties of this episode.

Edward's daughter Fanny was experiencing anxiety of a different nature – a romantic nature. Having encouraged the courtship of John Plumtre, she discovered that, now she was secure of his affection, she no longer valued it. She chose her aunt Jane as confidante, and long intimate letters passed between the two. Though she thought very highly of John Plumtre, not to marry without love was Jane's counsel.

Whilst Fanny dithered, Anna marched obstinately into a future which seemed by no means assured of happiness or prosperity. Ben had done nothing about improving his situation, and the only home he could offer her was a shared one with his brother Edward at Hendon. To escape from the dissatisfaction of her present home seemed as much her motive as anything. James had tried to dissuade her, had imposed a period of waiting – but, finding she was as determined as ever, gave his consent to the marriage taking place on 8 November.

Even the wedding ceremony had about it an unpropitious air, according to this account by Caroline:

My sister's wedding was certainly in the extreme of quietness, yet not so as to be in any way remarked upon or censured, and this was the order of the day.

The bridegroom came from Ashe Rectory where he had hitherto lived with his brother; and Mr and Mrs Lefroy came with him and another brother, Mr Edward Lefroy. Anne Lefroy the eldest little girl was one of the bridesmaids and I was the other. My brother came from Winchester that morning, but was to stay only a few hours. We in the house had a slight early breakfast upstairs, and between 9 and 10 the bride, my mother, Mrs Lefroy, Anne and myself, were taken to church in our carriage. All the gentlemen walked. The weather was dull and cloudy, but it did not actually rain. The season of the year, the unfrequented road of half a mile, to the lonely old church, the grey light within of a November morning, making its way through the narrow windows, no stove to give warmth, no flowers to give colour and brightness, no friends, high or low, to offer their good wishes, and so to claim some interest in the great event of the day – all these circumstances and deficiencies must, I think, have given a gloomy air to our wedding. Mr Lefroy read the service, my father gave his daughter away. The clerk, of course, was there, though I do not particularly remember him, but I am quite sure there was no-one else in the church, nor was anyone asked to the breakfast, to which we sat down as soon as we got back.

I do not think this idea of sadness struck me at the time, the bustle in the house and all the preparations had excited me, and it seemed to me a festivity from beginning to end.

The breakfast was such as best breakfasts then were: some variety of bread, hot rolls, buttered toast; tongue or ham and eggs. The addition of chocolate at one end of the table, and the wedding cake in the middle, marked the speciality of the day. I and Anne Lefroy nine and six years wore white frocks and had white ribband on our straw bonnets, which, I suppose, were new for the occasion. Soon after breakfast, the bride and bridegroom departed. They had a long day's journey before them, to Hendon; the other Lefroys went home: and in the afternoon my mother and I went to Chawton to stay at the Great House, then occupied by my uncle Captain Austen, and his large family. My father stayed behind for a few days and then joined us. The servants had cake and wine in the evening, and Mr Digweed walked down, to keep him company. Such were the wedding festivities of Steventon in 1814!

11

The tenderness of such a family

1815-17

Napoleon's escape from Elba brought Charles new employment; he was despatched to the Adriatic in command of the *Phoenix* to give chase to a squadron of Murat's ships sailing under the Neapolitan flag, whose purpose was to support the Emperor's last bid for power.

With the decisive victory of Waterloo came a time of national glorification, and Frank enjoyed a share of the honour when he was nominated a companion of the Most Honourable Order of the Bath at its institution in June 1815.

While the famous battle was raging, Caroline was convalescing after a near-fatal attack of bilious fever which struck her just before her tenth birthday. The Austen children seemed remarkably immune from the infant mortality rates of the times. Her recovery was celebrated in a set of verses written by her brother Edward to his 'darling Caroline'.[1]

Within a year of her marriage their sister Anna and her husband Ben moved back into family territory, leasing part of Wyards, a pleasant red-brick farmhouse just outside Alton. There the first child of the next generation was born on 20 October 1815. Christened Anna Jemima, she was always known by the second of her two names.

Four days after the birth of his first granddaughter was safely over, James received a letter announcing the serious illness of Henry.[2] It was sent by Jane, who was staying at Hans Place to see *Emma* through the press. What had begun as a slight indisposition with Henry had grown gradually more alarming and now, afraid for his life, she alerted all his relations and begged her brother to join her.

James and Mary drove immediately to Chawton, where Mary was deposited to keep Mrs Austen company, Martha being away at the time. The next day James and Cassandra travelled anxiously to London. For about a week Henry was believed to be in danger, but at the end of that period there was a favourable change, and he began to make a slow recovery.

James returned home, Cassandra continuing in town for a further month and Jane for two. During Cassandra's absence Mary and Caroline remained at Chawton cottage. Whilst they were there, Mrs Frank gave birth to a fourth son, Herbert Grey, on 8 November. This was the first child to be born at Chawton Manor for a hundred years.

Cassandra's place with Jane was now taken by Fanny Knight, the whole family rallying round to see Henry – and one another – through his illness. In addition to looking after her brother, Jane had much to occupy her with *Emma*. She had changed publishers and for this novel was dealing with John Murray. 'He is a rogue, of course, but a civil one,' she told Cassandra. 'He offers £450 but wants to have the copyright of M.P. & S & S included ... He sends more praise however than I expected.' With Henry still weak, not only the proof-reading but the chivvying and settling of all details fell to her share. She had been betrayed into a tiresome correspondence with the pompous James Stanier Clarke, librarian to the Prince Regent, and, moreover, had been invited (that is to say commanded) to dedicate *Emma* to the Prince, who admired her novels warmly and kept a set in each of his residences.

But for such fame and aggrandizement Jane cared nothing. Her family, and her own created people, were all to her. 'Sweet amiable Frank! why does *he* have a cold too?' she wrote to Cassandra on 26 November, adding, 'Thank you very much for the sight of dearest Charles's letter to yourself. How pleasantly and how naturally he writes! and how perfect a picture of his disposition and feelings, his style conveys! – Poor dear fellow!' Charles was about to put to sea again in the *Phoenix*.

Henry was still paying court at Hanwell. As he began to feel better, he spent two days there 'very quietly and pleasantly' and meeting with 'the utmost care and attention'.

He was well enough for Jane to return home on her fortieth

Jane Austen

Chawton before the pond was drained, with the Austens' cottage on the left

Chawton Great House

Captain Charles Austen

Caroline Austen

The Reverend Henry Austen

Fanny Knight, water-colour by Cassandra Austen

Mersham-le-Hatch in 1825, home of Fanny, Lady Knatchbull

Edward Knight the younger

Lady Austen, née Martha Lloyd

Emma Smith, later
Mrs Austen-Leigh,
sketched by her sister
Augusta

Catherine, daughter of
Sir Francis Austen

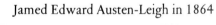

A sketch by Catherine Austen based on family life at Portsdown Lodge in 1836

Anna Lefroy in 1845   Jamed Edward Austen-Leigh in 1864

Fanny, Lady Knatchbull

Catherine Hubback, née Austen

birthday, and *Emma* was published the same day. A copy reached Charles just as he sailed; later he wrote to thank his sister: '*Emma* arrived in time to a moment. I am delighted with her, more so I think than even with my favourite *Pride & Prejudice*, and have read it three times in the passage.'[3]

Another copy was lent to Anna, with the note: 'As I wish very much to see *your* Jemima, I am sure you will like to see *my* Emma, and have therefore great pleasure in sending it for your perusal.' *Emma* was reviewed anonymously, favourably and at length by Sir Walter Scott in the *Quarterly Review*.

Two disasters marked the beginning of 1816. On 20 February the *Phoenix* went down off the West Indies. The crew were all saved, and as the pilot was on board, no blame attached to Charles – but nevertheless it was an unfavourable circumstance to lose a ship, and with the war over, Charles knew only too well that his prospects of getting another command were remote.

Then on 6 March came the blow of Henry's bankruptcy. It was a complete surprise to them all. The enforced neglect of affairs occasioned by Henry's long illness had doubtless contributed to a general crisis beginning with the failure of the Alton branch.

Caroline's reminiscences affirm that Henry 'had been living for some years past at considerable expense but not more than might become the head of a flourishing bank and no blame of personal extravagance was ever imputed to him'.

Edward Knight and Mr Leigh Perrot instantly lost the very large sums for which they had stood surety. Coming immediately on top of the legal settlement, this was a heavy stroke for Edward to bear, but he did bear it without recrimination or loss of regard for Henry. Mrs Leigh Perrot, by contrast, never forgave her unfortunate nephew – even though she and her husband were rich beyond their needs and had no family dependant upon them.

James and Frank Austen both lost several hundred pounds which they had bound to Henry for some army agency together with small personal sums. Most of the family were therefore involved in Henry's collapse, and there was not one that did not suffer mental anxiety, if not actual financial hardship. For the bank's employees, and for Henry's servant who had lost all her life's savings, there was

much anguish to be felt. Fortunately most of the family banking
had remained with Hoares of Fleet Street, where it had always been
– otherwise there might have been literal destitution.

Caroline states:

> To my uncle himself it was ruin – and he saw the world before him to
> begin again. In about a fortnight he came to Steventon, *apparently*, for
> it *truly* could not have been, in unbroken spirits. I believe he had even
> then decided on taking orders.
>
> Now the old learning was to be looked up, and he went to Oxford to
> see about taking the necessary degree. He had very good abilities, and
> such as were always ready for use – fond of all sorts of reading.
>
> Examinations were not over strict in the year 1816, so that altogether
> no difficulties opposed his entrance into the profession to which he now
> turned with all the energy of a sanguine, elastic nature. He was, I see,
> many times at Steventon this year, and then it was, I suppose, that I got
> to like him so very much, as I remember but little of him previously.

Henry Austen was forty-five this summer as he contemplated
embarking on this, his third career. As a clergyman he was not likely
to be anything but poor, for he could expect no preferment. But it
was an honest living and one for which he found he had a taste.
London and his old style of life went unmourned, as he looked to
the future with optimism and confidence. Perhaps the only thing to
be regretted was the collapse of his matrimonial plans; in his
changed circumstances he could hardly ask Miss Moore or any
other lady to be his wife.

The shock of Henry's bankruptcy following the ordeal of his long
illness took their toll on Jane's strength, and from about this time
her health began to fail. James too knew himself to be declining
physically.

In May Jane and Cassandra paid a visit of health and pleasure to
Cheltenham, where Jane tried the waters. Later in the summer
Charles, his daughters and the Palmers visited Broadstairs and felt it
did them all good. Little Harriet was prone to headaches, which was
a perpetual source of worry.

Perhaps to give Edward the chance of a more profitable tenancy,
or perhaps to economize on his own expenses, Frank left the Great
House this year and took lodgings in Alton. Mary was pregnant
again. 'Mrs F.A. seldom either looks or appears quite well. – Little

embryo is troublesome I suppose,' Jane told Cassandra on 8 September.

Anna's family too was increasing fast. On 27 September was born Julia Cassandra, just eleven months after her sister. Poor Anna had no leisure for novel-writing now. But all James' children had a literary gift, and both Edward and little Caroline were emulating their sister and aunt. Jane had encouraged Anna with a judicious, kindly mixture of criticism and praise. Her opinion of Edward's efforts, however, because expressed in a letter to Cassandra, was evidently sincere: 'Edward is writing a novel – we have all heard what he has written – it is extremely clever; written with great ease and spirit; – if he can carry on in the same way, it will be a first-rate work, and in a style, I think, to be popular.' This seems to imply she was thinking of eventual publication. She herself had just finished *Persuasion* and had put it aside, satisfied for the time being but not wishing to hurry it into print.

She was becoming increasingly fond of Edward. On her birthday she wrote to 'give you joy of having left Winchester'. Many Winchester schoolboys took the Chawton road on their way to and from the college, and she told him: 'Charles Knight and his companions passed through Chawton about 9 this morning ... Uncle Henry and I had a glimpse of his handsome face, looking all health and good humour.'

She added, 'We think Uncle Henry in excellent looks ... and we have the great comfort of seeing decided improvement in Uncle Charles, both as to health, spirits and appearance. – And they are each of them so agreeable in their different way, and harmonize so well, that their visit is thorough enjoyment.'

In December Henry was ordained by the Bishop of Salisbury and instituted into the curacy of Chawton. It is recorded that he was disappointed not to be examined in Greek, as he was rather proud of his scholarship, particularly at his time of life.

Though incumbents were free to choose their own curates, no doubt Henry owed this appointment to the influence of Edward. He was the patron of the living of Chawton, which was presently held by John Papillon of Kent, and designed eventually for one of the younger Knight boys. Edward's efforts to secure even a small income for Henry – the stipend was £54.12s.0d. per annum – are proof of his unwavering brotherly friendship despite his own financial loss.

In January James broke a bone in his leg during a riding accident and, being laid up on the sofa for several days, took the opportunity to teach Caroline chess. Edward paid a visit to Chawton, and Caroline received a letter from Jane written on the 23rd of the month:

> We were quite happy to see Edward, it was an unexpected pleasure, he makes himself as agreeable as ever, sitting in such a quiet comfortable way making his delightful little sketches. – He is generally thought grown since he was here last, and rather thinner, but in very good looks … Uncle Charles, I am sorry to say, has been suffering from rheumatism, and now he has got a great eruption in his face and neck – which is to do him good however – but he has a sad turn for being unwell. – *I* feel myself getting stronger than I was half a year ago, and can so perfectly well walk to Alton, *or* back again, without the slightest fatigue that I hope to be able to do both when the summer comes. – I spent two or three days with your uncle and aunt lately, and though the children are sometimes very noisy and not under such order as they ought and easily might, I cannot help liking them and even loving them, which I hope may be not wholly inexcusable in their and your affectionate Aunt J. Austen.

To her friend Alethea Bigg Jane wrote the following day, giving an optimistic account of her own health and continuing with news of the Steventon family:

> We have just had a few days' visit from Edward, who brought us a good account of his father, and the very circumstance of his coming at all, of his father's being able to spare him, is itself a good account. He is gone to spend this day at Wyards and goes home tomorrow. He grows still, and still improves in appearance, at least in the estimation of his aunts, who love him better and better, as they see the sweet temper and warm affections of the boy confirmed in the young man … Anna has not been so well or so strong or looking so much like herself since her marriage as she is now; she is quite equal to walking to Chawton, and comes over to us when she can, but the rain and dirt divide us a good deal … Anna's eldest child just now runs alone, which is a great convenience with a second one in arms, and they are both healthy nice children – I wish their father were ordained and all the family settled in a comfortable parsonage house. The curacy only is wanting I fancy to complete the business. Our own new clergyman is expected here very

soon, perhaps in time to assist Mr Papillon on Sunday. I shall be very glad when the first hearing is over. It will be a nervous hour for our pew, though we hear that he acquits himself with as much ease and collectedness, as if he had been used to it all his life.

Shortly after this visit to his grandmother and aunts, Edward went up to Exeter College, Oxford, where he obtained a Craven Founder's Kin Fellowship which was worth £25 p.a. for fourteen years. A spirit of reform was in the air, and the universities were beginning to baulk at these ancient privileges. What with this, and the fact that one of the links in the Craven pedigree could not be verified except by personal testimony, Edward experienced some difficulty in getting the award. The question is touched on humorously in a letter from Jane to Caroline dated 14 March: 'I hope Edward is not idle. No matter what becomes of the Craven Exhibition provided he goes on with his novel. In that, he will find his true fame and his true wealth. That will be the honourable Exhibition which no V. Chancellor can rob him of. – I have just received nearly twenty pounds myself on the 2nd Edition of S & S – which gives me this fine flow of literary ardour.'

Two other nephews, Henry and William Knight, aged twenty and nineteen respectively, now visited Chawton cottage. During February and March Jane wrote three times to their sister Fanny, long letters of mixed family news in which the boys figure: 'And now I will tell you that we like your Henry to the utmost, to the very top of the class, quite brimful. – He is a very pleasing young man. I do not see how he could be mended. He really does bid fair to be everything his father and sister could wish; and William I love very much indeed, and so do we all, he is quite our own William – Henry is generally thought very good-looking, but not so handsome as Edward. – I think *I* prefer his face. – William is in excellent looks, has a fine appetite and seems perfectly well.' And in a later letter, after Henry had left them to travel to France: 'William and I are the best of friends. I love him very much. Everything is so *natural* about him, his affections, his manners and his drollery. He entertains and interests us extremely.'

Fanny was again in romantic perplexity. There was a new suitor on the scene, James Wildman of Chilham Castle; but now that the rejected Mr Plumtre had turned his attentions to another young

lady, Fanny began to wonder whether she *had* loved him after all.
Jane wrote affectionately:

> You are inimitable, irresistible. You are the delight of my life. Such
> letters, such entertaining letters as you have lately sent! Such a
> description of your queer little heart! – Such a lovely display of what
> imagination does. – You are worth your weight in gold, or even in the
> new silver coinage. – I cannot express to you what I have felt in reading
> your history of yourself ... It is very, very gratifying to me to know you
> so intimately. You can hardly think what a pleasure it is to me, to have
> such thorough pictures of your heart. – Oh! What a loss it will be when
> you are married. You are too agreeable in your single state, too
> agreeable as a niece. I shall hate you when your delicious play of mind
> is all settled down into conjugal and maternal affections ... And yet I do
> wish you to marry very much, because I know you will never be happy
> till you are ...

In another letter she wrote:

> Single women have a dreadful propensity for being poor – which is one
> very strong argument in favour of matrimony, but I need not dwell on
> such arguments with *you*, pretty dear, you do not want inclination. –
> Well, I shall say, as I have often said before, do not be in a hurry;
> depend upon it, the right man will come at last; you will in the course
> of the next two or three years, meet with somebody more generally
> unexceptionable than anyone you have yet known, who will love you
> as warmly as *he* did, and who will so completely attach you, that you
> will feel you never really loved before. – And then, by not beginning
> the business of mothering quite so early in life, you will be young in
> constitution, spirits, figure and countenance, while Mrs William
> Hammond is growing old by confinements and nursing.

She could have used (and very likely had in mind) Anna for her
example. There was a strong suspicion that Anna was pregnant
again, as some of the following remarks show, although, as it
happened, this was a false alarm; 'Ben and Anna walked here last
Sunday to hear Uncle Henry, and she looked so pretty, it was quite
a pleasure to see her, so young and so blooming and so innocent, as
if she had never had a wicked thought in her life – which yet one
has some reason to suppose she must have had, if we believe the
doctrine of original sin, or if we remember the events of her girlish
days.'
Three weeks later it was: 'Anna has a bad cold, looks pale, and

we fear something else. She has just weaned Julia. – How soon, the difference of temper in children appears! – Jemima has a very irritable bad temper (her mother says so) – and Julia a very sweet one, always pleased and happy. – I hope as Anna is so early sensible of its defects, that she will give Jemima's disposition the early and steady attention it must require.'

And ten days later: 'Anna has not a chance of escape; her husband called here the other day, and said she was pretty well but not equal to a long walk; she must come in her donkey carriage. – Poor animal, she will be worn out before she is thirty.'

There was mention of two other nieces; first Fanny's own sister, Cassandra Knight: 'What a comfort that Cassandra should be so recovered! – It is more than we had expected. – I can easily believe she was very patient and very good. I always loved Cassandra, for her fine dark eyes and sweet temper.'

But there was less happy news of Charles' Harriet: 'Our fears increase for poor little Harriet; the latest account is that Sir Everard Home is confirmed in his opinion of there being water on the brain. – I hope heaven in its mercy will take her soon. Her poor father will be quite worn out by his feelings for her. He cannot spare Cassy at present, she is an occupation and comfort to him.' Ten days later: 'Now, the reports from Keppel Street are rather better, little Harriet's headaches are abated, and Sir Everard is satisfied with the effect of the mercury, and does not despair of a cure. The complaint I find is not considered incurable nowadays, provided the patient be young enough not to have the head hardened. The water in that case may be drawn off by mercury.' This is the only mention we have of any Austen child undergoing one of the horrifying remedies so many eighteenth- and nineteenth-century children were subjected to.

Of her own physical state she wrote on 23 March: 'Many thanks for your kind care for my health; I certainly have not been well for many weeks, and about a week ago I was very poorly, I have had a good deal of fever at times and indifferent nights, but am considerably better now, and recovering my looks a little, which have been bad enough, black and white and every wrong colour. I must not depend upon being ever very blooming again. Sickness is a dangerous indulgence at my time of life ... Aunt Cass is such an excellent nurse, so assiduous and unwearied! – But you know all that already.'

Fanny had enquired whether her aunt meant now to publish the early work *Susan*, whose eponymous heroine had undergone a change of name. 'I will answer your kind questions more than you expect. Miss Catherine is put upon the shelve for the present, and I do not know that she will ever come out; – but I have a something ready for publication, which may perhaps appear about a twelvemonth hence. It is short, about the length of Catherine.' The next letter added: 'Do not be surprised at finding Uncle Henry acquainted with my having another ready for publication. I could not say No when he asked me, but he knows nothing more of it. – You will not like it, so you need not be impatient. You may *perhaps* like the heroine, as she is almost too good for me.'

All the while that she was writing these long letters to Fanny, and other playful ones to Caroline and Cassy, Jane was not only suffering from an increasingly debilitating malady – now identified as Addison's disease – but creatively working on a new novel full of high spirits and fun – a novel that made a special point of mocking hypochondria.

Both Motley Austen and his eldest son Francis Lucius had died in 1815, the Kippington property passing to the second son, Colonel Thomas Austen, who had served in Ireland; now, on 17 February 1817, Motley's widow died, and distantly though they were related, the ladies of Chawton cottage put on their 'old black gowns' for her.

The death of a nearer and more important connection – that of Mr Leigh Perrot, on 28 March – perhaps justified new mourning, and certainly 'proper-edged notepaper'. He had been ill some little time. Five days before his death Jane wrote to Fanny: 'Indeed I shall be very glad when the event at Scarlets is over, the expectation of it keeps us in a worry, your grandmama especially; she sits brooding over evils which cannot be remedied and conduct impossible to be understood.' Impossible now to understand what Jane had in mind – but one thing was certain, that Mrs Austen's chief hope of something in the way of fortune for herself or her children depended upon her rich childless brother, and that the opening of his will was awaited in considerable suspense. As executor, James was summoned to Scarlets to perform this task.

It would be very acceptable to Mrs Austen and her daughters to receive a legacy, however modest, which would secure their independence and relieve the burden they must feel themselves to be on others. And there was scarcely an Austen son who would not have been grateful for some small capital sum to help him with his expenses. Henry was bankrupt, James and Frank had both lost money, the latter being obliged to cease the allowance to his mother now that he had a large family to support; Charles had always been poor, and even wealthy Edward had suffered proportionable losses in recent years. Perhaps Edward expected nothing, but certainly all the others hoped for some alteration in their circumstances from their uncle's will.

To quote *Sense and Sensibility*: 'His will was read and, like almost every other will, gave as much disappointment as pleasure.' Indeed it is hard to see who received any pleasure except for the widow, who kept everything for her life and could dispose of most of it as she chose thereafter. James had always been regarded as his uncle's heir, but he was not now to step into Scarlets, or even into any money. A legacy of £24,000 was designed for him but was to wait for his aunt's death. Should James predecease her, the sum was to go to his heirs. Those of Mrs Austen's younger children who survived their aunt were to get £1,000 apiece. Mrs Austen herself was not mentioned. Scarlets and the bulk of the fortune were left to Mrs Leigh Perrot absolutely – and her capriciousness and easily offended nature were notorious. Scarlets might end up out of the family altogether – perhaps amongst her own relations.

On 5 April James Leigh Perrot was buried in Wargrave churchyard. The following day Jane wrote to Charles:

Many thanks for your affectionate letter … I am ashamed to say that the shock of my uncle's will brought on a relapse, and I was so ill on Friday and thought myself so likely to be worse that I could not but press for Cassandra's returning with Frank after the funeral last night, which she of course did, and either her return, or my having seen Mr Curtis, or my disorder's choosing to go away, have made me better this morning. I live upstairs however for the present and am coddled. I am the only one of the legatees who has been so silly, but a weak body must excuse weak nerves. My mother has borne the forgetfulness of *her* extremely well; – her expectations for herself were never beyond the extreme of moderation, and she thinks with you that my uncle always looked forward to surviving her. – She desires her best love and many thanks for your kind feelings; and heartily wishes that her younger children had more, and all her children something immediately. My aunt felt the value of Cassandra's company so fully, and was so very kind to her, and is poor woman! so miserable at present (for her affliction has very much increased since the first) that we feel more regard for her than we ever did before ... As for your poor little Harriet, I dare not be sanguine for her. Nothing can be kinder than Mrs Cooke's enquiries after you and her, in all her letters, and there was no standing her affectionate way of speaking of your *countenance*, after her seeing you. – God bless you all. Conclude me to be going on well, if you hear nothing to the contrary.

This letter is endorsed, 'My last letter from dearest Jane C.J.A.'. Her illness was increasing in severity. On 22 May she wrote to a friend, Anne Sharp, that she had been confined to bed since 13 April. A surgeon from the hospital at Winchester had been called in since the Alton apothecary was at a loss, and this Mr Lyford had succeeded in alleviating some of the symptoms.

The consequence is, that instead of going to town to put myself into the hands of some physician as I should otherwise have done, I am going to Winchester instead, for some weeks to see what Mr Lyford can do farther towards re-establishing me in tolerable health. – On Saturday next, I am actually going thither – my dearest Cassandra with me I need hardly say – and as this is only two days off you will be convinced that I am now really a very genteel, portable sort of an invalid. – The journey is only 16 miles, we have comfortable lodgings engaged for us by our kind friend Mrs Heathcote who resides in Winchester and we are to have the accommodation of my elder brother's carriage which will be sent over from Steventon on purpose. Now, that's a sort of thing which Mrs J. Austen does in the kindest manner! – But she is still in the main *not* a liberal-minded woman, and as to this reversionary property's amending that part of her character, expect it not my dear Anne; – too late, too late in the day; – and besides, the property may not be theirs these ten years. My aunt is very stout. – Mrs F.A has had a much shorter confinement than I have – with a baby to produce into the bargain. We were put to bed nearly at the same time, and she has been quite recovered this great while.

The baby referred to was Elizabeth, born at Alton on 15 April.

Jane's letter to Anne Sharp is full of praise for her family's support: 'How to do justice to the kindness of all my family during this illness, is quite beyond me! – Every dear brother so affectionate and so anxious! – and as for my sister! – Words must fail me in any attempt to describe what a nurse she has been to me. Thank God! she does not seem the worse for it ... I have not mentioned my dear mother; she suffered much for me when I was at the worse, but is tolerably well. – Miss Lloyd too has been all kindness. In short, if I live to be an old woman, I must expect to wish I had died now; blessed in the tenderness of such a family, and before I had survived either them or their affection.'

Five days later she wrote to her nephew Edward Austen at Oxford from Mrs David's house in College Street: 'Our lodgings are very comfortable. We have a neat little drawing room with a bow-window overlooking Dr Gabell's garden. Thanks to the kindness of your father and mother in sending me their carriage, my journey hither on Saturday was performed with very little fatigue, and had it been a fine day I think I should have felt none, but it distressed me to see Uncle Henry and William Knight who kindly attended us on horseback, riding in rain almost all the way.'

But Jane continued inexorably to weaken, and the next account Edward received was from his father:

I grieve to write what you will grieve to read: but I must tell you that we can no longer flatter ourselves with the least hope of having your dear valuable Aunt Jane restored to us. The symptoms which returned after the first four or five days at Winchester have never been subdued and Mr Lyford has candidly told us that her case is desperate. I need not say what a melancholy gloom this has cast over us all. Your grandmamma has suffered much; but her affliction can be nothing to Cassandra's. She will indeed need to be pitied. It is some consolation to know that our poor invalid has hitherto felt no very severe pain, which is rather an extraordinary circumstance in her complaint. I saw her on Tuesday and found her much altered but comparatively cheerful. She is well aware of her situation. Your mother has been there since Tuesday and returns not till all is over, how long that may be we cannot say. Lyford said he saw no signs of immediate dissolution but added that with such a pulse – 120 – it was impossible for any person to last long. And indeed we cannot wish it – an easy departure from this to a better world is all that we can pray for. I am going to Winchester again tomorrow. You may depend upon early information when any change takes place ...[4]

Jane died on 18 July, attended to the last by Cassandra. 'I have lost a treasure, such a sister, such a friend as never can have been surpassed, – she was the sun of my life, the gilder of every pleasure, the soother of every sorrow, I had not a thought concealed from her, and it is as if I had lost a part of myself,'[5] Cassandra wrote to Fanny Knight in the immediate aftermath. As for Mrs Austen, she confessed she was 'in great affliction' for she had never given up hope that this the first of her children to die would recover.[6]

The funeral at Winchester Cathedral was attended by Jane's brothers Edward, Henry and Frank and by her nephew Edward Austen who came from Oxford to represent his father. James was himself too ill to make the journey, but he wrote a poem[7] on the death of his brilliant sister. It is a revealing composition. Generously though he praised her character, her

Fancy quick and clear good sense
And wit which never gave offence;
A heart as warm as ever beat,
A temper, even, calm and sweet ...

his subsequent words betray both the typically male fear that, if a woman is preoccupied with literature, she is bound to neglect her *real* duties, and a suggestion of personal envy that it had been a female member of the family, not one of the highly educated males – not himself – who had turned promise into achievement. The family, he wrote,

Saw her ready still to share
The labours of domestic care,
As if their prejudice to shame
Who, jealous of fair female fame,
Maintain that literary taste
In woman's mind is much misplaced,
Inflames their vanity and pride,
And draws from useful works aside ...

In September James suffered a particularly serious attack of illness and the following month decided to try a change of air at Worthing, accompanied by Cassandra, herself in need of some restorative after the physical and mental stresses of the year.

12

We left our home with sad hearts

1818-22

To distract the grieving Fanny, Edward took her and her next sister Lizzy on a visit to Paris, where they were joined by their brother George, who introduced to them a friend also holidaying in the city.[1] His name was Edward Royds Rice. He was twenty-seven years old, handsome, clever and rich, with a beautiful home at Dane Court in Kent. Fanny was twenty-four and Lizzy seventeen. 'How remarkably pretty your sister is,' he is reputed to have said to George as they left the house; it was Lizzy he spoke of.

He pursued the acquaintance when they all returned to Kent, and the young couple were married on 6 October 1818. It was the first wedding at Godmersham but passed with very little fuss, 'although', according to their daughter Caroline, 'my mother and father were said to be the handsomest couple who ever went to church'. When the company returned to the house, the bridegroom went out shooting with the bride's brothers, while the bride herself, with her sister Marianne, 'walked all round the chicken houses, and climbed up to the top of the cowhouses to say goodbye!'[2]

Earlier in the year, Jane's two novels still in manuscript were taken off the 'shelve' and published under titles probably chosen by Henry, *Northanger Abbey* and *Persuasion*. Henry also composed a short 'Biographical Notice' of his sister with which to preface the set of four volumes. This satisfied whatever small degree of public curiosity had been aroused, and for the next fifty years family privacy went unchallenged by any interest in Jane's life, while her reputation as a novelist advanced hardly at all.

The first of her nieces to be born after her death was given the names of the two heroines of these posthumous novels. Frank and

Mary were enjoying another spell at Chawton House, where their daughter Catherine Anne was born on 7 July 1818 and christened under the portrait by Romney of Mrs Knight, whose name she likewise bore.

This was the twenty-fifth grandchild of Mrs Austen, whose third great-grandchild also arrived this year. George Benjamin Austen Lefroy was born at Lasham, a little village between Alton and Basingstoke, where Ben had at last accepted a curacy. The story is told that at his ordination the bishop asked him only two questions – first, if he was the son of Mrs Lefroy of Ashe, and second, if he had married a Miss Austen.³ The year after George's birth the family moved again, to a Lefroy family living at Compton, near Guildford, Surrey.

Little George was the last of his grandchildren whom James was to live to see. His health continued to deteriorate. It could not have been helped by his aunt Leigh Perrot's behaviour in the spring of 1818. Only a year after her husband's death, she was already proving that the family fears of her capriciousness were not unfounded. James wrote to his son at Oxford on 28 April:

> I must now tell you some news at which you will surely be surprised, for I was. My aunt has withdrawn the annuity of £100 a year which she and my uncle had allowed me for these eight or nine years past. The ostensible reasons are her own *poverty* and my having £200 a year to support T. Leigh – of which I certainly clear more than half, but who is very unlikely to live long. The real reasons I leave you to guess.
>
> In consequence of this we have determined to take Caroline from school at Midsummer and your mother has persuaded me not to enter our carriage this year. No other alteration will be necessary so do not let this vex you. Your sister's superiority to her school-fellows makes her leaving school no great loss.

To this unwelcome communication Edward replied immediately:

> I am very sorry and certainly surprised at this last motion of Mrs L. Perrot, but I have long thought too meanly of her, to be much astonished at any fresh instance of want of feeling or of hypocrisy. So much for your reduction of income: now for the effects it is to have: this subject I cannot so easily dismiss and though you tell me not to vex myself about Caroline's removal from school, and though (if that removal *must* take place) it is certainly very proper and philosophical to

find out as many reasons as we can for thinking it rather a good thing
that it should be so, yet I cannot help considering it as a great and
serious evil: I am sorry that the weight should fall so heavily on her;
and still more so that it is out of my power to take *much* of it on myself;
I cannot possibly offer to give up anything in the money way, for I have
not a farthing more than is absolutely necessary, but in *expense at home* I
may give up considerably: if I were to give up hunting for the next year
or two, there would be no occasion for more than two horses which
with keep and tax and other little concomitant expenses would be, I am
sure, a considerable saving; giving up hunting would be no great
sacrifice, I am not so *exclusively* attached to it as I was, and till I take my
degree, I shall never find it an evil to have more time left for reading;
but it is nonsense talking about sacrifice; if it were much greater, it
could make no difference; it must be done, if any good could result
from it; I am sure it is highly improper I should be *indulging myself* with
my own horse in sports while you cannot afford to give my sister the
necessary education of a gentlewoman.

Only let me beseech you to reflect (that if one must be given up)
how disproportionate is what I should lose, compared with what
Caroline's loss will be. I shall lose a doubtful good ... she will forgo a
certain and inestimable advantage ... The same causes which would
prevent her remaining at Winchester must equally prevent the
possibility of travelling for masters. I could not sit easy on my horse – if
by giving him up I could secure Caroline a continuance of
instruction ...

I have not been writing all this long letter to be thanked. I have made
the proposal that it may be *accepted*; if it *can be*, for heaven's sake *let it be*
... Pray do not say a word about this to Caroline herself.

We do not know whether the offer was accepted, but for the
moment Caroline remained at Miss Burney's school in Kingsgate
Street, Winchester, where she had been a pupil since the previous
August.

James' letter to Edward had also contained news of Henry. He
had been offered an appointment as chaplain to the British Embassy
in Berlin, at a very low salary, but he was inclined to accept as it
might lead to something better. The offer had come his way
through Henry Walter, grandson of George Austen's half-brother
William Hampson Walter, fellow of St John's College, Cambridge.
Five years previously Jane had met a St John's man who 'spoke very
highly of H. Walter as a scholar. He said he was considered as the

best classic in the University. How such a report would have interested my father!' Jane had written.

Henry Austen's appointment presumably included some teaching as he went to thank Mr Walter and to 'rub up his own mathematics and algebra', according to James. However, in his next letter, there is different news: 'he has given up all thoughts of going to Berlin. The Bishop has sent so favourable an answer to the application of his Alton parishioners that your uncle says he feels it an imperative duty to remain among them. It is no doubt highly gratifying, and preferment so gained will be most honourable; but between ourselves I think he is running a great risk. The Bishop's life must hang by a thread, and in relinquishing his appointment he gives up a certainty – but we will hope that all is for the best.'

However, changeable Henry changed his mind yet again and did go to Berlin for five months; his signature is missing from the Chawton registers for that period.

In the summer of 1818 James decided to try a change of air again. A tour down the River Wye was planned. Like Jane, James had read with great enjoyment William Gilpin's book on picturesque beauty. Caroline wrote of this period:

He had a delight in natural scenery, and pleased himself with the idea of following Gilpin's footsteps along the banks of that 'gentle river.' He was interested in making all the arrangements for our tour but as the time approached for our starting, he felt it would be too much for him and the plan was altered, we were not to go so far as to reach the Wye, and we were to be away only a week, and we fell short even of this, but we *did* set off – my father and mother and myself.

We made Chawton the beginning of our tour, *he* thinking it right that if well enough to go anywhere, he should go and see his mother. His attention to her during all my recollection was great, especially so, considering that it was always an effort to him to leave his own home. Not many months ever passed, without his riding over to Chawton, and he gave up this habit very unwillingly. I *can* remember latterly his setting off once or twice to go there, and turning back after a few miles, because he felt unequal to going on.

We now stayed one night at my grandmother's, and it was the last time that the mother and son ever met. The next day we went on to Southampton, stayed there some hours, and at the close of a lovely summer's evening, got to Lyndhurst, where we slept.

They saw Stonehenge and spent a night at Amesbury, but further plans were abandoned, as James by now felt so unwell he was anxious only to be home. The next day therefore they turned towards Steventon, stopping a little while at Salisbury and reaching the Rectory by dinner time. A few days later Caroline returned to school.

James made some notes on what they had seen, concluding: ' "We travel," Gilpin observes, "for various purposes," and he enumerates several; but none, if I remember them right, was exactly my purpose. I travelled to get health, i.e. in the rational expectation that the woods and heaths of the New Forest would brace relaxed nerves, and the motion of a post-chaise rectify a disordered stomach. I had however some better motive to direct my route and determine my time; I went *where* I did to see my mother, whom I had never visited since my long illness, and I went *when* I did, that I might have Caroline's company. In the pleasure I expected from these circumstances I have felt no disappointment.'⁴

On 23 December Caroline left school for good. She was 13½ and an extremely clever child, as indeed were all James' offspring, but whether the decision was made because she had truly outgrown all the school could offer her, or for financial reasons, is not recorded.

That James did have money worries at this time is certain. He had too much reason to fear that his own life would not be prolonged much further, and the situation of his widow and children, deprived of their home and reduced to a very small income indeed, was not pleasant to contemplate. If only he had come into his uncle's £24,000 immediately! A great weight would then have been removed from his mind.

But though his aunt wrote him two letters couched in affectionate terms that January, she did nothing to help him. The first letter was written to assure him that her appointing another executor besides himself showed no lack of confidence in him but was occasioned by reports of his ill health; she concluded: 'From the difference in our ages *I* cannot be expected to survive you, but life is so uncertain that as we none of us know which of us may be called on first to resign it, it may do no harm to prepare for any change ... from my heart do I pray that many, many years of life and comfort may be in store for you ... I frequently wish I could see and know more of your young people – but *your* ill-health and *my* uncompanionable spirits seem to keep us asunder.'

The second letter from Scarlets refers to the disposal of some Kent property, the residue of William Austen's holdings there, and now required to pay off Henry's creditors: 'I am grieved that you should have so much vexation, nor would I have Henry's feelings (if he does feel) for more than he has occasioned us to lose by his imprudence ... when I reflect on what might have been the consequences if the Stoneleigh settlement had not occasioned us such an increase of property as to enable us to bear up against our losses, I am thankful it is no worse. Where would my pretty Scarlets have gone then? I wish you thought as fondly of this place as I must ever do – perhaps as it is the only house I have known for more than fifty years I may be partial to it as you may be to Steventon.'

There were powerful hints contained in these two letters which it behoved James not to ignore. To give his son any chance of inheriting Scarlets (for James must have accepted that he himself was unlikely to outlive his aunt), it was necessary to improve her acquaintance with Edward – to visit her and make her feel courted and to show some signs of regard for her beloved home. Perhaps through Mary's influence the old lady had been too much neglected. Amends must be made.

The idea of travelling was not pleasant but, to obtain the maximum benefit from the exertions entailed, James decided to combine a visit to Scarlets with a stay in London in order to seek medical advice. The Steventon family set off in June, accompanied by Cassandra, who also wished to consult a good doctor.

After a fortnight in town, the party left for Scarlets. Edward and Caroline were obliged to make the journey by public coach, which arrived first. Caroline records: 'The coach put us down at the entrance to the lane and my brother and I walked up to the house, and had to introduce ourselves to its mistress, whom I had never seen before, nor he, since the days of his early childhood.'

Caroline's account continues: 'We stayed ten whole days and then got home again ... My father grew worse almost daily, getting by degrees to take his meals in his own room, and living very much apart ... His craving to be out of doors could only be gratified by sitting out in a bath chair, almost daily for several hours during the autumn, in one particular spot, sunny and sheltered. He was visited by all his relations.'

When it got too cold outside for sitting still, his devoted manservant rigged up a kind of litter in which, with the aid of another man, he used to carry James about. Indoors, he spent much of his time drawing and composing poetry. On 17 November he became much worse, and he never left his bed afterwards. Edward was summoned from Oxford, and on 13 December 1819 James died at half past eleven at night.

He was buried in Steventon churchyard in a spot he had long chosen for himself. The funeral was attended by his son and his four brothers.

Almost immediately, Mrs Leigh Perrot showed the inconsistent kindness and generosity of which she was capable by offering to allow her sister-in-law £100, as compensation for the loss of income that she knew Mrs Austen must suffer on the death of one of her sons. Mrs Austen replied on 4 January 1820:

I sincerely thank you for your letter and its very kind contents; most thankfully do I accept your generous offer, such an addition to my income will be most acceptable at this time, and I will thank you if you will order Messrs Hoare every *half year* to place the money to my account, for he is my banker, and receives my dividends, amounting to not quite £116 a year: this sum, with a little land at Steventon, which I let for £6 a year is the whole of my own property, my good children having supplied all the rest.

My dear departed James always paid me £50 a year, and for the last two years had added to it by insisting on my retaining the dividends of my brother Thomas' money now standing in my name in the old South Sea Stock, almost £40 a year. Henry and Frank also paid me the same until the last four years, Charles I am sure would have done the same had he the power – from the unfortunate spring of 1816 poor Henry had hardly anything for himself. Frank also was so much a loser that he was unable to make me any remittance, but last year when he removed a part of his property he would have renewed it, but I declined it, on account of his large and increasing family, promising to apply to him if I found it necessary ...

Mr Knight is most kind and liberal: he allows me £200 a year, gives me my house rent, supplies me plentifully with wood and makes me many kind presents – and often asks Cassandra if she is sure I have enough, as if I had not he would most willingly give me more, but that

I should be sorry to apply for, well knowing that though his income is large, his family is large also, and with four grown up sons, it must be an expensive one, and he has moreover lately had great demands for considerable sums of money. Your generosity my dear sister will prevent me from ever having to apply to him: it will also enable me to pay my brother Thomas' dividends to Mrs James Austen, to whom I am sure it must be most acceptable.

Mr Knight I am sure will be very glad to be of any use to you, he has a most active mind, a clear head, and a sound judgement, he is quite a man of business. That my dear James was not – classical knowledge, literary taste and the power of elegant composition he possessed in the highest degree; to these Mr Knight makes no pretensions. *Both* equally good, amiable and sweet-tempered ...

Since I wrote the above the party from Steventon has arrived, consisting of Mrs J. Austen, Caroline, and Miss Lloyd – she has been staying at Steventon the last fortnight: dear Edward came yesterday. Mrs J.A. is as well as can be expected, a good deal agitated at our first meeting. I believe she and Caroline will spend a week with us. Edward leaves us on Thursday, having promised to spend a few days with his sister at Compton. She desires to be kindly remembered to you, and talks of writing to you tomorrow, she has not yet written to anybody. Frank and Mary are both confined to the house with very bad colds, fortunately hers is not attended with a cough, which would shake her very much in her present situation, for she expects to be confined for the ninth time, the end of this month or very beginning of the next. All your relatives here unite in love and every good wish, in which Miss Lloyd begs to join.

Frank and Mary's fifth son Edward Thomas was born at Chawton on 28 January. At Compton there was a third daughter for the Lefroys, Fanny Caroline; and another Fanny also arrived to swell the ranks of Mrs Austen's great-grandchildren: Fanny Margaretta Rice, whose brother Edward Bridges Rice had been born the previous year.

Mrs James Austen and Caroline returned from Chawton to Steventon only to supervise the packing and make their farewells. The living of Steventon, in the gift of Edward Knight and designed eventually for his son William, was given to Henry to hold for two or three years until his nephew was ready to take it. This was an arrangement which would not have satisfied James' scruples – but to Henry it was very welcome. Distasteful though it must have been to him to gain so much by a brother's death, he was suddenly provided with a home and an income on which he could afford to consider marriage. To boost his income still further, he resolved to emulate his father and take pupils.

Whilst James' widow and daughter remained in their old home, Henry rode over from Chawton to take the services at Steventon, but it was not convenient, particularly in the depth of winter, and besides, he had quickly secured two or three pupils and needed a house to receive them. Mary and Caroline agreed to leave by the end of January. They had reason to feel they had been swept out of their home in a literal as well as a figurative sense, for a great thaw flooded the cellars and so dampened the ground-floor rooms that they were obliged to flee upstairs for the last week.

We left our uncle Henry in possession [Caroline wrote]. He seemed to have renewed his youth, if indeed he could be said ever to have lost it, in the prospect before him. A fresh life was in view, he was eager for work – eager for pupils – was sure very good ones would offer – and to hear him discourse you would have supposed he knew of no employment so pleasant and honourable, as the care and tuition of troublesome young men. He was also looking forward secretly to his own marriage ... This we did not know of as certain, but his intention had been guessed in the family for some time. He was always very affectionate in manner to us, and paid my mother every due attention, but his own spirits he could *not* repress, and it is not pleasant to witness the elation of your successor in gaining what *you* have lost – and altogether although we left our home with sad hearts, we did not desire to linger in it any longer.

Edward of course returned to Oxford, and his mother and sister were offered a temporary home in Gay Street by an old friend of Mary's, Mrs Hulbert. 'The City of Bath by lamplight, as we approached, was a beautiful sight,' recalled Caroline.

On 11 April Henry took a second wife in Miss Eleanor Jackson. She was niece to the rector of Chawton, her mother, Sarah, having been a Papillon from Acrise in Kent. Her father lived in Chelsea and had been a slight acquaintance of Henry's in his London days.

Eleanor's age at the time of the marriage is unknown, but she almost certainly belonged to a later generation than her husband. From the brief glimpses we get of her character she seems to have been demure, dutiful, pious – she later published a pamphlet of questions and answers on the Old Testament aimed at her husband's semi-literate parishioners[5] – and contented with her lot: a true nineteenth-century wife where Eliza had been a thoroughly eighteenth-century one, perhaps it would not be too fanciful to say. Without doubt Eleanor's was the temperament better suited to being the helpmeet of a poor country clergyman – one wonders indeed how poor Eliza would have coped with Henry's drastically changed circumstances had she lived to endure them. Eleanor was approved of in the family, and Henry became as devoted to her as he had ever been to Eliza.

This was a year of marriages. At the age of twenty-seven Fanny Knight, having dithered her early youth away and possibly lived to regret the rejection of Mr Plumtre's love, at last made up her mind to accept a husband. Her choice would surely have surprised a little her aunt Jane, for it fell on Sir Edward Knatchbull, ninth baronet of Mersham-le-Hatch in Kent, Member of Parliament and a widower with six children. One would have supposed Fanny had had enough of being a surrogate mother – and one would dearly like to know whether she accepted Sir Edward in a spirit of desperation and because in worldly terms it was a good match, or whether, as one hopes, she really felt for him that love which she had always longed to experience.

And then, on 7 August, Charles married his sister-in-law Harriet Palmer. This was an entirely natural, almost inevitable union; luckily for them the Deceased Wife's Sister Act had not yet been brought in – that cruel piece of legislation which must have caused misery to thousands of couples who later found themselves in the same situation as Harriet and Charles. They had been thrown so much together, and she had become so much a mother to his three daughters (for little Harriet had recovered her health), that their mutual affection was the not surprising result. We know little of *her* virtues, but she may have been as pretty and as gentle as her sister Fanny; we *do* know that it was very hard for anyone not to love Charles. Indeed, what might have delayed the marriage so long – Fanny had been dead six years – was the thought of the children who would inevitably follow, for Charles lived in a chronic state of poverty.

Perhaps what encouraged them to marry now was the appointment of Charles to a post involving coastal defence in north

Cornwall. To live as economically as possible, they made their first home in a cottage at Padstow.

The Frank Austens too moved to the sea this year, leaving Chawton Manor for a rented house at Ryde on the Isle of Wight.

Mary, Caroline and Edward, having still no settled home, spent most of the summer visiting relations. From Chawton Edward escorted his aunt Cassandra on a week's visit to Ryde. On July 29 comes an enigmatic entry in his diary: 'Rode to Winchester (from Chawton) met Mr and Mrs H. Austen at the Black Swan – resigned my claim to the French estate.' It is known that Henry never recovered anything of his first wife's property in France, but presumably his buoyant spirits had given him hopes of it at this stage, and perhaps his loss of James' money would have rendered a claim by Edward valid.

In November Edward obtained his degree and henceforward Mrs Leigh Perrot made him the generous allowance of £300 a year. Without it, indeed, the little family could hardly have made a home for themselves, for Mary's resources were pitifully slight. Now they were able to rent a small house at Speenhamland. It seems to have been Mrs Leigh Perrot's intention to enable the young man she now regarded as her heir to live in a becoming manner – that is, as a leisured young gentleman. Edward had ordination in mind, but Mary Crawford-like, she did not approve this. Meanwhile, he now had the means to hunt again, a pastime that was one of the enduring loves of his life; he kept a horse for himself and a pony for Caroline. He also made his sister a personal allowance of £20 a year.

On 28 May 1821 the first of Charles' second family was born, and given his father's two names, Charles John. At Dane Court there was a new baby, Henry. And on 12 December at Ryde Mary produced her tenth child, Frances Sophia.

Three days later Thomas Leigh was buried at Monk Sherborne. He is mentioned in the letter which Mrs Austen wrote to Mrs James Austen on 24 March 1822:

Our little party are much as usual, I grow weaker and more infirm every day, but I am able to walk about the house, or creep about the garden. I never go beyond it – and do a great deal of patch-work. Yes, the lawyers have at last settled that I am to have half my late brother's property, but we are not yet in possession of the money, as the stock cannot be sold till the

South Sea books are open, which will be early next month: this acquisition of wealth comes to me just at the right time, as it will make me amends for what I lose by the reduction of the 5 per cents …

Of our own family I have not much to say – all well at Godmersham, we expect Mr Knight and his son William very soon after Easter. The Knatchbulls are in town, Fanny better than she has been but not near so well as her friends wish her to be. The large family at Ryde in good health, the family indeed is not quite so large as it has been, Frank being at the Naval College, where he was going on remarkably well, and Henry with his uncle at Steventon, he is also going on well, his uncle says he is an excellent scholar for his age. Our relatives at Padstow give a prety good account of themselves, they look forward to some weeks' holidays, which are to commence in May. Keppel Street and Chawton are the places to be visited; when they go back they mean to take Cassy and leave the two other little girls. We have not heard from Compton for some time.

Mary also received a letter[6] from Charles, who wrote to her on 5 May from Padstow. Like his sister Jane before him, he was assiduously reconciling himself to a move that was really unwelcome.

Though we are not violent correspondents I feel convinced that you take an interest in all that concerns me, and therefore I shall never fail communicating to you any event of consequence which occurs to us and change of residence, and from one county to another, may I think he deemed so. A few days ago we were agreeably surprised by the receipt of an order to remove to Plymstock near Plymouth at Midsummer, to hold the same appointment there that I have done here. There is no doubt a good deal of trouble and some expense attending this change, but not so much as would be the case if the furniture we have in this house was our own.

The neighbourhood we are going to holds out the prospect of many advantages – a fine country, an excellent and cheap market at Plymouth, and instruction for the girls which was not to be obtained here. The roads too are much better than the Cornish ones, and my district not above half as long. We shall however leave our nice cottage here with a certain amount of regret; we have passed near two years in it with a great comfort and have made some friends amongst our neighbours whom we shall be really sorry to part from.

Plymstock is only two miles from Plymouth and we have great hopes that Mr and Mrs Palmer will leave town and fix themselves there or in our immediate neighbourhood. However the change may turn out I shall have the satisfaction of knowing that I had nothing to do with it, the Admiralty having made the arrangements for the benefit of the service and not to please me.

Our party in this house is now but small consisting only of our two selves and little Charles, for we sent Harriet and Fanny up to Keppel Street yesterday under the charge of a friend and chaperoned by Mrs Gammon – ci-devant their maid Mary – Cassy you know has been there all the winter. We intend following ourselves about the 20th and I hope to be allowed there till it is time to join my new district. Though we have not the trouble of packing furniture we have plenty to do preparatory to quitting the house and were very glad of the opportunity of getting the children out of the way. They have certainly benefited by their stay in Cornwall, and so has my better half. I was never better, and our boy is the picture of health, so we have great cause to be thankful.

I hear from Chawton that they expect the pleasure of seeing your young folks ere long. I shall be happy if circumstances admit of my getting a peep at you during my visit to Hampshire. Anna seems disposed to have a house full of children! I was sorry to hear of the diminution of your income by the death of our unfortunate uncle. I too have had a very considerable reduction in mine, both by my salary being curtailed, and the paying off the 5 per cents in which my little all was placed.

Anna's fifth daughter, Georgiana Brydges, was born in 1822 – Brydges was Ben's mother's maiden name – and Charles' own second son, George, on 12 December of that year.

William Knight was approaching the age when he would be ready to take over the Steventon living, and Henry was therefore pleased to accept the offer of a curacy at Farnham, which carried a salary of £75 'with surplice fees averaging £35 and vicarage house, garden and offices'.[7] It was stipulated that the curate must reside in the parish as the vicar, Henry Warren, lived almost thirty miles away in Sussex, where he held another living.

Henry Austen was instituted into the curacy of Farnham on 1 August 1822.

13
Dreams of affluence
1823-28

Farnham presented a considerable contrast to the tranquil rural parishes in which the clerical Austens had hitherto earned their livelihoods. A sizeable and populous town with a large church, Farnham owed its prosperity chiefly to a flourishing brewing industry – which was not enough, however, to prevent the workhouse being always fully occupied. In effect the acting vicar, Henry had plenty of work to do, and in 1823 he added to his responsibilities the superintendence of the ancient Free Grammar School. Here, like his father before him, he put his outstanding scholarship at the service of the local youth. His reward was not only the master's salary but the opportunity to augment it by accepting private pupils.

Jane had expressed the view that 'Henry writes very superior sermons,' and his talent gained him invitations to preach not only in his own locality. A sermon which he delivered in the parish church of Clifton, Bristol's fashionable suburb, was published[1] 'at the request of many of the congregation', as was one which he gave in Farnham itself.

On the title page of the Clifton sermon, Henry is described as being also 'Domestic Chaplain to the Right Hon. The Earl Morley'. The Earl was an old friend from Henry's more affluent days, whose wife had been amongst the first to praise *Emma*. Since the Earl's seat was at Saltram, near Plymouth, Henry was hardly a domestic chaplain in the correct sense of the term. Almost certainly this was another instance of an old friend helping him over his difficulties; Henry had the ability to inspire loyalty and friendship of this order.

Another clerical connection of the family to move into a new parish was Ben Lefroy, whose eldest brother died in 1823, bequeathing him the living and extremely handsome parsonage house of Ashe, which had been built by their father. At last Anna had a truly comfortable home and income for her growing family.

On 29 May her brother and cousin, Edward Austen and William Knight, travelled by public coach to London where they were examined and ordained by the bishop, Dr Tomline. During their two days in town the young cousins lodged at an inn, and both evenings were spent by them at the theatre – ordination being not yet the solemn affair the Victorians were to make it.

William, of course, had the living of Steventon to step into. He was an extremely fortunate young man, for not only was there an excellent stipend waiting for him as soon as he required it but his father offered to pull down the old-fashioned rectory and build him a better! And so the old Austen home was swept away, quite without remonstrance it would seem, and William's smart new residence built on a different site.

The other newly ordained cousin, Edward Austen, had no such prospect to tempt him to flout his great-aunt's known wishes. He took holy orders out of the promptings of his conscience, and from a dislike of being idle and useless, even though he thereby risked losing Mrs Leigh Perrot's favour. She was continually changing her mind, making promises and then retracting them, hinting one minute that she would make Edward her heir, and the next that it was to Frank she intended to leave Scarlets. Both men bore her caprices with patience, equanimity and as much indifference as they could muster.

Indeed, Frank had soon a misfortune much worse to bear than the whims of an unreasonable old lady. On 14 July 1823, in their Gosport lodgings, his wife died a few days after giving birth to their eleventh child. It was a tragedy with many echoes of 1808 and the fate of Elizabeth Austen. Frank noted tersely in his memoir: 'It would be impossible and needless to describe the deep agony of the bereaved.'

The baby boy, who was christened with Mrs Leigh Perrot's maiden name, Cholmeley (Frank was perhaps not *wholly* disinterested), survived only a few months, dying on 11 January 1824. But there were ten other motherless children to raise, and

Frank now devoted himself to their care and education. Just as Fanny had been her widowed father's help and consolation, so was sixteen-year-old Mary Jane to be Frank's. On 25 May of the following year he was awarded the rank and pay of Colonel of Marines in the Woolwich division, much to Mrs Leigh Perrot's satisfaction. It now seemed more and more likely that Frank would be her heir.

Edward's star seemed to be fading, and he was quite resigned to the fact. He accepted the curacy of Newtown, a little village near Newbury, and two days before his uncle's promotion moved with Mary and Caroline to a house which they rented there for £20 a year. It was a humble enough situation for Edward, but his determination evidently impressed his aunt, who grew rapidly reconciled to his choice of profession. Eventually, to console him for the loss of Scarlets, she decided to present him with a handsome living. On 6 September 1826 she wrote to him in a fit of generosity:

> My intention being to serve you in any way most agreeable to you, I give you full permission to try at either Ashe or Deane, and you cannot be more happy in the possession of either, than I shall be in securing to you a comfortable residence. When I mentioned Ashe it was in consequence of having heard that the house was an excellent one; perhaps too good for the living, but as your fortune in future might enable you to live in a good house, I thought this rather an agreeable circumstance than otherwise; in addition to this I too much feared that Mr Lefroy, although so young a man, was in such a state as to cause alarm to his friends. I had an idea too that Ashe was a better living ...

Poor Ben Lefroy, though certainly in ailing health, was not yet ready to die and make way for his brother-in-law, who seems to have followed up neither of these suggestions but who shortly afterwards, according to his pocket-book, 'rode to Blendworth to look at the living which had been advertised'. However, either Edward did not like it or his great-aunt did not like it for him, or perhaps she backed down from her promise, because Edward remained a lowly curate at Newtown.

On the more affluent side of the family, the six sons of Edward Knight were beginning to take up their allotted roles. Two were to be clergymen, two soldiers and two gentlemen of leisure. In the latter category came the two eldest, Edward and George, who after

Oxford had been sent together to finish their education in Germany, principally at Dresden, of which their father had happy memories.

George was given an allowance to live on, but it was Edward, of course, who stood to inherit all the property and who, because his father owned two fine estates, came into one of them immediately upon his marriage, without waiting for that father's death.

Edward Knight married in 1826 Mary Dorothea – who was the eldest daughter by his first wife of Fanny's husband, Sir Edward Knatchbull.[2] The young couple became the new and permanent master and mistress of the Great House at Chawton, which now enjoyed a settled family of owner-occupiers in residence at last.

Here Edward developed into the perfect English country gentleman, after the style of Mr Knightley. He became remarkable for 'his great courtesy, his dignified bearing, his invariable and hearty kindness and good temper and above all his uprightness and appreciation of honour, truth and duty'. As well as being 'an intelligent and keen sportsman and an unrivalled horseman', he was 'openhearted, hospitable and generous, endowed with considerable abilities, and a good sense which seldom failed him; a staunch and loyal friend, unswerving in the support of whatever he believed to be right, and just, and incapable of anything that even savoured of meanness or deception'.[3]

His first son, Edward Lewkenor, was born on 25 January 1827. The second name harked back to the complex ancestry of Chawton Manor; Jane Austen would surely have approved the young parents thus 'proving and strengthening their attachment to the place'.

Fanny Knatchbull was herself now a mother. After five years of childless marriage, she began her family, at the age of thirty-two, with the birth of Fanny Elizabeth in 1825; a second daughter, Matilda Catherine, arrived the following year.

Of the six Knight brothers, it had in fact been the fourth, William, who was the first to marry. Like his uncle Henry and his grandfather George Austen before him, he was able to do so because he had a home to offer his bride at Steventon Rectory. In 1825 he married Caroline, eldest daughter of John Portal of Freefolk Priors in Hampshire. The Portals were old friends and neighbours of the Austens, and the beautiful dark eyes that ran in the family had often been admired by Jane.

The new rectory at Steventon began to fill up with children, starting with Elizabeth Caroline, who was born on 17 July 1826. In a family remarkable for its longevity, she held the record, living to be 101, her life encompassing all the Victorian era, and ending amid the startling changes which followed World War I.

Only comparatively rarely was an Austen infant lost – but Charles seems to have been the unluckiest in parenthood as he was in worldly prosperity. In 1824 his two-year-old son George died, and the next year Harriet gave birth on 12 May to a daughter – the only Jane Austen of her generation – who lived just two months.

Nursing a baby at least ensured a reasonable gap before the next one came; without this safeguard, Harriet was soon pregnant again, and on 16 April 1826 Henry was born. However, further increase in the family was prevented now by a four-year separation between the parents, and thus its final tally stood at three girls by the first marriage, and two surviving boys by the second.

It was ten years since Charles had been at sea, but the Admiralty, deciding that he had been punished long enough for the loss of the *Phoenix*, now appointed him second in command of the *Aurora*, which for the next two years served on the West India station suppressing the slave trade. By the excellent performance of his duties Charles sufficiently redeemed himself to be removed to the *Winchester*, in the same waters, as Flag Captain to Admiral Colpoys.

Charles never saw his mother again. Mrs Austen, who in recent years had been prone to remark that she thought God had forgotten to come for her,[4] died on 17 January 1827 and was buried at Chawton. Cassandra replied to Philadelphia's letter of condolence, writing from Frank's home at Gosport on 14 February:

> For the last year and half my mother had been confined almost entirely to her bed, which to a person of her active habits must of itself have been a great evil, and in addition to this, not a day passed without her suffering severe and increasing pain, which was latterly so acute and so unremitting, that I assure you my most earnest prayer to the Almighty was that she might be released. My dear mother was 87 last September, a great age for a person who had been ailing for the greatest part of her life! Her constitution was certainly a wonderful one and so were the powers of her mind likewise, for her faculties remained unimpaired to the last and even her cheerfulness continued till a very late period of her existence.

My brother Henry was our frequent visitor during the last few weeks and Mr Knight had left us only just before Christmas and if my mother had felt the slightest wish of seeing them, they would any of them have come at the shortest notice and as it was they all came to me as soon as every thing was over. All at least who were in England, for my youngest brother Charles is so unfortunate as to have the command of a frigate in the West Indies.

Nothing can exceed the kindness which I have received from each of them in every instance in which they have an opportunity of showing it, and I am fully aware that I have still a great many blessings to be thankful for. Thanks to my brother Knight, I shall still be able to occupy the same comfortable cottage at Chawton which has been our home for seventeen years past ...

My letter is full of blunders, which require an apology and I am sure you will admit the one I am about to make. I am at present writing in a room in which half a dozen nephews and nieces are repeating their different lesons of geography, arithmatic etc and though I must approve of the manner in which they and their father employ their mornings I cannot but acknowledge that a school room is not the most favourable field for letter writing, at least to such a crazy head as mine.

The family circles of my brothers are now too large for me to enter into a particular description of them, I can only say in general that they are well and prosperous. My brother Knight has now two sons and two daughters married, all of whom have children, so the family does not at present seem likely to come to an end.

To this letter Cassandra added a postscript: 'My address in future will be Mrs C.E. Austen.' This was the title customarily adopted by middle-aged or elderly spinsters who found themselves head of their households.

And it was soon to be a household of one, for although Cassandra remained for the rest of her life at the cottage – where she devoted herself more and more to good works among the poor, finding an especial interest in teaching their children – she before long found herself the only one so remaining out of the four females who had set up house together there so joyously in 1809. The year after her mother died, she was deprived of the companionship of Martha Lloyd by a circumstance which she could hardly grieve over.

A fate befell Martha which at the age of fifty-six she must have long ceased to expect – she was sought in marriage. It happened as the result of another marriage: that of Frank's eldest daughter Mary

Jane, who on 10 June 1828 became the wife of George Thomas Maitland Purvis RN, of Blackbrook Cottage, Fareham.

Frank, anticipating that his younger children would miss the motherly care of their grown-up sister, and that he himself, as he expressed it in his memoir, would find 'his situation very lonely after his daughter's marriage, he selected as his second wife a lady he had long and intimately known and considered almost a sister, Miss Martha Lloyd, the elder sister of his eldest brother's second wife, and who being several years older than himself made it improbable that there should be any child of such a union, which considering the number he had had by his first marriage seems to have been much wished. He was married on the anniversary of his first marriage' – that is, on 24 July 1828, the ceremony being performed at Winchester.

Of Martha Frank further wrote: 'Joined to the profession of much good sense, she possessed the blessings of a sweet temper, amiable disposition, ladylike manners, and, what is of far greater importance, a mind deeply impressed with the truth of Christianity.'

As many a father in the same situation has found before and since, Frank's belief that his children would welcome as much as he did the presence of a new mistress in their home was naïve and unrealistic. The boys were often away, at school or naval academy or university or sea; but for the girls it was hard to accept, as a replacement for their lively, affectionate sister, a rigid old lady whose ideas were from another century. Catherine in particular, whose spirited and independent nature was already in evidence at the age of ten, conceived a strong antipathy towards her stepmother. In this role, Martha was to fail as miserably as her sister Mary had done thirty years before.

One must hope that Frank himself at least found solace in the companionship of his new wife, for by marrying her he unwittingly destroyed his chances of inheriting Scarlets. Mrs Leigh Perrot was outraged to a degree that surely could not have been foreseen. 'This is a year of marriages – but all have not been so hard of digestion as the Gosport arrangements,' she wrote to Edward Austen. Her objection is not clear. Perhaps it was simply that Frank had omitted to consult her beforehand. Perhaps Martha came in for her residual dislike of Mary – yet she did not scruple to express her disapproval to Mary's son. Mrs Leigh Perrot was a thorough-going snob and may have imagined some deficiency on that score – but Martha was well connected on her mother's side, at least; and in any case, Edward bore the same blood. Was it simply Martha's age that the even older lady found so distasteful?

Whatever the reason, it was Edward who benefited from his uncle's fall from favour. And when Edward himself happened to become engaged, just two months after the obnoxious marriage, to a young lady of whom nothing bad could be said, his good fortune was pretty well assured.

Edward Austen had known Miss Emma Smith for several years, for she was one of the nieces of Mrs Chute at whose house, 'The Vyne', he was always a welcome visitor. Indeed, the Chutes were old friends of the James Austens, and it had been Mrs Chute who had written to Emma Smith's mother some thirty years before, describing Edward's mother as a newly married woman.

Despite possessing a surname which would have drawn forth the scorn of that other snob Sir Walter Elliot, Emma was of good family. Her father, who had died in 1814, had been a Member of Parliament – as had been her maternal grandfather and her uncle William Chute. Emma had grown up at the splendid family estate of Suttons, in Essex, and at their town house in Portland Place. These properties were now occupied by her eldest brother, Sir Charles Smith, who had inherited a baronetcy through the maternal line. (Their mother's maiden name had also been Smith.)

The widowed Mrs Smith lived with her two younger sons and six daughters at Tring Park in Hertfordshire. They were indeed an extremely affectionate and outgoing family, all possessing that warmth of heart which Edward so much valued, and a ready sympathy with their fellow creatures that he had not before witnessed to such a degree.

Edward himself was exceptionally attached to his two sisters – but he was born to be one of a large family and, in that sense, had been deprived of his birthright. Now he had found it, and the key to it in the person of a pretty and amiable young lady, who had the sense to fall in love with a man who could hardly fail to make an excellent husband.

Having met her often at her aunt's house, Edward was invited to Tring Park for the first time in September 1828. He arrived on the 12th, preached at Tring church on the 14th, and on the 16th Emma recorded in her diary: 'This day proved one of the most important in my life. We read *Emma* in the morning. After luncheon Mamma and Fanny went to call on Mrs Badcock. We all walked towards the woods at Terrets and during the walk I was engaged to marry Mr Austen. On our return home Mamma was spoken to and most kindly gave her consent. I afterwards walked with him in the shrubbery.'⁵

Edward immediately sent off the momentous news to Newtown, whence both mother and sister wrote to Emma on 18 September. From Mary: 'The only possible regret I can feel is the losing the society of my son, to Caroline and me it will be a sad blank, but we must and shall derive the greatest pleasure we can desire in seeing him happy ... Will it my dear Emma be incorrect if I congratulate *you*, in having engaged the affections of a man, who, as far as human nature will allow, is free from fault? It must I am sure be satisfactory to Mrs Smith and yourself to know that his conduct never caused me an uneasy moment, and that you will find him kind and affectionate I can have no doubt.'

And from Caroline: 'Had I been to choose I could have fixed on no one that I should consider so well suited to him as yourself, and if you knew how inexpressibly dear this brother has always been to me, and how I have doted on him from my earliest childhood to the present time, you would feel that in speaking my approbation of your intended union I could not express myself in stronger terms – *You* of course think highly of him ... but it is not *yet* that you can know all the excellence of his temper and principles.'

Emma received yet another letter, from her aunt Mrs Chute, then travelling in Switzerland: 'I was aware two years ago of the decided preference which he gave you. I must consider your marriage with him as in some degree under my auspices as it was at my house you first met ... He certainly is a very agreeable companion, cheerful, lively, animated, ready to converse, willing to read out loud, never in the way and just enough of poetry and romance to please me and yet not to overlook sober reason.'

Mrs Chute did more than praise and congratulate: she offered to make the young couple a small annual allowance. Mrs Leigh Perrot, whom Edward had not omitted to inform, was equally forthcoming, writing on 20 September:

I thank you for your early communication on a subject which gratifies every feeling more than I can express. I have, indeed, always felt the most sincere regard for you; as well on your own account, as on your excellent father's – who had ever shown me the attention of a son. You may therefore well imagine how pleased I am that the event I have hoped for is likely to take place in your union with so truly amiable a character as you describe your Emma to be – but, Edward, you have told me just enough to prove I am a true woman, *as to curiosity*, for I want to know more ...

You ask me whether you may, in any arrangements made, consider as *certain the £300* a year which I have hitherto allowed you. Yes indeed you may; and I shall double that sum with the greatest pleasure. Mr Hoare shall receive my direction to this purpose on your marriage. As you have added (like a good son) to the income of your mother, I shall relieve you from any unpleasant feelings on her account, by asking her acceptance of £100 per annum, which Messrs Hoare shall pay her in half yearly payments – in the same manner as my later sister Austen received it. I trust this may free your mind from any uneasiness on her account.

On 3 October she wrote at greater length, and her readiness to imagine herself slighted and her tendency to 'whims and inconsistencies' are self-revealed:

You may perhaps recollect that considering myself not quite properly treated by some ill-adviser of your much valued father (who had never in his life omitted any friendly or affectionate proof of his regard to me) I had turned my thoughts towards Captain Austen as I was determined that Scarlets with the landed property which I had added to it, should never go from my generous husband's family – I had however never concealed from Captain Austen that such intention was by no means fixed; for many circumstances might occur which would induce me to dispose of it in a different manner. Scarlets has been too much endeared to me, from the association of true domestic enjoyment, to be left to the management of one whose professional duties might call him out of the kingdom, by which means it might have been *let*, or given up to children, or improper managers. When I have repeatedly represented the possibility of my altering my intention, I have been requested to make my intention known. One of the circumstances I had alluded to was, my dear Edward, the chance of your marrying, and thereby securing to *yourself* an amiable *wife*, and to my *favourite Scarlets* a proper mistress.

I think nothing can ever occur to make me regret the having so far opened my mind to you, or make me alter my present intention in your favour. Your open son-like statement to me called for this avowal of my determination.

On receipt of this letter Edward wrote to his fiancée, remarking on 'the share which *you*, though unseen by her, have had in fixing her decision in my favour. Well may the proverb say, "What is one man's meat is another man's poison." Marriage which has sunk my uncle has raised me in her favour. She says she is particularly gratified by the attention of Lady Northampton.' Emma's aristocratic connections were evidently appreciated by the capricious old lady.

Mrs Leigh Perrot's next letter is a pleasant trifle. It was written on 29 October: 'We have quite a summer's day – I have been enjoying my garden, and *creeping* about, notwithstanding my cold. – You I daresay are as happily engaged. – I have been reading *Emma* a second time; but I still cannot like it so well as poor Jane's other novels. Excepting Mr Knightley and Jane Fairfax, I do not think any one of the characters *good*. Frank Churchill is quite insufferable. I believe *I* should not have married him, had I been Jane. Emma is a vain meddling woman. I am sick of Miss Bates. *Pride and Prejudice* is the novel for me. Your *Emma* is a very different character, or I am much mistaken.'

Then it was back to business. In November she wrote:

The will made by your father I know nothing of but I have heard that the mortgage of £20,000, and Mr Leigh's bond for £4,000 is pretty nearly your fortune; as the legacies, duties etc will leave nothing considerable in the trust fund to yourself. I certainly shall wish that Scarlets, with the Dean Pit Farm (both of which your uncle left me) should go where he chose to leave the bulk of his funded property: as to Bearhill Cottage ... *that* I have not altogether made up my mind about, as to make that purchase I was obliged to lessen the legacy of £10,000 which your uncle left me; supposing that I had, in addition to that legacy, £5,000 of my own savings from his own liberal annuity, as well as several sums (very considerable) left me by my relations the Cholmeleys etc – all my property besides I have accumulated through my very inexpensive manner of living; and therefore I mean to think the more of my own family. You must therefore suppose that in case Scarlets is left to you, it is partly from my knowledge of the dependence I have on you for keeping it up *properly*; which the fortune you will inherit through your uncle, as well as that which your Emma will add to it, will enable you to do.

'*In case* Scarlets is left to you'? She was up to her old tricks again.

Meanwhile Edward received a letter from his uncle Henry, a letter which must have cost him some pride to write, though perhaps he was inured to such things by now. He wrote from Bentley, a village midway between Farnham and Alton. To this parish he had been appointed perpetual curate – the equivalent of vicar – in 1824, whilst still resident at Farnham. At first he had employed a curate at Bentley, although also active there himself, but in February 1827 he left Farnham, resigning both the curacy and the mastership of the school and settling at Bentley for the remainder of his clerical career. The letter[6] to his nephew is dated 22 November 1828:

I am aware that by a recent alteration of Mrs L. Perrot's mind (I hope she will not get into the way of altering often in future) you will be master of Scarlets one of these days. When your Uncle F. considered himself as standing a good chance of that property, he very kindly and quite voluntarily told me that (in such case) he should release me altogether from the £800 which he paid for me as joint surety with your dear father. N.B. – I have to his moment contrived to pay him the full interest regularly, though providence only can tell how much longer I shall have the means of doing it. Now although F. is the last person in the world to abate aught from his promise – yet as his prospective circumstances are *pro tanto* certainly and rather suddenly altered, I do not feel that I have any claim on him to make good his conditional promise.

Therefore without further preamble which would impugn your kind-heartedness I ask you to release me from the said debt of £800 – both principal and interest as long as I and Eleanor live – provided you do come into possession of Scarlets. After our death you and your assigns shall be paid the principal sum. We can give you ample and clear security for it. Finally should we become unexpectedly rich, you may be sure that no promise on your part would prevent us from as strict a discharge of the debt as if you had not promised. But my dreams of affluence, nay of competence, are closed ...

We cannot doubt that Edward, with his inherent good nature and in his new-found happiness and prosperity, agreed to his unfortunate uncle's request.

Edward's whole life was shifting rapidly into a different gear. He and Emma were invited by Mrs Smith to make their home at Tring Park, and this they gladly accepted. Not only could Emma scarcely bear to part from her family, nor they from her, but the offer would enable the young couple to save out of their income for future wants. There was plenty of space at Tring Park for the Austens to have their own set of rooms; it was a huge house which had cost Emma's great-uncle, Sir Drummond Smith, £80,000.

In order that Edward might not feel idle, he accepted the curacy of Tring, the value of which was only £20 per annum. The incumbent held three neighbouring livings, so there was plenty of help required.

Mrs Austen was the chief sufferer by this arrangement, losing the society of her beloved son. She declined travelling to Tring for the wedding, so Caroline was the only guest from his side of the family. Early in December Edward resigned his Newtown curacy, and on the 11th he escorted his sister to Tring. On 16 December he noted in his diary, 'Wedding day, went with dear Emma to Suttons.' She wrote in hers, 'We went to church at 10 o'clock, and Mr Fowle married Edward and me, for which I thank God.'

Her sister Augusta described the sartorial side of affairs: 'Caroline Austen and myself were in sentimental blue, the rest in all the youthful elegance of white muslin, pink ribbons and flowers – the bride … in white, looking, though I say it, as sweet and engaging in Madam Maradan's becoming construction of white crape, blond and orange flowers as she ever looked in her life. As to the gentlemen's upper and nether garments I need only say they were new and very appropriate in all points, except Mr Fowle's surplice, which was sadly besprinkled with iron moulds …'

Even the servants were given new clothes, and they danced in the hall to a violin while the wedding breakfast proceeded. 'Then,' Augusta continued, 'the bride took off her gay attire and wrapped in lilac silk and fur bade a hurried farewell to the many friends around her and set off at one o'clock in Mamma's chariot and four.'

The honeymoon was spent at Suttons and Pollard Place, and

they returned to Tring, where Caroline Austen was still a guest, by Christmas, when Edward took his first service at Tring church.

14
So many withered beech leaves
1829-53

Emma was introduced as opportunity afforded to the various members of Edward's scattered family. He took care that his formidable great-aunt should receive the first such attention. 'Mrs Leigh Perrot is not at all a stupid person,' Emma discovered, as if Edward had led her to believe otherwise; 'she is a ladylike little old woman and though for years she has been quite out of the world, yet she once lived in it and talks agreeably of past times.'[1]

Cassandra she described as 'a very nice delicate looking thin elderly woman with a good deal of conversation and kind and ladylike in her manner'. It seems to have been a matter of some surprise that Edward's female relations were so uniformly ladylike!

Of Edward himself Emma wrote to her aunt, when she had been married a few weeks: 'He is all, and a great deal more than I had fancied him, his temper is sweet to a very great degree and he is so good and has so much mind and talent.'

For the first time in his life Edward was living not only in luxurious surroundings and in liberal style but in the midst of a numerous and sociable family – the kind in which his heart delighted. But he would not be with in-laws for ever, and he and Emma set about creating their own large family with which to surround themselves in coming years.

Their first child was born on 26 September 1829 and diplomatically given the name of Cholmeley. Three wealthy people were selected as his sponsors: Mrs Leigh Perrot, Edward Knight and Sir Charles Smith.

If only increasing happiness and prosperity seemed in store for Edward, his sister Anna's share of comfort and plenty was soon over. On 27 August Ben died, leaving her with one son and six daughters – for two more girls had been added to the family, Louisa Langlois in 1824 and Elizabeth Lucy in 1827. Anna wrote in her pocket-book of 'My irreparable loss in the death of my dear husband, who died at Ashe after months of slow decay'.[2]

The fate of so many clergymen's widows now befell Anna, for she had to hurry out of her home while her grief was still fresh. On 13 November she left Ashe and went to live with her brother-in-law Edward Lefroy near Basingstoke, in a village called West Ham. Henceforward her life was to be a continual struggle against penury and ill health.

Another bereavement occurred in the family in 1830 with the death of Frank's daughter Elizabeth, at the age of thirteen. Honours as well as sorrow visited Frank that year, for he was elevated to the rank of Rear-Admiral. His unluckier brother Charles was invalided home from the West Indies following an accident – from the effects of which, however, he did fully recover, once in the care of his wife.

In his memoir Frank expressed no regrets or recriminations regarding Scarlets but bore his shifting prospects philosophically, as one who had been brought up to expect no fortune except that which his own exertions could procure. However, Mrs Leigh Perrot, as inconsistent as ever, suddenly made him the gift of a large amount of money with which to buy himself an alternative home.

Exactly how this came about is not revealed in the memoir, which simply records that when he bought Portsdown Lodge it was 'thanks to the liberality of his aunt and godmother'. But Edward drily informed his sister Anna that Mrs Leigh Perrot had quarrelled with Frank 'in the most agreeable way possible, as she has paid him off with nearly £10,000 and told him she will have nothing more to do with him. She will find plenty of people ready to offend her, if she pays them so liberally for it!'

Portsdown Lodge lay at the eastern end of the Portsdown Hills which rise above Portsmouth Harbour: the perfect spot for an Admiral to live, with its magnificent views over Portsmouth, Spithead and the Isle of Wight. Indeed, it probably suited Frank a great deal better than Scarlets would have done – and he had the satisfaction of choosing it and remodelling it himself. As soon as the house was his, he embarked on improvements, personally supervising the workmen and characteristically interesting himself in every detail, until by early 1831 he had 'made it fit for a gentleman's home'. The lodge stood in its own grounds of thirty-five acres, part of which had once been a chalk pit, now transformed into a picturesque dell.

Of Frank's sons, his namesake had by now achieved the rank of lieutenant in the Royal Navy, and the fourth boy, Herbert, had just left the academy to begin his career at sea. Henry and George were both at Oxford – the former destined for the law, and the latter for the Church. Edward Thomas, the youngest, was still at school.

With this and other family news Cassandra brought Philadelphia Whitaker up to date in a letter written on 20 January 1832.

I write now to answer your kind enquiries and give you some account of my branches of the family. First for myself, I continue to live in this cottage which I have now inhabited more than twenty years, and I can say with thankfulness that my health is tolerably good, better perhaps than I have any right to expect at my time of life, and considering that I have never been otherwise than a little ailing. I have no constant inmate, but am frequently visited by brothers and nephews and nieces and am likewise a visitor in my turn.

I spent five months last year (from June till November) at Godmersham and have since passed a fortnight at Steventon, of which place one of my Knight nephews is Rector. My brother of that name is still residing in the midst of his large family, counting 22 grandchildren. Two sons and two daughters are married, the former are both of them settled in Hampshire, and the latter remain in Kent. Nothing more important has occurred amongst them for some years, than a regular addition to their respective nurseries.

My eldest brother left a son and two daughters. In the course of the last three years my nephew has married respectably and happily, and my eldest niece has become a widow. She is left, poor thing! with a large family, a narrow income and indifferent health. One of her daughters, a girl of fifteen, is at present my visitor.

Henry resides on his little piece of preferment between six and seven miles from me and is a very good neighbour. He makes an excellent parish priest, is indefatigable in his exertions and seems to have nothing to wish for but a trifling increase of wealth and better health to his excellent wife. His own health is on the whole good, as you will suppose when I tell you that he walked over one day this week to breakfast with me.

My brother Frank's life has I think been the most eventful of any of our family of late. In the year '28 he married first his eldest daughter and then himself. He chose for his second wife a very old friend of mine, who makes an excellent mother to his younger children. They were in great affliction two years ago by the death of one of them, a fine girl of thirteen, but time always heals such wounds, and there are still three left, one just grown up and two in the school-room. Four boys are out in the world (two at sea and two at college) and one is at school. My brother became an Admiral in the late promotion and is settled in a very comfortable house he has purchased near Portsmouth.

Charles lives likewise in the same neighbourhood. He is the fond father of three daughters and two little boys. I wish he were richer, but fortune has not yet smiled on him. I have now given you a brief account of relations for whom I am sure you feel an interest, though most of them you have never seen.

A new edition of Jane's works was projected in 1832 by the printer-turned-publisher Richard Bentley. This was the first time they had been reprinted since the original publication. For the sum of £250 Henry and Cassandra sold the copyright of all the novels with the exception of *Pride and Prejudice*, which belonged to Egerton and his successors.

On 6 February 1833 Cassandra wrote again to her cousin Philadelphia. Written in Charles' home in the village of Anglesey near Gosport, this was probably her last letter to Mrs Whitaker, who died the following year.

I passed the greater part of the year *thirty-two* at home, but I have begun *thirty-three* in a different style, having set off to pay visits on the 7th of January. I have already passed three weeks with my brother Frank at his house in the neighbourhood of Portsmouth and am now finishing my excursion by a visit to Charles who is settled at this place ...

I propose leaving them in the course of a few days and returning to my own cottage, which is about thirty miles distant. I shall of course miss the cheerfulness of a large family, but home always ought to have its comforts, and it certainly has for me, and although I have no inmate in my house, my nephew Edward Knight lives so near, that I never need be more alone than I like.

He is likely to have a large family – his stock already amounts to four, the eldest of whom is but just six years old. My possessions in great nephews and nieces are so extensive that I have done keeping an exact account of them. I know that there were five born in the course of last year and that a sixth made its appearance before January was completed in this.

No other family events have occurred since I wrote to you last. My brother Henry still continues to reside in his very small benefice about six miles from Chawton, and is happy in an excellent wife and moderate wishes ...

I am pleased to find that you still derive amusement from needlework. I am likewise a great worker and have varieties of knitting and worsted work in hand. My garden is also a constant object of interest and at suitable seasons of the year of employ likewise.

Cassandra was not the only spinster in the family with little to occupy her but needlework. Caroline, belonging to the next generation, was another. She had been a gifted child and a compulsive writer and might have been expected to emulate her aunt Jane and substitute the delights of a self-created world for the normal maternal occupations, once it began to seem that she would never marry. But Caroline early put away her novel-writing, and in 1833 she spent many hours working a whole armchair in tapestry for Edward. (He too had long ceased to write fiction – more understandable in view of his full life, but nevertheless a pity, since Jane had thought his talent so promising.)

The armchair was a gift on the occasion of the Edward Austens' moving house. When they first took up quarters at Tring, it had been reasonable to expect that, before their family was very large, Scarlets would be theirs. But by November 1933 Cholmeley had been joined in the nursery by Emma Cassandra (always known as Amy) and by Charles Edward, and a fourth child was on the way; yet still their great-great-aunt lingered on.

So a house at Speen, near Newbury, convenient for Mrs Austen and Caroline at Newtown, was taken. Edward had already given up the curacy at Tring, for he had contracted a complaint of the throat which for quite a long period – several years – made speaking difficult and both preaching and reading aloud, at which he had formerly excelled, impossible. The years at Speen were therefore rather idle and frustrating ones for Edward, though he had the pleasure of being much with his children as they developed and of welcoming two more to his hoped-for cricket eleven – Spencer and Arthur. In the spring of 1835 he made his first appearance in print, with a pamphlet on the subject of one of the most debated issues of the day: whether candidates for matriculation should be obliged to sign the Thirty Nine Articles. Edward reasoned not and that a simple affirmation of their faith would do.

In religion the Austens were straightforward unevangelical Anglican, and in politics thoroughly Tory. This was the party into which the minor gentry and professional classes were born, so to speak, while the Whigs drew their support from the aristocracy. So traditional and inbred was the Austen adherence to the Tory line that even the men of the family rarely felt the need to discuss politics.

In the general election of 1835 both naval brothers intended to vote against Palmerston, who was standing in the South Hants constituency. Frank's daughter Catherine, aged seventeen, took a lively interest in the proceedings. She was something of a 'new woman', with an independent spirit, zest and curiosity for life. Of Palmerston she wrote, forty years later: 'I remember him very well when he came to Portsdown canvassing for the county and Fanny and I were sent out of the room almost immediately and I always believed it was for fear he should canvass by kissing us – that being not an unusual way. I felt injured and defrauded not because I wanted a kiss, which, as I was a keen politician and, of course, a conservative, I should have refused, but because I wanted to hear what was said.'[3]

Catherine's eldest brother Frank had recently had the misfortune to lose the use of his right thumb and forefinger during an accident involving a powder horn on board the *Tweed*. This voyage to the West Indies was altogether ill-starred, for a quarter of the crew were lost through yellow fever, and the captain died on board, leaving Lieutenant Austen to take command for three months.

The next brother, Henry, who had been admitted to the Inner Temple in 1833, was called to the Bar in 1836. At the end of this year, on 29 December, their eldest sister Mary Jane Purvis died after only 8½ years of marriage, leaving five little children. Her death followed an illness of fifteen months, borne, her epitaph in Fareham church declares, with 'resignation and patience' due to the principles taught her by 'her excellent father'.

Once again, for Frank, the death of a beloved daughter preceded the acquisition of further honours. As 'one of Nelson's captains' he was awarded the KCB in the last investiture of the reign of William IV, on 28 February 1837. On 3 March, at her home in Berkshire, Mary Austen read the news of the Admiral's knighthood in the paper. Her sister, for more than half a century plain 'Miss Lloyd', was now elevated to 'Lady Austen'.

As Mrs Leigh Perrot sank into extreme old age, her letters became more and more retrospective and nostalgic. She was still capable, on 8 March 1835, however, of composing a paragraph that created more doubt than reassurance in Edward's mind: 'I think, *unless in my dotage*, I should never wish to leave this property from you – perhaps as I did change my mind you may be led to fancy I may again – but I do not believe I could leave it to a more affectionate or kind-hearted creature than I have ever found you. Your Emma too is all I could wish.'

By November 1836 it was clear the old lady was dying. Edward was sent for and, accompanied by Mary and Cassandra, travelled to Scarlets. Mrs Leigh Perrot was considered too weak to be told of their presence, and for three days they quietly waited in her house for her death, which occurred 'without a struggle'[4] at twenty minutes to nine on the morning of Sunday the 13th.

Her old servant, Hannah, showed Edward her mistress's will lying uncovered and unfolded in the drawer. Edward would not read it but sealed it up in the presence of his mother, his aunt and the servants and left it for four days until some relations of her own arrived; Edward all the time in perfect ignorance and suspense as to whether Scarlets was to be his or she had changed her mind in her 'dotage'.

On the 17th the will was opened and read and, as Mary Austen recorded in her pocket-book, 'found highly satisfactory to my dear Edward and I hope to every branch of *her* family'. Edward was to get Scarlets and sufficient capital to produce an income of five or six hundred a year, plus the £24,000 bequeathed by his great uncle. Mrs Leigh Perrot's own relations got £27,600 between them.

Mary and Caroline Austen moved into the house at Speen, which was larger and more comfortable than any they had inhabited since James' death, for now Edward could afford to make them a generous allowance. He and his wife and children took possession of Scarlets on 3 January 1837. Here they set about the long and enjoyable process of altering it to suit the needs of a growing family, and the tastes of a different generation. In the year that Victoria came to the throne, one of the first acts at Scarlets was to banish all the Chippendale and Sheraton mahogany furniture to the bedrooms and replace it with brand new items.

The inhabitants too were in a state of alteration – they had a new name to get accustomed to. Under the terms of his great-uncle's will, Edward had to take the name and arms of Leigh in addition to those of Austen, though he was free to choose in which order to couple the names. On 4 February at the Herald's office the arrangement was formalized at a cost of £150; henceforward this branch of the family was to be known as Austen-Leigh.

Sir Francis Austen was among those who benefited from the naval promotions made to mark Victoria's coronation in the summer of 1838. He was elevated to the rank of Vice-Admiral. The same year Charles, still a captain after forty-five years of service, put to sea in the *Bellerophon*, his two teenage sons, Charles and Henry, serving under him.

For Harriet Austen it was an anxious circumstance to have her husband and only surviving children in one vessel – and an ancient vessel too. The *Bellerophon* had her place in history, for it was this ship which had taken Napoleon on board during his attempt to flee the French coast after Waterloo. She had anchored in Torbay whilst awaiting orders from a perplexed government as to what to do with the wily old foe and had eventually conveyed him to his final exile on St Helena.

That was a quarter of a century before, and now the *Billy Ruffian*, as she was called by the seamen, was employed in different circumstances, as Britain confidently extended her empire and her influence in global affairs. Two years after taking command, Charles assisted in the bombardment of Acre, in Syria, which the British desired to free from Egyptian occupation. Part of his log for 3 November 1840 reads nonchalantly:

2.30. – Anchored astern of the *Princess Charlotte*, and abreast of the Western Castle, and immediately commenced firing, which the enemy

returned, but they fired high, and only two shots hulled us, hitting
no-one.

At sunset. – Admiral signalled 'Cease Firing,' up boats, and then
piped to supper, and sat down with the two boys to a cold fowl, which
we enjoyed much.

At 9 p.m. – A dish of tea, then gave my night orders and turned in.[5]

For his part in this successful campaign Charles was awarded the
Companionship of the Order of the Bath. Then, according to
O'Byrne's Naval Biographical Dictionary: 'On December 2nd
following, the *Bellerophon* was attacked by a violent gale and
nothing but the unparalleled exertions of the officers and crew,
guided by Captain Austen's able management, preserved her from
being cast away on the iron-bound shore of Syria, where, had she
been wrecked, not a soul could have been saved.' Well might
Harriet shudder! The entry continues: 'The Good Service Pension
was awarded to Captain Austen on August 28th 1840. The
Bellerophon was paid off in June 1841. He was promoted to the rank
of Rear Admiral on November 9th 1846.'

Meanwhile there was a wedding to celebrate between the two
naval branches of the Austen family. Fanny, the third daughter of
Charles, had two admirers among Sir Francis' sons: Frank and
Henry. The latter, a reluctant barrister with a talent for light verse,
composed an acrostic on his cousin's full name, Fanny Palmer
Austen, which begins:

Fanny! Since long in vain I have expected
An answer due from you to my last letter
Now I proceed to make you more my debtor
Not cross, though grieved; not sullen, though dejected
Yet much annoyed at being thus neglected ...[6]

Fanny continued to neglect poor Henry and in 1843 married his
sailor brother Frank. Perhaps Henry's light-hearted approach to life
did not appeal to her, or perhaps he had never seriously sought the
responsibility of a wife. He remained a bachelor all his life. His
attitude to his career is revealed in another of his rhymes:

Law – always hateful – most so when it winds

Its tangled meshes round unwilling minds
I hate the law – and Equity's a worse
More undefined, more arbitrary curse.

Much sympathy cannot be supposed to have existed between this
son and Sir Francis, whose ruling principles throughout his life had
been diligence, industry and self-discipline. Nor under the
circumstances is it altogether surprising to find Henry under-
employed:

So I a briefless barrister
Am haunted by a busy clerk
Who every morning comes with, 'Sir,
I should be glad, Sir, of some work.'

The marriage of the cousins Frank and Fanny produced no
children, and as neither of Fanny's sisters ever married, the line from
Charles' first wife descended no further.

Quite a different character from Henry was his friend and
colleague John Hubback, whom he brought to stay at Portsdown
Lodge. John came from a mercantile north-country background and
was the first of his family to achieve professional status; he was
ambitious and hard-working, with a promising future before him.
Soon he had fallen in love with Catherine, the most ardent, spirited
and imaginative of Henry's sisters – 'vivid' was the word her son
chose to describe her personality. She was captivated by John's
seriousness and strength of purpose. Their wedding took place at
Portsdown Lodge on 25 August 1842, with Edward Austen-Leigh
officiating.

London was of course the scene of John's endeavours, and the
young couple took a house in Torrington Square, Bloomsbury.
Their first baby lived only long enough to be christened with the
name of Catherine's lamented mother, Mary; but three healthy sons
arrived in quick succession.

Portsdown Lodge was rapidly emptying. The youngest son,
Edward, was now at St John's College, the last of the Austens to
enjoy the privilege of Founder's Kin, which was abolished by Act of
Parliament before the next generation came up. Catherine's
marriage had left just Cassandra and Fanny at home; they were to
remain spinsters and were soon to be Sir Francis' only companions,

for five months after Catherine's departure his second wife died.

Martha and Mary, the two sisters who had married Austen brothers, each as a second wife, went to their graves in the same year. Mary died after an illness of only twenty-four hours on 3 August 1843. The following day Edward wrote to his mother-in-law: 'We find an affecting note amongst her papers stating her conviction that her death would be sudden, and praying that she might be found prepared, adding that she would not mention this conviction for fear of distressing us and making Caroline afraid of ever leaving her. The funeral will be on Friday, at Steventon, where a vacant brick grave by the side of my father's has been waiting nearly 24 years for its tenant.'

The service was conducted by William Knight and attended not only by Edward and Cholmeley but by Emma, Anna and Caroline: a break with tradition instigated by Caroline, who was a dutiful daughter and independent-minded woman.

Population explosions – and occasional tragic losses – were now occurring in the Austen-Leigh family and in the Kent and Hampshire nurseries of Edward's Knight's children. The first baby ever to be born at Scarlets was a second daughter for the Austen-Leighs, named Mary Augusta after her two grandmothers. She was followed by four more brothers, Edward, Augustus, George and William, making ten children in all, although the youngest but one, George, died in July 1842 at six months old of whooping cough.

At Chawton Manor, the younger Edward Knight lost his beloved wife Mary Dorothea a little less than three weeks after the birth of their seventh child in February 1838. She died in London but was brought back for burial at Chawton. Her epitaph reads: 'Her afflicted husband caused this tablet to be erected to record his irreparable loss and in the hope that her children when they read these lines may call to mind and endeavour to imitate the virtues of a good and affectionate mother.'

The inscription on the north wall of the aisle at Chawton church goes on to lament another premature loss, the second which Edward sustained that year: 'In the same sacred place are laid the remains of her eldest son Edward Lewkenor who died at Tunbridge

Wells on the 19th day of May 1838 aged 11 years.'

Two years later Edward married again. His second wife was Adela Portal, aged twenty-two to his forty-six. She was the much younger sister of William Knight's first wife Caroline – who herself had died in childbed three years previously. Adela added nine more children to the tally at Chawton Manor, all five of her daughters bearing her unusual Christian name.

At Steventon Rectory, Caroline Knight had brought eight children into the world during her twelve years of marriage – and as one of her sons was to beget twenty-one children himself, there was no likelihood of the Knight name dying out. William next married Mary Northey, daughter of a canon of Windsor, but the three infant daughters of this marriage, Mary, Cecilia and Augusta, were all swept away by an epidemic in 1848, along with their poor mother. William's third wife was a widow, Lady Jane Hope, by whom he had no issue.

George Knight, the second brother, the one who had no paid occupation, remained childless. In 1837 he made a rather splendid match – with Hilare, Countess Nelson. She was the widow of the Reverend William Nelson, 1st Earl Nelson of Trafalgar and Merton, brother of the hero Horatio. George Knight was Hilare's third husband, her first having been her cousin Captain George Barlow.

Henry Knight, who reached the rank of Major in the 8th Light Dragoons, had two wives – and one child by each. First he married a cousin on his mother's side, Sophia Cage; their son Lewis was born in 1833. Three years later he wed Charlotte Northey, sister of his brother William's second wife; this marriage produced one daughter, Agnes.

Charles Knight, the fifth brother, became Rector of Chawton in 1837 on the death of Mr Papillon, but the comfortable rectory was rather wasted on him, as he never married. The youngest in the Godmersham family, Brook John, who was a Captain in the 6th Dragoon Guards, married Margaret Pearson of Gloucester Square, London, but the couple had no children.

Fanny, Lady Knatchbull, completed her family of seven – three daughters followed by four sons – in 1837. Her sister Lizzy Rice began childbearing earlier and ended it later, producing fifteen children by 1844. When they ran out of the classic English names which had been in the family for generations, the Rices resorted to such Victorian innovations as Cecil, Walter and Ernest. Lizzy was lucky indeed to survive so many births.

Her husband, Edward Rice, had become MP for Dover. Later he broke his back in a fall downstairs, and for the rest of his long life he was confined to a wheelchair. Nevertheless the couple enjoyed, in the words of their daughter, 'one of the most perfect lifelong attachments of sixty-two years'.

While Fanny and Lizzy were busy mothering, their three younger sisters remained for a long time unwed, until in 1834 the youngest of the trio, twenty-eight-year-old Cassandra (she of the beautiful eyes) married Lord George Hill of County Donegal, the fifth son of the second Marquess of Downshire. Two sons and two daughters were born before Cassandra's death in 1842. Five years later Lord George married her elder sister Louisa, the god-daughter of Jane Austen. The Deceased Wife's Sister Act had been in force since 1835, and this marriage had to be solemnized on the Continent. Louisa was forty-three when she thus flouted convention and risked scandal to marry her brother-in-law, and forty-five when she gave birth to her only child, George, who was, under British law, illegitimate.

Marianne, the middle sister, never married.

In 1839 the Reverend Henry Austen retired from Bentley and with Eleanor moved from one spa to another in quest of health and cheap living.

Far from settling into a well-earned retirement, his brother Sir Francis, who enjoyed a remarkably strong constitution, was after thirty years on shore suddenly called to active service again. Alone at Portsdown Lodge but for his two unmarried daughters, the prospect of another spell of useful employment and a change of scene evidently appealed, for in December 1844, at the age of seventy, he accepted the appointment of Commander-in-Chief of the North American and West Indian station.

It was a post admirably suited to the dignity and authority of his age, experience and rank, involving duties of an almost vice-regal nature, far removed from the hazards and hardships of his youthful service, though arduous enough for one of his years. With the job came two official residences, at Halifax, Nova Scotia, and Bermuda, plus extremely comfortable quarters on the flagship *Vindictive*. Such provision made it possible for him to be accompanied by his daughters Cassandra and Fanny, who would be useful to him on occasions of state and the giving and receiving of hospitality. During their absence Portsdown Lodge would be shut up. The sailing of the *Vindictive* was quite a family affair, for besides his daughters on board Sir Francis had one son, Herbert, as flag-lieutenant, and another, George (who combined the two favourite Austen professions of Church and Navy), as chaplain.

By March preparations were well in hand and the departure imminent, when Sir Francis' sister Cassandra arrived on a visit to Portsdown Lodge to wish him '*bon voyage*'. She was now seventy-two, 'a pale, dark-eyed lady with a high arched nose and kind smile, dressed in a long cloak and a large drawn bonnet, both made of black satin', according to the recollection of her niece Mary Austen-Leigh.

At their respective ages, Cassandra and Sir Francis knew that they could not depend upon meeting again; before his duty overseas was completed, one or other of them might well die. But the severance was to come sooner than expected. Whilst still at Portsdown Lodge, Cassandra fell suddenly ill.

Edward Austen-Leigh wrote from Scarlets to his sister Anna Lefroy: 'Caroline had a letter on Friday from Uncle Frank written from London not exactly proposing her going down to Portsdown, but so written as to induce her to propose it which she did by return of post. This morning brought an answer from Catherine written in her father's home (as he was returning home yesterday from town) thankfully accepting the offer and highly approving of her proposal of taking her maid with her to share the work. At the same time came to her a letter from Portsdown written by Uncle Henry on Friday giving a *helpless* account and leaving us to expect that the end will not be many days prolonged.'[7]

Caroline's reminiscences fill out the story:

1845. – In March, on the 17th, being much alarmed by bad reports of Aunt Cassandra, I went off to Portsdown Lodge – where she was lying in the last stage of weakness. She had gone there as well as usual to take leave of her brother and his family – for Sir Francis was on the point of sailing in the *Vindictive*, to take his command on the West India

Station. All the inmates had cleared out and were on board the vessel at Portsmouth when I got there. It was impossible for Uncle to delay his departure. He came over to see his sister once – that was all he could do – I found Uncle Henry left in charge. My Uncle Charles joined us ere long. On the morning of Saturday the 22nd Aunt Cassandra passed away at 20 minutes before 4. Her illness had begun with some sort of seizure in the head – and she had never rallied much; though her mind was not at all affected even up to the last. She was buried at Chawton on Friday 28th March.

As Edward wrote to Anna on Saturday evening, 29 March:

I have been attending Aunt Cassandra's funeral ... I went on Thursday and found in the cottage my Uncles Henry and Charles ... I dined with this party in the drawing-room (the coffin being placed in the dining-room) and slept at the parsonage – Uncle Henry struck me as very agreeable and not very old: Uncle Charles was kind, grave and thoughtful.

Next morning the ceremony took place and was all done between the hours of 10 and 11. Charles Knight officiated ... The day was fine, but the wind exceedingly boisterous, blowing the pall almost off the coffin, and quite sweeping away all sound of Charles' voice between the gate and church door. It also struck me as remarkably emblematic of her age and condition that the wind whisked about us so many withered beech leaves, that the coffin was thickly strewed with them before the service closed.[8]

The last inhabitant of Chawton cottage was gone. Nobody else in the family required it as a dwelling, and Edward Knight had it divided into three tenements for village people. So it remained for almost a century, until 1940, when it was purchased and restored by the Jane Austen Memorial Trust.

The three years of Sir Francis Austen's American command provided a mixture of incident and interest, action and socializing, which together made an agreeable last appointment to a long and distinguished career. His robust constitution saw him safely through the less pleasant aspects of his duty – such as carrying out an hour's inspection of the dockyard at Antigua in the tropical heat, surely enough to sap the strength of anybody in his seventies.

Sir Francis made his usual cool observation of the resident population. In the United States he found 'there was a sort of flippant air amongst the women which seemed rather at variance with the retiring modesty so pleasing in the generality of English women.'

In May 1848 he voluntarily relinquished his command and returned to Portsdown Lodge, and to further promotion to the rank of full Admiral. The following year, at the age of thirty-five, Cassandra died, leaving Fanny as mistress of the place.

But another daughter was soon to seek shelter under the paternal roof – for while her father was abroad, poor Catherine had been plunged into tragedy.[9]

Her husband, John Hubback, had worked hard to support his wife and children and to advance himself in his profession. In 1844 he had published *Evidence of Succession to Real and Personal Property and Peerages*, quite an achievement for so young a man. Briefs flowed in, perhaps more than he could cope with. Suddenly, in the summer of 1847, he suffered a complete mental breakdown, brought on, it was believed, by intense overwork.

At first there were high hopes of a cure. He had never been ill before, there was no insanity in his family, and there seemed every reason to suppose that with complete rest he would recover. When no sign of recovery came, Catherine took her husband and children on a courageous round of resorts in a pathetic attempt to find a cure. It must have been a frightening decision for her to make alone, to give up their home and professional contacts in London. First the little family went to Malvern, where they were visited by an anxious Sir Francis, newly returned to England. Malvern was fast becoming to the Victorians what Bath had been to the Georgians – among its regular visitors was Edward Austen-Leigh, seeking relief for his sciatica – but poor John Hubback received no benefit. Next the deep tranquillity of Wales was tried.

The longer John's illness persisted, the more frantic with worry must Catherine have become. Everything was at stake – the health of a beloved husband, the financial security of the family – but she was helpless to effect a remedy. She later wrote of 'the long weary suspense of watching the failing intellect in the dearest and most precious of our relations, of the terrible distress such afflictions bring in families'. Total responsibility for her children and husband fell on her, changing her from a vibrant, eager girl to a resourceful and grittily determined woman.

During the long stay in Wales, to distract herself from perpetual anxiety and in the hope of earning some money now that John's livelihood that failed, she turned to writing. She recalled the unfinished fragment of her aunt Jane's, as yet unnamed but later known as *The Watsons*, which she had often heard read aloud by her aunt Cassandra or stepmother Martha in the carefree days of her girlhood. Now she conceived the bright idea of completing it, along the lines which they had spoken of as being its author's intention.

Catherine did not have the abandoned manuscript to work from – she had to rely on her memory for the beginning of the novel and on her own creative powers for its continuation. She called her version *The Younger Sister* and dedicated it to the memory of Jane Austen from the authoress who 'though too young to have known her personally, was from early childhood taught to esteem her virtues and admire her talents'.

It was accepted for publication in 1850 by Newby of Cavendish Square, who had published the first novels of Trollope and of Emily and Anne Brontë. He had a parsimonious attitude to his authors – the two Brontë sisters had had to share £50 between them – but whatever sum he paid Catherine Hubback (who wrote under her married name), it was gratefully received, and she found sufficient encouragement to begin another novel, this time with plot and characters of her own invention.

There was need for every penny she could earn, for not only was John incapable of supporting his family but, because of the Married Women's Property Act, Catherine could not touch either the money she herself had brought into the marriage or the savings the young couple had since made, and she was therefore dependent for herself and her sons on the charity of her father.

John's behaviour was becoming increasingly uncontrollable, and by May 1850 Catherine, after three years of struggle and receding hope, had no option but to have him confined to an asylum. His former colleagues in the legal profession kindly contributed to the cost of a place at Brislington House in Bristol, run by the Quaker Dr Fox, whose humane approach to mental illness was well in advance of his time.

Catherine and her little boys found *their* asylum at Portsdown

Lodge. Providing his grandsons did not make too much noise and were well disciplined, obedient and respectful, the old Admiral loved to have them under his roof, and they would listen entranced to the many tales of naval exploits he could recount. John, the eldest boy, became particularly close to his grandfather, whom he later described as being in his recollection bent in figure, with a bush of white hair, keen, bright eyes and a kindly expression.

Within the next two years Sir Francis lost his three remaining brothers. First to die was Henry, in March 1850, at the age of seventy-nine. He had chosen to settle for his final years at Tunbridge Wells, in the county of his ancestors. It was from his retirement here that Henry wrote to his nephew Edward Austen-Leigh – whose interest in family history was highly developed – describing what he himself remembered and what he had heard tell of the early Austens, as far back as his lawyer great-uncle Francis.

Rear-Admiral Charles Austen enjoyed no such gentle close to his life of endeavour. Like Sir Francis, he was suddenly required for active service in his old age. He was appointed Commander-in-Chief on the East India Station in 1850, when he was seventy-one.

He left England by P & O steamer for Alexandria and crossed the desert to Suez by the overland route. Here he joined his flagship the *Hastings*, whose captain was his nephew and son-in-law Frank, and proceeded to direct a little imperial war against the unco-operative Burmese. Two other young relations were amongst the officers under his overall control – Lizzy's sons Edward Bridges Rice and George William Rice, both naval commanders.

In 1852 Charles contracted cholera. The war being in a favourable state to be left, he was persuaded to go to Calcutta where he recuperated at the home of the Governor-General. But when hostilities in Burma intensified, Charles insisted on returning to duty. Transferring his flag to an East India Company sloop, he made a voyage of reconnaissance up the Irrawaddy River as high as Prome, where he was obliged to wait for re-inforcements. Stranded in this unhealthy spot for two or three weeks, he lost the strength he had gained at Calcutta, and his cholera flared up again. On 6 October Charles noted in his log: 'Received a report that two steamers had been seen at anchor some miles below, wrote this and a letter to my wife, and read the lessons of the day.' The following morning he died, 'winning all hearts', according to a witness, 'by his gentleness and kindness, when struggling with disease'.

The expedition continued, and Prome was recaptured. Edward Rice commanded the naval detachment ashore, and in the assault his brother George received a wound from a musket ball passing in at the back of his hand and out at the wrist. The second Burmese war thus claimed the lives of two of George Austen's descendants – for George Rice eventually died of this wound, although not until the following March, when he was back home at Dane Court. He was twenty-five and had been mentioned in despatches for his bravery.

Charles was buried far from homely soil, at Trincomalee in Ceylon. The news of his death took some time to reach England, but when he heard of it, Edward Austen-Leigh turned back his pocket-book to 7 October and wrote: 'Died this day my good Uncle Charles.'

Charles' second surviving son, Henry, had predeceased him by two years. He died while with his regiment at the Cape of Good Hope as the result of a fall. Though he had begun his working life as a naval volunteer, at the age of seventeen Henry had changed careers and joined the army, eventually purchasing a captaincy in the 73rd Regiment of Foot.

Henry was unmarried, so the only grandchildren of Charles were the offspring of his namesake son, who had joined his uncle Francis on the *Vindictive* in 1847 and met, at the Commander-in-Chief's official residence at Halifax, Sophia de Blois, a Nova Scotian. Their marriage took place the following year and eventually produced five daughters and one son – in whom the name Charles John Austen was perpetuated.

In striking contrast to his brother's death on active service of a foul disease in an unhealthy climate, Edward Knight, who died at almost the same time, closed his life as peacefully and as comfortably as he had led it.

Until 18 November 1852 he continued his normal quiet routine established over a lifetime at Godmersham; his physique was becoming ever frailer but had not hitherto incommoded him. On that day, however, he felt unequal to taking his customary drive.

Early next morning, when woken by his servant, he asked to be left to sleep, as he felt so comfortable. Returning a little later, the servant thought his master was still asleep but, on approaching more closely, found that he had died.

A friend wrote of Edward's death: 'It strikes me as a characteristic end of his prosperous and placid life, and he will certainly leave on the minds of all who knew him an image of gentleness and quiet cheerfulness of no ordinary degree.'[10]

By settling at Chawton a quarter of a century before, the younger Edward Knight had transferred his allegiance from Kent to Hampshire and had no wish to uproot his large family now. So Godmersham Park was let and eventually, some twenty years later, sold out of the family altogether.

Another piece of the Knight inheritance was Steventon Manor, which ever since the Austens' connection with the place had been tenanted by Digweeds – successive generations of them. When the last Mr Digweed died, however, this property too was offered for sale by Edward Knight – and one who was interested in buying it was his cousin Edward Austen-Leigh.

To do so would have necessitated selling Scarlets – but his attachment to that place was not nearly so powerful as that which he felt for the village of his childhood and of his father's and grandfather's ministrations. Had there been fewer sons to educate and establish in the professions, Edward undoubtedly would have indulged the nostalgic and romantic side of his nature by carrying through this change, according to the opinion of his daughter Mary. He was seriously tempted – but seven boys to put through school was a strain on even his considerable resources, and the responsible father in him regretfully gave up the idea of returning to his roots and acquiring Steventon Manor.

A removal from Scarlets which would enable him to *save* money was an altogether more prudent proposition – and such an opportunity was now afforded him. His bishop thought so highly of his exertions at Knowl Hill, where he had helped build a church, putting up £2,000 of his own money, that he offered him wider scope for his clerical abilities in one of the best livings in his gift – that of Bray, just a few miles from Scarlets, where the lucky incumbent enjoyed not only a stipend of £500 per annum but a vicarage whose gardens stretched down to the River Thames.

Emma concealed her own reluctance to leave Scarlets and insisted that the decision be Edward's alone. It was made, after much contemplation, in favour of Bray, cheap living and hard work.

Scarlets was let to a Mr Littledale on a seven-year lease, during which period Edward hoped to recoup for his children's benefit the money spent on Knowl Hill church. However, after the luxury of Scarlets, Bray vicarage seemed rather cramped when called on to accommodate so large a family. Edward therefore immediately began spending on improvements – adding five bedrooms and a second stable and resiting the approach drive so that it did not cut through the churchyard, an arrangement which so offended his sensibilities that his acceptance of Bray had depended on the feasibility of this change.

Mary Austen-Leigh recorded in the life of her father which she wrote half a century later: 'The removal took place at the end of April 1853, and was of a patriarchal nature, for there were at least thirty people to be transported, including the family of Hale the gardener, and those of the butler and the coachman, who all had to be settled in neighbouring cottages. The horses, ponies, dogs, cows and farmyard stock came by degrees, but all had arrived before May the first.'

What his great-aunt and benefactress would have thought of this voluntary desertion of her beloved Scarlets after only sixteen years, and of letting it fall into the hands of tenants, the thing she had above all dreaded, was evidently not allowed to influence Edward's decision. Had she been able to foresee such a circumstance, it is inconceivable that she would have made him her heir.

15

There was so little to tell

1854-69

At the outbreak of the Crimean War in 1854, Sir Francis Austen was offered the appointment of Port Admiral at Portsmouth, with his flag on HMS *Victory*. It was a great honour, but at eighty years of age he felt unequal to performing the duties to his own satisfaction and so declined.

The armed services being, next to the Church, the favourite occupation of the male members of the family, many were the descendants of George Austen who served in the Crimea. No fewer than five of Lizzy Rice's nine surviving sons were involved in the war against Russia, making this an anxious time at Dane Court, especially as news was slow to reach England.

Of the five, two Rice brothers deserve special mention. Cecil, a captain in the Third Regiment of Foot, took part in the siege of Sebastopol and was the first British officer to investigate the place after its fall, having been sent by his General to find out whether the Russians really had evacuated it. Cecil Rice was awarded the Crimean war medal with bar and the Turkish medal for the Crimea.

His youngest brother Ernest joined the navy at the start of the war; he was just fourteen years old. At this tender age he truly received a baptism of fire, for his ship was heavily shelled as it neared the Russian coast. Ernest was flung to the deck and saved from injury by the bodies of other officers and men falling on top of him, twenty-six of whom were killed. The boatswain, pulling Ernest to his feet, told him, 'You are in command now, sir.'[1] It was the beginning of a distinguished naval career for the boy who eventually became Admiral Sir Ernest Rice KCB.

A youthful victim of the war was his cousin Charles Knight,

fourth son of Edward Knight of Chawton House and his first wife Mary Dorothea, at the age of twenty-one, as his inscription at Chawton church records: 'After distinguishing himself by his gallant conduct before the enemy on several occasions, and especially at the attack on the Rifle Pits on the night of the 19th of April 1855, he fell ill of a fever shortly after the taking of Sebastopol on the 8th of September, and died in Camp on October 2nd 1855. His many amiable qualities endeared him to the officers and men of his Regiment and … the premature close of a life so full of promise cannot but cause deep sorrow to his family …'

From Sir Francis Austen's division of the family, Mary Jane's son Reginald Purvis was disabled at Balaclava and only narrowly avoided amputation of a leg. He went on to become a Rear-Admiral, and his brother Herbert a Major-General – grandsons in the true tradition of their high-ranking grandfather.

Hitherto, trade had been eschewed by the Austens – at least, since the early days in Kent – but another of Sir Francis' grandsons, John Hubback, was at the age of fourteen offered an opening which, given his parents' circumstances, was too favourable to decline. His uncle Joseph Hubback was a grain merchant in Liverpool and, childless himself, invited his eldest nephew to join him with the possibility of a partnership in the future if hard work and a flair for business were shown.

Catherine welcomed this opportunity to secure a livelihood for at least one of her sons. To make a home for John, she left the comforts of Portsdown Lodge and, taking the two younger boys with her, moved to lodgings in Birkenhead. Here she was in uncongenial surroundings. She found little intellectual stimulation and made few friends. Her facility for writing, which had resulted in the publication of ten novels between 1850 and 1863, now failed her. Nevertheless, she could look back with some satisfaction on her achievement – in terms of independence gained and money saved if not of literary merit.

As a novelist she had been hard-working and prolific – but verbose and dull. After *The Younger Sister*, which, inspired by her aunt's beginning, had been not without humour and vitality, her writing fell off and her style became pedestrian, her plots long-winded, her characters repetitive. Despite these faults, her books were eagerly read by the growing ranks of middle-class young ladies at whom they were aimed and whose appetite for fiction was fed by a whole bevvy of minor female novelists.

Not that all Catherine's readers were youthful. The grandmother of Henry James was one of her known admirers.[2] In the mid-Victorian era, some perverse value judgements were made. *The Rival Suitors* published in 1857 was called by a reviewer 'the best of all Mrs. Hubback's novels and one which proves her to be nearly allied by genius as she is by blood to the first of English female novelists, Miss Austen'.

Within the family, however, Catherine's measure of success was somewhat resented. She was the only female among them to work for payment, and the unorthodoxy of her situation in life, though no fault of her own, was regarded with suspicion by some of the more sedate and conventional of her cousins. Neither maid, wife nor widow, she aroused uncomfortable feelings in their respectable Victorian breasts.

Though there were many lady novelists in mid-nineteenth-century England, both major and minor, they were invariably a shade or two lower on the social scale than the Austens. Perhaps this, perhaps the increasing sobriety of the age, resulted in something ambivalent about that generation's attitude to Jane herself.

Writing to one of her sisters, Lady Knatchbull – the Fanny Knight with whom Jane had passed 'delicious mornings', who had been to her 'almost a sister' and whose letters were 'the delight of my life' – proved herself transformed into a thorough-going Victorian dowager:

Yes my love it is very true that Aunt Jane from various circumstances was not so refined as she ought to have been from her talent, and if she had lived fifty years later she would have been in many respects more suitable to our more refined tastes. They were not rich and the people around with whom they chiefly mixed, were not at all high-bred, or in short anything more than mediocre and they of course, though superior in mental powers and cultivation, were on the same level as far as refinement goes – but I think in later life their intercourse with Mrs Knight (who was very fond of and kind to them) improved them both and Aunt Jane was too clever not to put aside all possible signs of 'commonness' (if such an expression is allowable) and teach herself to be more refined, at least in intercourse with people in general. Both the aunts (Cassandra and Jane) were brought up in the most complete ignorance of the world and its way (I mean as to fashion etc) and if it had not been for Papa's marriage which brought them into Kent and the kindness of Mrs Knight, who used often to have one or other of the sisters staying with her, they would have been, though not less clever and agreeable in themselves, very much below par as to good society and its ways.

It is hard to resist hating Fanny for this – hard at any rate not to feel a little twinge of satisfaction that Fanny's last ten years of life were clouded by senile dementia – which perhaps was creeping up on her even in the repetitiveness of this ghastly letter.

Others in the family still loved and reverenced the memory of Jane and yet were not unaffected by the climate of their times. Caroline's loyalty and devotion were unqualified, but an action she took in old age illustrates the regrettable plunge into hypocrisy and earnestness which the Victorians had made. For 27 April 1871 she records: 'Burnt, as I had long intended to do, all that remained extant of my childish writings. Lines on the death of Farmer Hyde the earliest, no date. Letter in verse to my brother at Winchester 1815. Comedy in verse the same year … A few scraps besides, all in verse … I pass this judgment. That they showed wonderful facility in rhyme and measure for a child of ten years old, but that they were flippant and in bad taste – an attempt at the comic, where comedy should not have been, and I wonder that they passed without rebuke.'

There seems reason to be thankful that Jane's hilarious early writings 'passed without rebuke', that she did not, as Fanny would have wished, 'live fifty years later' and that her comic genius was nurtured and allowed to flourish in the liberal and civilized atmosphere of Georgian England.

In 1860 Sir Francis Austen was appointed Senior Admiral of the Fleet, the topmost position in the Royal Navy.

During the same year that he achieved this supreme recognition of his services to his country, Sir Francis sold Portsdown Lodge to the Government, who desired it to form part of the line of fortification round Portsmouth Harbour. He remained in his old home as life tenant until his death five years later, on 10 August

1865. He was ninety-one and had outlived all his siblings by at least thirteen years, and his sister Jane by thirty-eight.

The Government offered a Service Funeral, complete with a detachment of Bluejackets for the last salute, but his sons declined, believing that their father would have preferred a simple burial at Wymering churchyard, attended only by his grandsons and themselves.

The two eldest of Sir Francis' sons, Frank and Henry, had predeceased him, dying in 1858 and 1854 respectively, but George, Herbert and Edward all came to Wymering to pay their last respects. George had married Louisa Tragett in 1851 and, relinquishing the naval chaplaincy, become Rector of Red Hill, just four miles from Portsdown Lodge, in 1856. He had five children.

Herbert married another Louisa in 1863 and retired from the Navy the following year, having reached the rank of Captain. He purchased Whitely Lodge near Reading, and there his two daughters and one son were born. The third brother, Edward, obtained the living of Barfreston in Kent in 1855 and the same year took a wife, Jane, who bore him three daughters.

Portsdown Lodge had now to be vacated, its last inhabitant, Fanny, disposing of its contents as she thought fit. Far away in Lancashire, Catherine was angry and upset to learn that Fanny, without consulting anybody, had burned all of Jane Austen's letters to their mother which their father had so carefully preserved.

Fanny went to live at Barfreston, where two years later her sister-in-law died, leaving the three little girls to her care. In their secluded rectory Edward and Fanny lived peaceably together, both surviving into the twentieth century.

Their sister Catherine had fewer but more eventful years left. In 1871, at the age of fifty-three, she set out to make a new life in America. Her son John was now a prospering grain merchant and had a family of his own. The next boy, Edward, had more need of her. He had gone out to California to try to live by farming and appealed to his mother to come and make a home for him. With an adventurous spirit and indomitable courage reminiscent of her great-aunt Philadelphia, she left home and friends behind her to begin again on a far continent.

As her letters to John and his wife Mary reveal, she relished every new experience and, in contrast to most disapproving matrons of her age, observed with fascination the difference in customs and characters she encountered. Her years in America were stimulating and satisfying ones.

In due course her third son, Charley, also emigrated, choosing to settle on a smallholding in Virginia. It was while she was on a visit to Charley that Catherine died, very suddenly, in 1877. Her husband survived her by eleven years, never recovering his sanity.

Meanwhile, at Bray, Edward Austen-Leigh settled comfortably into the role of Victorian parson and paterfamilias – the close counterpart of his Georgian grandfather, the Reverend George Austen.

Like his grandfather, Edward educated all his boys himself – but only up to the age of thirteen. Then, presumably loath to risk them all in one educational basket, he sent them off: Cholmeley to Winchester, Charles and Spencer to Harrow, Arthur to Radley, and Edward, Augustus and William to Eton. They were all notable scholars and achievers. With the exception of Spencer, who took up farming, all attended university – dividing themselves between Oxford and Cambridge on a similar principle.

In an age of muscular Christianity (and Edward had once considered actually going to live near Rugby in order that his boys might profit from Dr Arnold's style of education – but, having visited the place with such a view in mind, decided that he did not like the countryside or the climate), the seven boys were brought up to play as hard as they worked. The river flowing at the bottom of their garden encouraged bathing, boating and fishing; and as for cricket, their record could hardly have been more praiseworthy. All at university obtained their blue, and Spencer excelled even these, becoming so well known for scoring a century in any match he graced with his presence that people came from as far afield as Bristol in the expectation of seeing him repeat the achievement.

Gradually all thought of returning to Scarlets was abandoned, and in 1863 it was sold to the sitting tenant. Capital had not proved so easy to accumulate as Edward had somewhat naïvely supposed, and with his ever-increasing commitments he could not foresee ever being able to afford to live at Scarlets again. But what finally decided him to sell was need of cash for a specific purpose.

Cholmeley wished to leave the law, for which he had been trained, and purchase a partnership in a publishing firm, Spottiswoode & Co. Friends advised Edward to mortgage rather than sell, but his attachment to Scarlets had never equalled that of his great-aunt, and so the house that James Leigh Perrot had built just a century before passed out of the family for ever.

Presumably Cholmeley, who would have inherited Scarlets, had no objection to the arrangement or agreed with his father as to its prudence. His ambition realized, and settled into a business he found highly congenial, he married Melesina Chenevix, whose father shortly afterwards became Archbishop of Dublin. (Cholmeley and Melesina: amid the classic English names so much favoured by the Austens, and so confusing to us, it is a relief to record this distinctive coupling.)

Of the other Austen-Leighs, Spencer rented from the Duke of Devonshire a 550-acre farm in Sussex called Frog Firle, which he later purchased together with his brother Charles, who was Chief Clerk of Committees at the House of Commons. Their aunt Caroline came to keep house for these two bachelors at Frog Firle, ending her days being useful as she would wish and indulging in the pleasure of writing her reminiscences. All the other brothers had clerical or academic careers. Neither Amy nor Mary married.

Though fundamentally the same as his grandfather's, Edward Austen-Leigh's way of life differed in small but telling ways – due to the age in which he found himself rather than to any significant dissimilarity of character. Whereas George Austen had concerned himself solely with his parish and his family, Edward (perhaps because of improved communications) was active in a larger sphere, writing tracts and discussing the issues of the day with his bishop and other dignitaries. So much for work; as for domestic life, Edward and Emma had more servants to perform more basic tasks for them. They were further removed from the soil and the seasons, from the production of food and clothing, from all the practical aspects of life which had given real satisfaction to George and Cassandra and which had seemed to them not incompatible with the exercise of their intellectual faculties.

Among the young Austen-Leighs there was all the usual fun of a large, clever, affectionate family, with plenty of home-made entertainment, musical and verbal; the Leigh talent for light verse and word games was much in evidence. Nevertheless at Bray the tone of family life was a shade more earnest than it had been at Steventon in the last quarter of the previous century. But it was the tenor, rather than the underlying moral values, which differed.

One of the few points of ethical judgement in which a real difference *can* be identified was the question of hunting. Though there is no record of the Reverend George Austen's having hunted, he allowed all his sons to do so from an early age, even those designed for the Church. By Edward's time, a sporting clergyman was regarded as unseemly. Hunting was one of his delights, but he gave it up – not because his own conscience found it wrong, for he could see no harm in it, but because he was persuaded by others that he would lose influence among his parishioners if he offended their ideas of propriety. Thus was Georgian tolerance – or laxity, as the age which came after saw it – whittled away.

Perhaps it was in a spirit of vicarious enjoyment that Edward wrote in 1864 his *Recollections of The Vine Hunt*[3], which was printed for private circulation. And then, as his daughter Mary records in her own memoir of her father:

> The ease and swiftness with which it had been written, showed that no powers of composition were lost, and possibly this may have encouraged him to undertake, a few years later, another work, for which a strong desire had at times been expressed by his family – a memoir of his aunt, Jane Austen. He had been accustomed to answer, when urged on the subject, that, as there was so little to tell, it appeared to him impossible to write anything that could be called a 'life'.
>
> At length, however – that is to say, early in 1869 – he agreed to put down what little there was to say. His interest grew as he wrote; he appealed to other members of the family, some of whom had long been unseen by him, and received assistance from several quarters in the form of letters and manuscripts ...
>
> He also went for a night to Hampshire, first visiting Deane, his birthplace, where he inspected the register, and then going to Steventon, one mile further on, the birthplace of his Aunt Jane, and the spot where she and he had in their respective generations grown up to womanhood and manhood. It must to him have been a deeply interesting renewal of old associations and familiar haunts, unseen for many years. The old rectory had been pulled down, and its successor, in

which he spent one night with his cousin, the Rev. William Knight, had been rebuilt upon another site; but the landscape, the church, and the old manor house were still the same. 'Walked about Steventon grounds, old and new, by myself,' is the entry in his diary. It was for him the last sight of that old and beloved early home, the picture of which he was about to paint on behalf of the lovers of Jane Austen.

The memoir was begun on March 30, 1869, and was finished early in September. Mr Bentley, the publisher, brought it out on December 16.

The book was written in Edward's old age but has a freshness of expression and grace of style hardly compatible with declining or unexercised powers. So well received was it that he was persuaded to bring out a second edition, including some of Jane's hitherto unpublished fragments. Mary continues: 'The sum which the two editions brought him amounted, I think, to about £80. Some of this he employed in placing a brass tablet to his aunt's memory in Winchester Cathedral, and the remainder he divided among such of his relations from whom he had received assistance as would agree to accept it.'

In researching his book, Edward had been able to indulge his interest in the past, particularly in the past of his own family; in writing it, he dwelt much on the subtle changes which had overtaken the rural middle classes even during his own lifespan. Whilst expressing no regret for the passing of the old ways, he painted a sympathetic picture of the background which had produced his brilliant aunt, whose remembrance he had fondly cherished for fifty years.

Edward died in 1874, Emma in 1876; Anna in 1872 and Caroline in 1880. Edward's book had both satisfied and helped to create a growing interest in and admiration for Jane Austen – her life and her work. His was the first loyal drop in the flow of words about her which in the next century was to reach the proportions of a torrent. The family pride in her was now revived.

Even Lord Brabourne, son of the monstrous Fanny, and the most eminent in public life of all George Austen's descendants (he was Liberal MP for Sandwich from 1857 to 1880, when he was raised to the peerage, and was Under-Secretary first for Home Affairs and then for the Colonies, and a Privy Councillor), found it by no means beneath him in 1884 to edit and publish Jane Austen's letters to his mother.

At the other end of the (limited) Austen social spectrum from Lord Brabourne, John Hubback of Liverpool, who shared Edward Austen-Leigh's fascination for the past and who never outgrew the influence of his remarkable grandfather (though like Sir Francis he lived to his nineties), collaborated with his daughter Edith in 1904 to write *Jane Austen's Sailor Brothers*, which traces the careers of both Frank and Charles.

Thereafter professionals took over the 'industry', which inevitably concentrated on the genius of the family, or at most the lives of others as they overlapped hers; while the many interesting histories which made up the whole Austen saga – made it so representative of its era and place in society – remained neglected. This study has been an attempt to remedy that neglect and to do justice both to the individuals and to the family as an entity.

Appendix

The great-grandchildren of
George and Cassandra Austen

The line from William Austen, born in 1701, descended through his son George. George Austen and his wife Cassandra had eight children, thirty-three grandchildren, and one hundred and one great-grandchildren. Of the latter, seventeen were the grandchildren of their son James, fifty-eight of Edward, twenty of Frank and six of Charles.

So prolific, robust and long-lived was this line that in the middle year of the nineteenth century, one hundred and fifty years after the birth of William Austen, he had over ninety descendants *living*.

The name of Austen, however, was not perpetuated to the degree suggested by so large a number of great-grandchildren. Change of surname and descent through the female line resulted in only five of this generation being males called Austen. And of these five, just three had sons to carry on the name.

These three are asterisked in the following table of the great-grandchildren of George and Cassandra Austen.

THROUGH JAMES AUSTEN
Anna Austen married Ben Lefroy
Anna Jemima 1815-55
Julia Cassandra 1816-84
George Benjamin 1818-1912
Fanny Caroline 1820-85
Georgiana Brydges 1822-74
Louisa Langlois 1824-77
Elizabeth Lucy 1827-95

James Edward Austen-Leigh married Emma Smith
Cholmeley 1829-99

Emma Cassandra 1831-1902
Charles Edward 1832-1924
Spencer 1834-1913
Arthur Henry 1836-1917
Mary Augusta 1838-1922
Edward Compton 1839-1916
Augustus 1840-1905
George Raymond 1841-2
William 1843-1921

THROUGH EDWARD KNIGHT
Fanny Knight married Sir Edward Knatchbull
Fanny Elizabeth 1825-45
Matilda Catherine 1826-60
Alice Sophia 1828-49
Edward Hugesson 1829-93
Reginald Bridges 1831-1911
Richard Astley 1832-75
Louisa Susanna 1834-74
Herbert Thomas 1835-1922
William Western 1837-64

Edward Knight married firstly Mary Dorothea Knatchbull
Edward Lewkenor 1827-38
Wyndham William 1828-1918
Annabella Christiana 1830-44
Georgina Elizabeth 1832-64
Philip Henry 1835-82
Charles Ernest 1836-55
William Brodnax 1838-96
Edward Knight married secondly Adela Portal
Elizabeth Adela 1841-96
Edward Brook 1843-44
Montagu George 1844-1914
Charles Edward 1846-1912
Henry John 1848-79
Adela Louisa Cassandra 1849-?
Adela Mary Margaretta 1852-1912
Helen Adela 1853-79

Ethel Adela 1856-1913

Henry Knight married firstly Sophia Cage
Lewis Edward 1833-86
Henry Knight married secondly Charlotte Northey
Agnes Charlotte 1837-1927

William Knight married firstly Caroline Portal
Elizabeth Caroline 1826-1927
Gertrude 1827-1916
Frederic William 1828-1902
Edward Bridges 1829-78
Richard 1830-66
Emily born and died 1832
Arthur Charles 1833-1905
Louisa 1837-1911
William Knight married secondly Mary Northey
Mary 1843-8
Cecilia 1844-8
Augusta 1845-8

Elizabeth Knight married Edward Royd Rice
Edward Bridges 1819-1902
Fanny Margaretta 1820-1909
Henry 1821-48
John Morland 1823-97
Elizabeth Louisa 1824-1916
Marianne Sophia 1825-1909
George William 1927-53
Charles Augustus 1828-1905
Cecil 1831-1917
Caroline Cassandra 1835-1923
Walter Brook 1837-92
Arthur 1838-61
Ernest 1840-1927
Florence Mary 1841-1910
Lionel Knight 1844-1929

Louisa Knight married Lord George Augusta Hill
George Marcus Wandsbeck 1849-1911

Cassandra Jane Knight married Lord George Augusta Hill
Arthur Blundell George Sandys 1837-?
Augustus Charles Edward 1839-1908
Norah Mary Elizabeth ?-1920
Cassandra Jane Louisa ?-1901

THROUGH FRANCIS AUSTEN
Mary Jane Austen married George Thomas Maitland Purvis
George Thomas Maitland 1829-80
Mary Renira 1830-?
Herbert Mark Garret 1831-?
Francis Reginald 1833-95
Helen Catherine 1835-?

George Austen married Louisa Tragett
Mary Louisa 1852-1925
Frances Heathcote born and died 1854
Francis George Heathcote 1857-85
Ernest Leigh 1858-1939
Arthur Robert 1860-1939*

Herbert Grey Austen married Louisa Lyns
Alice Mary 1863-1945
Ella Frances 1865-1935
Frederick William 1873-?*

Catherine Anne Austen married John Hubback
Mary born and died 1843
John Henry 1844-1939
Edward Thomas 1846-1924
Charles Austen 1848-1924

Edward Thomas Austen married Jane Clavell
Janet Rose 1856-1946
Flora 1859-?
Mary Jane 1867-1942

THROUGH CHARLES AUSTEN
Charles John Austen married Sophia de Blois
Jane 1849-1928
Emma Florence 1951-1939

Frances Cecilia 1853-1923
Charles John 1855-96*
Edith 1857-1942
Blanche Frederika 1859-1924

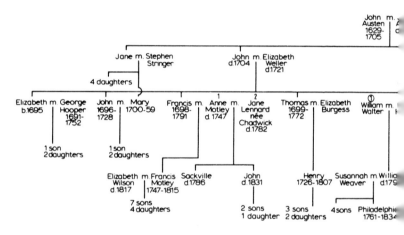

John m. ...
Austen | ...
1629- | d
1705

Jane m. Stephen   John m. Elizabeth
     Stringer   d.1704 | Weller
                                        d.1721

4 daughters

| Elizabeth m. George | John m. Mary | Francis m. | 1 Anne m. | 2 Jane | Thomas m. Elizabeth | ① William m. |
| b.1695 | Hooper | 1696- | 1700-59 | 1698- | Motley | Lennard | 1699- | Burgess | Walter |

Elizabeth m. George   John m. Mary   Francis m.   1   Anne m.   2   Jane   Thomas m. Elizabeth   ① William m.
b.1695   Hooper   1696-   1700-59   1698-   Motley   Lennard   1699-   Burgess   Walter
          1691-   1728   1791   d.1747   née   1772
          1752   Chadwick
                                             d.1782

1 son   1 son
2 daughters   2 daughters

Elizabeth m Francis   Sackville   John   Henry   Susannah m. Willia
Wilson | Motley   d.1786   d.1831   1726-1807   Weaver | d.179
d.1817 | 1747-1815

7 sons   2 sons   3 sons   4 sons
4 daughters   1 daughter   2 daughters   Philadelphi
                                                           1761-1834

          1   First Wife
          2   Second Wife
          ①   First Husband
          ②   Second Husband

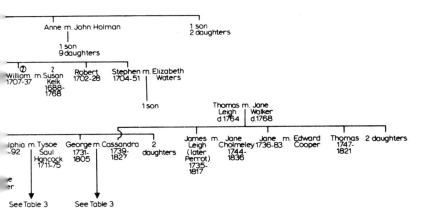

Anne m. John Holman
1 son
9 daughters

1 son
2 daughters

① William m. Susan Kelk 1688-1768
1707-37

Robert 1702-28

Stephen m. Elizabeth Waters 1704-51
1 son

Thomas m. Jane Leigh Walker d.1764 | d.1768

...lphia m. Tysoe Saul Hancock 1711-75
~92

George m. Cassandra 1739-1827 1731-1805

2 daughters

James Leigh (later Perrot) 1735-1817 m. Jane Cholmeley 1744-1836

Jane 1736-83 m. Edward Cooper

Thomas 1747-1821

2 daughters

See Table 3

See Table 3

Table 1 The Austens of Kent

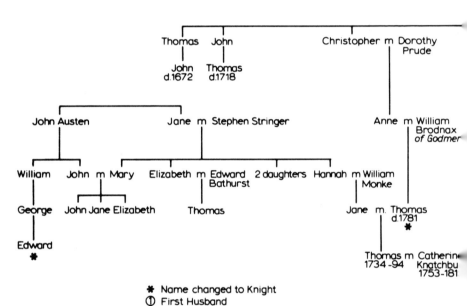

Thomas John   Christopher m Dorothy
                                    Prude

John   Thomas
d.1672 d.1718

John Austen   Jane m Stephen Stringer   Anne m William
                                                   Brodnax
                                                 of Godmer

William John m Mary   Elizabeth m Edward 2 daughters Hannah m William
                           Bathurst   Monke

George John Jane Elizabeth   Jane m. Thomas
                         Thomas   d.1781
Edward   *
✻

                                           Thomas m Catherine
                                           1734 -94 Knatchbu
                                                  1753-181

✻ Name changed to Knight
① First Husband
② Second Husband

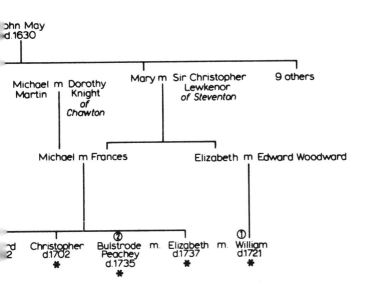

ohn May
d.1630

Michael m Dorothy   Mary m Sir Christopher   9 others
Martin   Knight   Lewkenor
          of   of Steventon
          Chawton

Michael m Frances   Elizabeth m Edward Woodward

⌐d   Christopher   ②   ①
 2   d.1702   Bulstrode   m. Elizabeth m. William
            ❋   Peachey   d.1737   d.1721
                     d.1735   ❋   ❋
                       ❋

Table 2 The Knight Inheritance

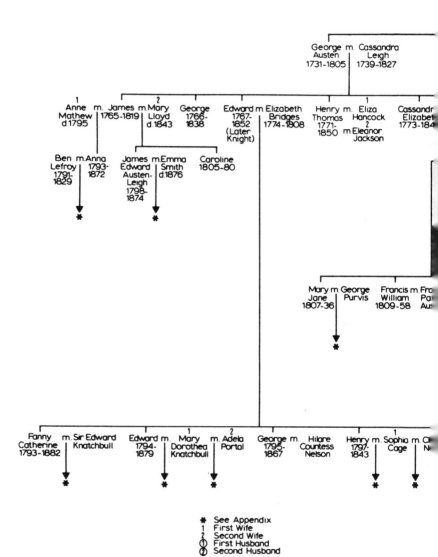

George m. Cassandra
Austen   Leigh
1731-1805 1739-1827

          1
Anne   m. James m. Mary   George   Edward m. Elizabeth   Henry m. Eliza   Cassandr
Mathew   1765-1819 Lloyd   1766-   1767-   Bridges   Thomas   Hancock   Elizabet
d.1795   d.1843   1838   1852   1774-1808   1771-   2   1773-184
                              2   (Later   1850 m Eleanor
                                              Knight)   Jackson

Ben   m.Anna   James m.Emma   Caroline
Lefroy   1793-   Edward   Smith   1805-80
1791-   1872   Austen- d.1876
1829   Leigh
                 1798-
                 1874

                                   Mary m.George   Francis m.Fra
                                   Jane   Purvis   William   Pai
                                   1807-36   1809-58   Aus

          1   1   2
Fanny   m.Sir Edward   Edward m. Mary   m. Adela   George m. Hilare   Henry m. Sophia m. C
Catherine Knatchbull 1794-   Dorothea   Portal   1795-   Countess 1797-   Cage   N
1793-1882   1879   Knatchbull   1867   Nelson   1843
                                1

                    ❋ See Appendix
                    1 First Wife
                    2 Second Wife
                    ① First Husband
                    ② Second Husband

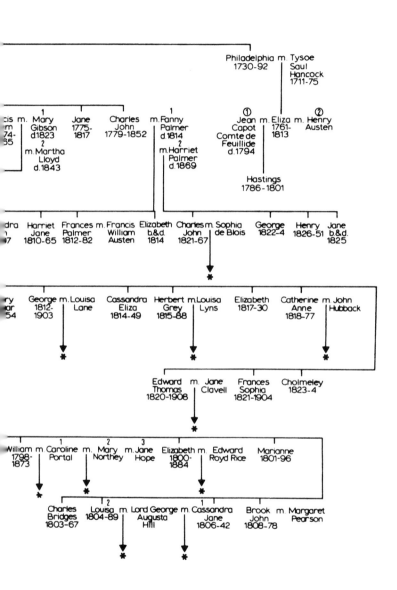

Philadelphia m. Tysoe
1730-92   Saul
             Hancock
             1711-75

cis m. Mary   Jane   Charles   1 m.Fanny   ① Jean m. Eliza   ② m. Henry
m.   Gibson   1775-   John   Palmer   Capot   1761-   Austen
74- d.1823   1817   1779-1852   d.1814   Comte de 1813
65   2   Feuillide
     m.Martha   m.Harriet   d.1794
     Lloyd   Palmer
     d.1843   d.1869   Hastings
                                                              1786-1801

dra   Harriet   Frances m.Francis Elizabeth Charles m. Sophia   George   Henry   Jane
n   Jane   Palmer William   b.&d.   John   de Blois 1822-4   1826-51   b.&d.
7   1810-65   1812-82 Austen   1814   1821-67   1825

                                              *

ry   George m.Louisa Cassandra Herbert m.Louisa Elizabeth Catherine m. John
ar   1812-   Lane   Eliza   Grey   Lyns   1817-30   Anne   Hubback
54   1903   1814-49   1815-88   1818-77

       *   *   *

              Edward   m. Jane   Frances   Cholmeley
              Thomas   Clavell Sophia   1823-4
              1820-1908   1821-1904

                          *

William m. Caroline m. Mary   m. Jane   Elizabeth m. Edward   Marianne
1798-   Portal   Northey   Hope   1800-   Royd Rice 1801-96
1873   1   2   3   1884

   *   *   *

       Charles   Louisa m. Lord George m. Cassandra   Brook m. Margaret
       Bridges   1804-89   Augusta   Jane   John   Pearson
       1803-67   2   Hill   1   1806-42   1808-78

                     *   *

References

*Where full title details are not given below, see
Bibliography*

Chapter 1
1. *Austen Papers*
2. Thomas Fuller, *A Church History of Britain* (1837)
3. William Page (editor), *The Victoria History of the Counties of England*, Kent Volume III (St Catherine Press, 1932)
4. Richard Arthur Austen-Leigh, *Pedigree of Austen* (Spottiswood, Ballantyne & Co Ltd, 1940)
5. *Austen Papers*
6. John Recker, *A Short History of the School and Almshouses of Sir William Sevenoke* (1913)
7. *Dictionary of National Biography*, Volume VI

Chapter 2
1. *Tonbridge Associations* – for all local information in this and the following chapter
2. *Jane Austen's Letters* – all quotations from the Chapman edition
3. *Austen Papers*
4. *Jane Austen in Kent*
5. *Warren Hastings*

Chapter 3
1. *Austen papers*
2. *Minor Works*
3. *Austen Papers*
4. *Warren Hastings*
5. Mark Bence-Jones, *Clive of India* (Constable, 1974)

6. *Tonbridge Associations*
7. D.C. Somervell, *History of Tonbridge School* (Faber & Faber, 1947)
8. *Austen Papers*
9. *Chawton Manor* – for all information concerning the Knight inheritance and genealogy

Chapter 4
 1. *Catherine Hubback*
 2. *Memoir of Jane Austen*
 3. *A Goodly Heritage*
 4. *Austen Papers*
 5. *Austen Papers*
 6. *Catherine Hubback*
 7. William Jarvis, 'Some Information about Jane Austen's Clerical Connections', *Annual Report*, 1976
 8. *Jane Austen's Letters*
 9. *Austen Papers*
10. *Austen Papers*

Chapter 5
1. *Austen Papers* – for this and following letters from Eliza Hancock
2. G.D. Squibb, *Founder's Kin* (Clarendon Press, 1972)
3. Elizabeth Jenkins, 'Some Banking Accounts of the Austen Family', *Annual Report* 1954
4. *Memoirs of Sir Francis Austen*
5. *Chawton Manor*
6. *Chawton Manor*
7. *A Goodly Heritage*
8. *Jane Austen in Kent*
9. *Memoirs of Sir Francis Austen*

Chapter 6
1. Eliza de Feuillide, *Austen Papers*
2. Lady Bridges, quoted in *Brabourne*
3. Lady Bridges, quoted in *Brabourne*
4. *Caroline Austen's Reminiscences*
5. William Jarvis, 'Some Information about Jane Austen's Clerical Connections', *Annual Report* 1976

6. *Jane Austen's Letters*
7. Anna Lefroy, quoted in *Jane Austen, Her Homes and Her Friends*
8. *Caroline Austen's Reminiscences*
9. *Caroline Austen's Reminiscences*
10. Henry Austen, *Austen Papers*
11. *Austen Papers*, Appendix 1
12. George Sawtell, 'Four Manly Boys', *Annual Report* 1982
13. *Sailor Brothers* – for all information about the careers of Frank and Charles
14. Quoted in *Sailor Brothers*
15. *Jane Austen's Letters*
16. *The English Militia*
17. *Caroline Austen's Reminiscences*

Chapter 7
1. *Memoir of J.E. Austen-Leigh*
2. Unpublished manuscripts of the Rev. James Austen owned by the Jane Austen Memorial Trust, Chawton
3. *The English Militia*
4. *Austen Papers*
5. *Austen Papers* – for all letters to and from Jane Leigh Perrot.

Chapter 8
1. Anna Austen, quoted in *Jane Austen, Her Homes and Her Friends*
2. *Sailor Brothers*
3. *Austen Papers*
4. *Austen Papers*
5. *Caroline Austen's Reminiscences*

Chapter 9
1. *My Aunt Jane Austen*
2. *Sailor Brothers*

Chapter 10
1. Letter from one of Anna's daughters to Cholmeley Austen-Leigh
2. *Caroline Austen's Reminiscences*
3. *Austen Papers* – for all letters from Cassandra Austen to Philadelphia Walter
4. *Austen Papers* – Appendix IV
5. Account by the Rev. Arthur Loveday, son-in-law of Anna Lefroy

and grandson of one of the Hinton sisters, quoted in *Caroline Austen's Reminiscences*

Chapter 11
1. *Memoir of J.E. Austen-Leigh*
2. *Caroline Austen's Reminiscences*
3. Quoted by Jane Austen in 'Opinions of *Emma*', *Minor Works*
4. *Austen Papers*
5. *Jane Austen's Letters*
6. Letter from Mrs Austen quoted by Fanny Lefroy, *Temple Bar* February 1883
7. Manuscript in the Fellows' Library, Winchester College

Chapter 12
1. *Jane Austen's Kindred*
2. *Jane Austen's Kindred*
3. *Memoir of J.E. Austen-Leigh*
4. Quoted in *Caroline Austen's Reminiscences*
5. Winifred Midgley, 'The Revd Henry and Mrs Eleanor Austen', *Annual Report* 1978
6. *Austen Papers*
7. Winifred Midgley (see note 5) for this and subsequent information on Henry's career at Farnham

Chapter 13
1. A copy of the sermon is in the Bristol Reference Library
2. *Jane Austen's Kindred* – for all the genealogical information on this and subsequent generations of the family
3. *Hampshire Chronicle*, 5 November 1879
4. *Memoir of Jane Austen*
5. *Memoir of J.E. Austen-Leigh* – for this and following letters to Emma
6. *Austen Papers*

Chapter 14
1. *Memoir of J.E. Austen-Leigh* – for all letters from Emma
2. Helen Lefroy, 'Strangers', *Annual Report* 1982
3. *Catherine Hubback*
4. From Mary Austen's pocket-book, quoted in *Caroline Austen's Reminiscences*

5. *Sailor Brothers*
6. *Catherine Hubback*
7. *Memoir of J.E. Austen-Leigh*
8. *Austen Papers*
9. *Catherine Hubback*
10. *Chawton Manor*

Chapter 15

1. *Jane Austen's Kindred*
2. Henry James, *Autobiography, A Small Boy and Others* (W.H. Allen, 1956)
3. James Edward Austen-Leigh, *Recollections of the Early Days of the Vine Hunt by a Sexagenarian* (1865)

Bibliography

Annual Reports of the Jane Austen Society, 1949 to the present year, William Dawson.

Caroline Mary Craven Austen, *My Aunt Jane Austen* (Jane Austen Society, 1952)

James Edward Austen-Leigh, *Memoir of Jane Austen* (Richard Bentley, 1870)

Mary Augusta Austen-Leigh, *Memoir of James Edward Austen-Leigh* (privately printed, 1911)

Richard Arthur Austen-Leigh (editor), *Austen Papers 1704-1856* (Spottiswoode, Ballantyne & Co Ltd, 1942)

William Austen-Leigh and Montagu George Knight, *Chawton Manor and Its Owners* (Smith, Elder & Co, 1911)

Edward, Lord Brabourne (editor), *Letters of Jane Austen with Introduction and Critical Remarks* (Richard Bentley, 1884)

R.W. Chapman (editor), *Jane Austen's Letters to Her Sister Cassandra and Others* (Oxford University Press, 2nd Edition 1972)

R.W. Chapman (editor), *The Works of Jane Austen*, Volume VI, Minor Works (Oxford University Press, 1954)

Keith Feiling, *Warren Hastings* (Macmillan, 1954)

Constance Hill, *Jane Austen, Her Homes and Her Friends* (John Lane, 1902)

John and Edith Hubback, *Jane Austen's Sailor Brothers* (The Bodley Head, 1904)

David Waldron Smithers, *Jane Austen in Kent (Hurtwood, 1982)*

George Holbert Tucker, A Goodly Heritage (Carcanet, 1983)

J.R. Western, *The English Militia in the Eighteenth Century: The Story of a Political Issue 1660-1802* (Routledge & Kegan Paul, 1965)

Unpublished Sources

'Caroline Austen's Reminiscences' – manuscript owned by the Jane Austen Memorial Trust, Chawton, Hampshire

'The Memoirs of Sir Francis Austen'

Joan Corder, 'Jane Austen's Kindred', genealogical tables tracing the descent from Jane Austen's brothers together with reminiscences of later generations of the family. Typescript lodged with the Royal College of Arms.

G.P. Hoole, 'Tonbridge Associations of Jane Austen's Family'

Diana and David Hopkinson, 'Catherine Hubback – A Life'

Index

Whether by marriage or by adoption, many characters in this history changed their name during the course of the narrative. In the index they appear under the final name by which they were known. Maiden names are given in brackets, and other former names are also indicated therein.

Not infrequently, the same Christian name passed from father to son; in these cases, small Roman numerals have been used to distinguish the different generations.